On the Persistence of the Japanese "History Problem"

In Japan, people often refer to August 15, 1945, as the end of "that war". But the duration of "that war" remains vague. At times, it refers to the fifteen years of war in the Asia-Pacific. At others, it refers to an imagination of the century-long struggle between the East and the West that characterized much of the nineteenth century. This latter dramatization in particular reinforces long-standing Eurocentric and Orientalist discourses about historical development that presume the non-West lacks historical agency. Nearly seventy-five years since the nominal end of the war, Japan's "history problem" – a term invoking the nation's inability to come to terms with its imperial past – persists throughout Asia today.

Going beyond well-worn clichés about the state's use and abuse of discourses of historical modernity, Koyama shows how the inability to confront the debris of empire is tethered to the deferral of agency to a hegemonic order centered on the United States. The present is thus a moment one stitched between the disavowal of responsibility on the one hand, and the necessity of becoming a proper subject of history on the other. Behind this seeming impasse lie questions about how to imagine the state as the subject of history in a postcolonial moment – after grand narratives, after patriotism, and after triumphalism.

Hitomi Koyama is a University Lecturer at Leiden University, The Netherlands.

Interventions

Edited by Jenny Edkins
Aberystwyth University

Nick Vaughan-Williams
University of Warwick

The Series provides a forum for innovative and interdisciplinary work that engages with alternative critical, post-structural, feminist, postcolonial, psycho-analytic and cultural approaches to international relations and global politics. In our first 5 years we have published 60 volumes.

We aim to advance understanding of the key areas in which scholars working within broad critical post-structural traditions have chosen to make their interventions, and to present innovative analyses of important topics. Titles in the series engage with critical thinkers in philosophy, sociology, politics and other disciplines and provide situated historical, empirical and textual studies in international politics.

We are very happy to discuss your ideas at any stage of the project: just contact us for advice or proposal guidelines. Proposals should be submitted directly to the Series Editors:

- Jenny Edkins (jennyedkins@hotmail.com) and
- Nick Vaughan-Williams (N.Vaughan-Williams@Warwick.ac.uk).

'As Michel Foucault has famously stated, "knowledge is not made for understanding; it is made for cutting" In this spirit The Edkins – Vaughan-Williams Interventions series solicits cutting edge, critical works that challenge mainstream understandings in international relations. It is the best place to contribute post disciplinary works that think rather than merely recognize and affirm the world recycled in IR's traditional geopolitical imaginary.'
Michael J. Shapiro, University of Hawai'i at Manoa, USA

On the Persistence of the Japanese "History Problem"
Historicism and the International Politics of History
Hitomi Koyama

Ontological Entanglements, Agency and Ethics in International Relations
Exploring the Crossroads
Laura Zanotti

For more information about this series, please visit: www.routledge.com/series/INT

On the Persistence of the Japanese "History Problem"

Historicism and the International Politics of History

Hitomi Koyama

Routledge
Taylor & Francis Group

LONDON AND NEW YORK

First published 2018
by Routledge
2 Park Square, Milton Park, Abingdon, Oxon OX14 4RN

and by Routledge
711 Third Avenue, New York, NY 10017

Routledge is an imprint of the Taylor & Francis Group, an informa business

© 2018 Hitomi Koyama

British Library Cataloguing-in-Publication Data
A catalogue record for this book is available from the British Library

Library of Congress Cataloging-in-Publication Data
A catalog record has been requested for this book

ISBN: 978-1-138-08972-3 (hbk)
ISBN: 978-1-315-10906-0 (ebk)

Typeset in Times New Roman
by Apex CoVantage, LLC

Kan-san e

Contents

Figures

Acknowledgments

A dandelion seed nestles in red soil, sequestered apart from the busy street and is given time. Before long, concrete is poured atop. I want to thank Renee Marlin-Bennett for reminding me that there is an option other than withering, Jennifer Culbert for constant support and encouragement, P.J. Brendese for patiently going through multiple drafts, and Sibagro for having cultivated such a space for a weed to grow at Johns Hopkins. Fragments of this book were written and shared over the years in many places among endearingly critical companies both near and afar, in Baltimore, Sydney, and Kyoto, and at various conference sites in International Studies Association and American Political Science Association, and in workshops at Yonsei University in Seoul, at Kyoto University in Kyoto, and at the National Taiwan University in Taipei. I thank Nicola Parkin and Jenny Edkins at Routledge Interventions Series for publishing this book, and Himadeep Muppidi and Mustapha Pasha for putting me in touch with Jenny. I am indebted to the generous research funding offered by Ryukoku University's Afrasian Research Centre in Kyoto, and to be offered a space to finish the manuscript in an abandoned library in southern Kyoto. Thomas J. Mathew has been a patient copyeditor and pleasure to work with. Earlier versions have been thoughtfully edited by Casey McNeill, Timothy Vasko, Greg Sesek, and Mariam Banahi. More raw versions of my writings and thoughts have been in the making over countless exchanges with my intellectually generous cohorts in Baltimore. I am fortunate to be at Hopkins at a time when I could easily bump into Nobutaka Otobe, Aditi Saraf, Tulio Zille, Ben Meiches, Chad Shomura, Dot Kwek, Derek Denman, Alex Barder, Nate Gies, Andrew Brandel, and Daniel Levine. A special thanks goes to Osamu Koshimizu at San'nin-sha Publisher in Kyoto who introduced me to Suga Syuichi at Hanazono University, who generously gave me the permission to take photographs of his collection of wartime and postwar textbooks. Part of the chapters is based on the reuse of an earlier publication at *Contexto Internacional: Journal of Global Connections*, "Historicism, Coloniality, and Culture in Wartime Japan" Vol. 38 (3) Sep/Dec 2016 http://dx.doi.org/10.1590/50102-8529.2016380300003, the licensor is not represented as endorsing the use made of the work. Carrying out a book project while on the road without anchor would not have been possible without the support of Ching-Chang Chen, Shine Choi, Kosuke Shimizu, Cameron Shepherd, L.H.M. Ling, Mustapha Pasha, and Barry Buzan.

I would like to thank my family for their support and patience, despite the subject of my work being a thorny issue for contemporary Japan. Finally, I would like to dedicate this book to Mr. Abe Kang. The grace and generosity you extended to my family in Virginia sustained me at moments when the world felt too fraught with hate, thoughtless words, and violence. You were fighting to breathe till the very last moment and left with grace as I was still holding your hand. I wish I could have thanked you in person today. I miss you.

Introduction

Rethinking persistence in impatient times: the international politics of history in East Asia

One serves upward of forty to sixty men a day in a war zone where she does not speak the local language, thereby rendering her both captive and dependent. Some men use condoms, others do not; her vagina is swollen, and at the height of war she also had to serve as caretaker for these same soldiers who at times disparaged women's bodies (Tanaka, 2002). These women endured the day's transition to another night and day without the hindsight that we have today, that this would end in 1945.

After 1945, they are abandoned amid the resumption of civil war in China or independence movements elsewhere, and for those who made it back home alive, there awaited patriarchy and the social shame of no longer being a virgin. Years of servitude and multiple forced abortions often rendered the bodies barren. Some tell their stories, whereas others cannot bear to.

The majority of these women came from impoverished families in Korea, which at the time of war was under Japan's colonial domination, and many others from the regions that fell under Japanese rule. They are called the "comfort women" (Soh, 2008; Yoshimi, 1995). Contemporary Japanese national history textbooks neither go into these graphic details nor reflect on the enduring consequences of what happened to these women since 1945 when accounting for the history of "comfort women", and this is if there is any mention at all.[1]

As both the survivors and perpetrators as well as those who experienced war in Asia are near the end of their biological lives, those who were born after 1945 in recent years have become visibly impatient with the persistence of what many have come to call Japan's history problem in the past few decades. The history problem in this context pertains to disputes both among and within mostly Asian states over how the past – especially Japanese colonialism and imperialism – is to be narrated and thereby acknowledged.

The impatience of those born after 1945 is symbolized in the phrase "final and irreversible resolution" deployed by Japanese Prime Minister Shinzo Abe in the December 2015 joint announcement with former South Korean President Geun-hye Park to resolve the "comfort women" issue for good.[2] The surviving "comfort women" in South Korea were never consulted by President Park (Maeda ed., 2016). On first glance, the phrase appears as the Japanese government's attempt at forestalling any future demand by the Korean government. Nonetheless, the term was inserted by the South Korean representative during the negotiation meeting that took place in January 2015 as a way to hedge the Japanese representative from backing away from progress made on the terms of the apology in the future ("Summary of Analysis of Japan-ROK Agreement on 'Comfort Women' Issue". *Yomiuri Shinbun*, December 28, 2017). In the undisclosed part of the agreement, the Japanese representative also demanded that the South Korean representative no longer use the term "sex slave" to refer to these women, and also sought to ask that the government withhold support of civic groups that seek to commemorate these victims in the world (ibid).

Against such sovereigns' claim over their rights to resolve the matters of history, in December 2016 a South Korean civic group placed in front of the Japanese Consulate in Busan a statue that symbolizes the women who had to work as military sex slaves. This is in addition to a statue that was already erected across the Japanese Embassy in Seoul, which Abe had been pressuring Park to remove. The 1-ton statues materially defy the ephemeral nature of the human body and, therefore, upset those who are seeking to wait out for the remaining survivors to pass away from the scene.

In December 2017, a new statue was unveiled in the Philippines, a first for the country, to remember what happened.[3] This news came amid the move by the Mayor of Osaka to terminate its sister-city relations with the city of San Francisco for allowing a statue commemorating the "comfort women" to be erected. While this is not the only crime committed by Japan, the question of how to account for the "comfort women" in post-Cold War Japan has come to symbolize the persistence of Japan's history problem.

The solution appears simple. Many have asked why Japan cannot just apologize and move on, or to follow the German model with regard to the Holocaust survivors. I have asked this myself. Technically, there are the Murayama and Kono statements on "comfort women" that express remorse for what had happened in the past, which the current Japanese Prime Minister Shinzo Abe claims to inherit from his predecessors.

When Prime Minister Tomiichi Murayama sought to pass a Diet Resolution for the fiftieth anniversary of the end of the war in 1995, the content was rendered ambivalent by the time it passed through the Diet. The survivors who decided to accept monetary reparation from the Asian Women's Fund – a state and privately funded hybrid institution that began distributing money from 1996 and which has since disbanded in 2002 – also received letters from the Japanese Prime Minister (Onuma, 2007). The letter begins with a carefully guarded wording that "in cooperation with the Government and the people of Japan, offers atonement from the Japanese people to the former wartime comfort women, I wish to express my personal* feelings as well" – the term personal was omitted from the 1998 versions on, thereby navigating an ambiguous relation to the subsequent paragraph that states that "[a]s Prime Minister of Japan, I thus extend anew my most sincerely apologies and remorse to all the women who underwent immeasurable and painful experiences and suffered incurable physical and psychological wounds as comfort women" – the initial insertion and deletion of the term personal attests to the wavering figure of the sovereign representative practice, that is both personal and public, simultaneously.[4]

Nonetheless, what stands out within the Asian perception of Japan is a sense of inconsistency. Murayama's minister of environment Arata Sakurai made a statement a year before, in 1994, that the Greater East Asia War had no intent to invade. He then resigned shortly afterward. A few months before that, under Prime Minister Tsutomu Hata, the minister of law, Shigeto Nagano, stated that the Rape of Nanjing is a hoax. He too had to resign afterward.

On other fronts, bilateral initiatives between Japan and South Korea as well as with the People's Republic of China have been taken to bring together national historians from both sides to discuss how to write history. Issuing of state apology and inclusion of formerly excluded actors in history, as well as the addition of formerly silenced narratives in national history, while politically contentious, appear both rational and inevitable.

Yet while the periodic expression of apologies by Western states such as New Zealand, the Netherlands, and Canada over settler colonialism and massacres of indigenous populations and past colonial rule has prompted many to consider our age the "age of apology" (Gibney, Howard-Hassmann, Coicaud, and Steiner, 2009), apology alone is inadequate. As Lind demonstrates, it quite often backfires in the form of domestic backlash against attempts at coming to terms with the past, thereby further leaving "Japan's" stance ambivalent (Lind, 2010).

A state-centric discourse invites attention to sovereign claims to exemption from external intervention. Tellingly, opinion polls in the immediate aftermath of a series of then Prime Minister Junichiro Koizumi's sequential visits to the Yasukuni Shrine, indicated that national opinion was polarized between those who agreed with the statement that because such visits would upset Japan's neighbors, the Prime Minister should not go, and those who agreed with another statement that the Prime Minister should have the right to act as he sees fit because Japan is a sovereign state (2002: 461).[5]

The latter logic, which equates Chinese and South Korean protests against prime ministers and high-ranking ministers visiting Yasukuni Shrine as an infringement of Japanese sovereignty, also informs the argument by right-wing commentators in Japan that the Chinese and South Korean states are merely instrumentalizing the history problem in the pursuit of respective national interests. In the process, the voices of the survivors are silenced, thereby reducing the ethical weight of the debates on how to talk about history. What this quick sketch shows is how those who seek to right history and to deny history both converge upon this consolidation of the state as the sovereign subject, though the former critique it, and the latter sanctify it.

In postwar Japan there has been a consistent attempt to rebut revisionist efforts to commandeer the history problem (Ienaga, 2003 Takahashi, 2005). Nationalistic history in modern Japan has glorified war and colonial rule, and seeks to rectify the exclusion or euphemisms that have been deployed to whitewash the past. Against the logically consistent argument that what Japan did was wrong and hence must apologize until the victims forgive, the nationalist argument constantly invokes the geopolitically and historically specific predicament of Japan, that it exists under the "American shadow" (Kato, 1995).

The postwar constitution was written by dozens of Americans in a matter of days and imposed during the Occupation that lasted until 1952. Article 9 of this imposed constitution renounces Japan's sovereign right to use military force to resolve international dispute. With the advent of the Cold War, then Prime Minister Shigeru Yoshida entered into a security alliance with the United States, thereby effectively locking Japan into a permanent state of dependency.

The United States also dictated who Japan could normalize relations with. So communist states were excluded from signing the San Francisco Peace Treaty in 1952 by which the Western powers dictated Japan's geopolitical future.[6] Much of this predicament is well documented in John Dower's classic work, *Embracing Defeat* (2000). To this, historian Toshikazu Inoue adds, "not only democracy, but even our post-war history is given by America" (2015: 5).

One can take a normative approach and reject this context and claim that such a predicament cannot absolve Japan from dealing with its past. Yet the two positions, one asserting a moral response toward past wrongs, and the other emphasizing the extenuating force of contemporary circumstances, are locked in a stalemate, even as the survivors dwindle in numbers.

The search for a solution often short-circuits into a technical discourse that reduces the history problem to whether the state is to offer apology or to placate those who object to such an approach as unreasonable or conservative and illiberal. It normalizes the sovereigns' claim upon historical narratives and abnormalizes the detractors in turn. Against these impatient moves, this book asks how the history problem between Japan and its neighbors persists, and what the persistence unveils about the broader contours of the politics of history in the contemporary global context of a post-historical present, that is, to *be* after history.

This being after history implies multiple subjects and subjectivities – be they the state, the survivors, the Japanese – with one being pitted against another quite often. Depending on the kind of subject invoked, any argument could be turned on its head. For example, it might be argued that Japan cannot consistently apologize because it has evaded being a subject that could be held accountable in postwar years. This is one latent thesis, most notably posited by literary critic Norihiro Kato, that frames the postwar debates on the history problem.

Yet this thesis that emphasizes the need of a subject who may be held responsible betrays the expectation of others who consider, to the contrary, that there is no I without the Other. This raises a question: how does one being's assertion of being a subject in turn implicate others and vice versa, and what if these are juxtaposed against others, forming a cluster whereby between these cacophony of assertions, occluded histories are produced? In other words, how can we re-vision persistence beyond bilateral self-other relations, and instead as historically generated clusters?

While I do not want to negate the symbolic import of building a national dialogue over how to include the "comfort women" as a part of Japanese history, I do want to place the persistence in the broader context of how global existence and coexistence have increasingly been theorized after the model of a liberal sovereign being the subject of history. This re-centers the state in an age when nationalism is understood to be a dangerous path to partake of, and grand narratives are no longer deemed viable or desirable. This is the purpose of this book.

This can be visualized in the way that the chapters to follow are organized, to show how histories are occluded by geopolitics within what Ann Laura Stoler calls the "conceptual, epistemic, and political architecture" of imperial debris (2016: 10). Stoler does not deal explicitly with the Japanese empire, but I find the metaphor of architecture useful to convey the contours of this book.

Imagine a building that collapsed after an earthquake. The remnant of the first floor is clustered against the second, and third. The construction of the pillars was temporally sequenced, the first had to be built first, and then second, yet the material blocks are set against one another in the present, in the state of simultaneity despite having their origins at different times in the evolution of the building.

Each part is built with different geopolitical formations in mind, and is marked by it. You hear a voice within the debris. To reach in is to consider the historicity of each of the components that are blocking the way toward the voice, to understand the history behind each of the materials at hand and to see how, in the present, they are compounded upon and against each other.

To come back to the issue at hand, my point is quite simple: what is meant by the "problem" in the "history problem" depends on the historical context and period. It is geopolitically informed at different scales and in different time periods, and while differentiated, there nonetheless are impacts of the presence of these pillars in the debris.

To understand the impasse, we need to map out the architectural blueprint and the ad hoc additions that inevitably become incorporated into the blueprint, as ideas are put to practice on ground, to ask how the first floor was built, and then the second, how the pipe plan affected the bird's decision to build the nest, and how the attempted solution for the first floor may in fact be what is preventing the pillar on the third floor from collapsing completely. Plans and contingencies and the material limit of each component makes the architecture assume the form of what is built. Yet each is also implicated at different levels of ephemerality as well as endurance.

What I want to visualize through writing is how sediments of the past are rarely completely gone. And when we speak of a material, we may have many different assumptions about how this is to be used and to what ends. Sometimes, the issues faced at different time periods could be eerily familiar. Inoue's lament that even Japan's postwar history was given by the United States strikes a note similar to Ranajit Guha's indictment of the role of British history in eliminating Indian history (2002). What unites the two is the observation that a particular historical subjectivity is denied by the dominant power that writes history, be it in the name of the empire or the world – which are often equated.

The persistence of the history problem is often posed as a question of how to navigate and create consistency between national and world history through a rational account of the past. By contrast, this book attempts to show how this navigation is not so straightforward when world history is understood as being

Eurocentric, both in the past at the turn of twentieth century in Westernizing Japan, and in the present post-Cold War East Asia.

I want to map out the clustering of geopolitical formations in the plural, and how those from different time periods are interlocked with one another, creating a shadow for some, and crushing others slowly, over time. This is why I conceive of the project as the *politics* of history, rather than over truth claims or facts – where truths and facts, by definition, are anti-political (Arendt, 1968). To see it as a history of the international politics of history is to further complicate the layered image of geopolitical formations. And to think of a ruin in the aftermath of an earthquake is to recognize how the past is never entirely in its past.

A particular passage written by Norihiro Kato anchors this study:

> Since then [the Asia-Pacific War], sorrow no longer unites us . . . it shatters us apart. We are given a predicament by losing the war where unless we find another answer, we cannot go forward . . . yet behind this experience lies a kind of worldliness.
>
> (2005: 287)

I returned to the same passage over and over in the past decade, because I read it as an invitation to think of both the specificity of Japan's "history problem" and the ubiquity of the international politics of history in the broader postimperial and postcolonial context.

How does history become a political problem? While historiographical approaches to the study of history is of import, this book looks at how Japan fits into what Robert Young calls the "problem of the Hegelian model, particularly of a historicism which presupposes a governing structure of self-realization in all historical processes" (1990: 3).

What specifically is the implication of performing a paradox where self-realization is *structured*, what becomes of its legacies and memories, and how do these in turn bind the present? How does the dominance of structure – be it local, regional, or systemic – impact the pursuit of responsibility, which, by definition, presupposes the free will and agency of a subject? As the function of the Introduction is to introduce a subject, convey its stake, and invite readers to join this road less taken, I begin with an episode about the "twilight zone" of history.

The "twilight zone" of history and the discourse on decolonizing history

In *The Age of Empire: 1875–1914* (1989), historian Eric Hobsbawm begins with an account of how his mother traveled to Egypt, and met his father there, under the larger historical circumstance of the British empire. Had the British not occupied Egypt, Hobsbawm would not have been born. To study the British empire as a historian and as a British subject is to navigate through this "twilight zone between history and memory", where personal memory of family history and imperial history can never be fully dissociated (1989: 3).

While he acknowledges that it is possible to cultivate a relationship with a past much further back in history, Hobsbawm nonetheless asks how this more immediate distance from the past tends to invoke intensive affect in the form of contentions over how to write the past on all sides. He observes that discussions of Stone Age history seem much more detached, whereas the debates on recent empires feels much more charged, tense, and intense.

It is charged because the personal and the political, and by extension, collective history and collective memory short-circuit. And this concept and geography of the collective widely vary in the age of empire and its aftermath. Treatment of recent empires resides in this liminal zone. For Hobsbawm, it is the British empire. For me, it is the Japanese empire.

I was born in Tokyo. My family first moved to Virginia, then back to Tokyo, then to New York, and then to California in the 1980s and 1990s. My father worked for a large Japanese corporation, and this demanded that our family had to relocate at short notice according to the whims of the company headquarters.

Silicon Valley in the 1990s was on the verge of its boom and, given its strategic import, we were assigned to move there in the mid-1990s after living in New York for less than a year. I joined a local art studio, and it was there that I met an elderly Taiwanese woman. Upon giving my name, a common one in Japan, she began speaking to me in fluent Japanese. She was visibly upset when I asked her where she learned the language, as this signaled my ignorance of Japan's colonization of Taiwan.

That was high school. I attended university afterward, taking courses on Japanese history along with courses in political science as a way to fill the lack that my question to the woman had exposed. What does it mean to speak about history as a Japanese in the postcolonial present? From the frequent moving I knew the category "national" was a highly problematic fiction to say the least. But I simultaneously knew it also was not.

On finishing university, I took a course in Mandarin Chinese, and it was then that my parents revealed to me that my grandfather grew up in Taiwan, as the colonizer. While I was relieved to learn that he was too young to be drafted into the military, the news reinforced my unwillingness to rebut the question of how to respond to history with the claim that I was not born yet and, therefore, had nothing to do with the past.

My family offered me tuition support on the precondition that I take my grandfather back to visit the sites of his childhood memory: Taipei, and Taichung, in postcolonial Taiwan. To learn of my own heritage in relation to the problem of how to narrate and speak of history while being aware of the artificiality of the collective identity in question furthered the sense that I could not resort to double-speak in what I write. That is, I must place both my grandfather and the elderly Taiwanese woman in the intended audience.

To a significant extent, this book is my attempt at responding to the Taiwanese woman, and many more like her, about this "twilight zone" of history. Japan's "history problem", broadly put, is a problem of how to relate to this "twilight zone". But unlike Hobsbawm, I approach the twilight zone from a vantage point at the intersection of international relations, which presumes the nation-state as an agent-subject of history, and of the politics of postcolonial history that continually re-centers the state despite the awareness of how subject-centrism occludes the presence of Others, at the expense of historiography.

Globally, in the same decade that I encountered the elderly Taiwanese woman, in 1991, Korean survivor Kim Hak-sun, herself a victim of imperial sex slavery, demanded that the Japanese government recognize its responsibility in running the wartime military brothel system. The abstract question of how to come to terms with the past and to critically engage with state control over the historical narrative assumed a concrete aspect in the image of her face, which was reprinted in millions of newspaper headlines, her eyes piercing through the camera lens. And this face demanded a response from none other than the "Japanese" in post-imperial, postcolonial, Japan.

The period in which I became cognizant of the question of how the past is to be remembered and spoken of coincided with the period when Japan's "history problem" took a global – and no longer international – dimension. This distinction is relevant. The term international presumes state-to-state relations, and in those terms, most of Japan's former victim states have normalized their relations with Japan. (North Korea is the sole country which has not normalized relations with Japan to this day.)

The globalization of the history problem, in part, has to do with the demise of the Cold War framework. But it is also partially connected to the transnational diaspora and networks of advocacy groups that re-visioned the past in terms of human rights violations, thereby circumventing the language of the nation-state. Within Japan, the military presence of the United States has for long dominated the political imagination of war. Yet there is an inner self-reflection too, prompted by the awareness of Japan's complicity in the U.S. war in Vietnam.

In the 1970s there was a steady stream of writing aiming to come to terms with the past. But the domestic movement seldom had impact beyond its borders until the mid-1980s and 1990s, when the democratization of Taiwan, South Korea, the demise of the communist ideology in the People's Republic of China, the new-found international attention to wartime violence against women in the aftermath of Bosnia and Yugoslavia, the attendant rise of the feminist discourse in newly democratized nations, and the defusing of the military standoff between the two Chinas and two Koreas as well as the broader tension between the United States and Russia spelled the end of the grip that "high politics" and politics among nation-states had over the history problem. Much of the regulation of the narration of the past since 1945 has pivoted around the weighty presence of the United States in the Asia-Pacific, and this was beginning to change in the 1990s.

The term "history problem *[rekishi mondai]*" in the contemporary context refers to disputes among and within East Asian states over how the past – and especially Japanese colonialism and imperialism – is to be narrated and thereby acknowledged by Japan in history textbooks as well as in symbolic practices by leaders. What appear to be mundane practices congeal into what Michael Billig calls "banal nationalism" (1995), underwriting the implicit reproduction of colonial attitudes into a contemporary atmosphere that has become ever more receptive to (re)militarization (Shigematsu and Camacho, 2010).

Especially for Japan's neighbors, the Japanese attitude toward its militarist past is closely associated with how Japan is to act in the future. The assumption here is that if one does not learn from history, one is bound to repeat it. For centuries, major historical texts in East Asia contained in their titles the Chinese character for mirror. Therefore, how the Japanese state treats its national history is closely scrutinized not only for the interest in the past, but also for the future.

Japanese textbook authors must undergo an evaluation process conducted by the Ministry of Education, which is now renamed Ministry of Education, Culture, Sports, Science and Technology (MEXT), and school districts are to choose from several state-approved textbooks for their respective curricula. Given state involvement in the evaluation process, regardless of the actual adoption rate of the specific textbook, Japan's neighbors see the approval of controversial textbooks as state endorsement of the content.

One of the textbook controversies that took place in the 1980s concerned the *Asahi News* report that the authors were asked to alter the term "invasion" to "advancement" in their description of Japanese imperialism in China (Narita, 2012: 214). The lexical change was understood to water down the gravity of Japan's crimes. And it is not only the content of national history textbooks that is being problematized by China and South Korea.

Statements made by high-ranking ministers and the decision of the Prime Minister of Japan to visit the Yasukuni Shrine (a Shinto shrine which since 1987, in theory, includes the souls of Class A war criminals, therefore rendering any visit thereafter a defiance of the Tokyo War Crimes Trial) have all been subject to scrutiny by victim states. The shrine visits have been met with Chinese and Korean protests, and the discontent over how history is narrated in Japan has led to cancellations of summit meetings and anti-Japanese demonstrations at the turn of the century.

In this way, historical memories of what Japan had done and how Japan has yet to come to terms with its imperial past continue to constrain regional politics to this day. The end of the Cold War and the rise of the human rights discourse further meant that questions of how to deal with history are no longer the sole province of the sovereigns. Despite the recent joint announcement by Prime Minister Shinzo Abe and President Geun-hye Park to resolve the issue "irreversibly" in December 2015, mutual distrust between Japan and South Korea and Japan and China continue to be anchored in this thorn called the history problem.

Furthermore, it is not only the democratization of former authoritarian states that adds complexity to the history problem. Both Japan and Germany were democratized immediately after 1945, so within these respective states, too, the relationship between the state and history have undergone decades of interventions by historians and civil society. After World War II, there is a worldwide effort at demythologizing the state in school textbooks and curriculums, most notably in Germany and Japan and in the so-called First World (Schissler and Soysal, 2005).

Within Japan, historian Saburo Ienaga's three-decade-long critique of state control over education is anchored in his remorse that history writing, in part, was responsible for sending his students to the war front (2003). Historians, educators, and ordinary Japanese have continued to seek ways of coming to terms with, and to also, thereby, judge the past (Narita, 2012). This is to say that the "who" who constitute the subject of history in postwar Japan has diversified to include women and children, to acknowledge the agency of the formerly excluded and the poor (Nagahara, 2003).

The proliferation of subjectivities in turn implicates the role of the state, both decentering and re-centering the state as the sovereign subject of history. The amplified question is this: *what does it mean to speak of the state of history?* The term "state of history" is strategically left ambivalent. It could be read in two ways: the sovereign nation-state as depicted in history, or as the state of history's relationship to the state.

Furthermore, how do we speak of the state of history after philosophy has begun to deconstruct the notion of the subject (Cadava, Connor, and Nancy, 1991)? The association of "who" and the subject is by no means straightforward in philosophy. It is even less so in the discipline of international relations. Depending on the analytical method deployed, the state could be either a unit following behavioral law or a supposedly conscious agent-actor that is the subject (Schroeder, 1994).

To be sure, the concept of sovereignty itself is relational and to a significant degree dependent on recognition from other sovereigns, as well as the population within the territory the sovereign claims control over (Bartelson, 1995; Howland and White eds., 2009). In international politics, the sovereign nation-state is presumed to be the unit or the agent-subject of history (Hobson, 2000).

The rationale for such a presupposition and how it became ubiquitous cannot be understood apart from the history of the breakdown of the hold of the Church and the Holy Roman Empire (Spruyt, 1994) and the expansion and "discovery" made by the European powers. These occurred in tandem with European imperialism, as well as the ways in which sovereigns proclaimed independence from the Holy Roman Empire by drawing a line between the traditional and the modern (Fasolt, 2004; Osbourne, 1995; Young, 1990).

Edward Said observes that it is in the age of empire "in which the novel form and the new historical narrative become preeminent, and in which the importance of subjectivity to historical times takes firm hold" (1993: 58). For Ranajit Guha, too, the appropriation of history by the West is part and parcel of Western domination of the world (2002). The implicit dichotomy here is the contrast between the West and the non-West, or the rest, where Japan is sometimes presumed to be Western, and at other times, non-Western.

While the positioning of Japan remains unresolved, the fact that Japan was an imperial power stands. But so does the notion that Japan at the turn of the twentieth century sought to assert agency in history in response to Western denial of Japan as an equal partner in world politics. What is then needed is a questioning of how efforts at resisting the West ironically replicates the same structure of violence it originally sought to critique.

The relationship between imperialism and assertion of the state as the sovereign subject of history in turn raises the conundrum of how to engage with the question of norms. This is to ask how to theorize the responsibility of a state that claims to be the sovereign subject of history toward its past as an empire when the tide of post-1945 politics of history has been to de-link the two.

While Alexander Wendt's influential formulation (with caveats) of the "state as a person" (2004) continues to inspire recent studies on ontological security and insecurity which emphasize the role of identity and recognition, not all theorists share this premise. As Roxanne Doty aptly puts it, Wendt's formulation of state as person is informed by "desire all the way down", – that is, the desire to see the world in orderly and, therefore, order-able manner (2000: 139).

To take this further, a normative discourse *needs* a coherent state. In more practical terms, the victims' turn to the state and legal measures to seek redress re-centers the state (Brown, 1995). This is because to speak of responsibility for war, the state must be imagined as an agent-actor, a subject. Here, the demand for the specificity and concreteness of the state as an agent-actor, the subject of world history, is pitted against the decades-long movement to deconstruct the state.

What *is* a state? Behind this benign question lies the politics of epistemology and ontology that the presupposition of the state as an agent implies. Namely, what is the nature and property of the agent, and what is its relationship to the structure (Wight, 2006)? Indeed, everyday language reinforces the usefulness of seeing the state as an actor in social relations rather than a unit in a system.

Not a day passes without hearing phrases like "Russia will be advancing . . ." or "South Korea will respond with a . . .". This book is no exception in this respect. Yet I argue that attending to the persistence of Japan's history problem elucidates the general limit of leaving this empirical as well as ontological question off the hook. What I explicate in later chapters is the necessity of considering the agent-structure relationships and presuppositions in the discipline of international relations (IR) because of their ethical implications.

Historically, too, the scope of the "who" has varied, and sociologists, anthropologists, and historians have effectively documented that the nation-state is a social construct (Anderson, 1991). While the myth of the homogenous nation took root immediately after decolonization (Oguma, 2002) and manifested in the form of Nihonjin-ron (the idea that Japanese are unique and different), sociologically, Shunya Yoshimi observes that, at least by the 1990s, the concept of "Japanese" could no longer be presupposed within the geographical confines of Japan (2010).

It is this inability to presuppose who the Japanese are that vexes alike both conservatives, such as Prime Minister Shinzo Abe, and those who stand for reconciling with Asia. The collective phrase, "as Japanese", was, and continues to be, suspect, "externally". Many in Asia – notably the two Koreas and the People's Republic of China as well as Singapore – continue to fear the resurgence of Japanese nationalism, yet the response to the history problem has to come from none other than those who identify with Japan.[7]

Furthermore, this demand to respond "as Japanese" all too often has compartmentalized the question of how to think of national history and whether to offer or withhold state apology. While apologizing is of import, the focus on the national question in turn has effectively led the stories of the survivors to become captive to the state, thereby reducing their stories to state instrumentalization of the past as a "history card" (Nakanishi, 2005). On the one hand, the appeal to the state appears to empower the nationalists, yet on the other, the accusation that the state has a self-interest in using the past denies the ethical claims of the survivors.

The rationale for reconstructing the history problem as an architectural debris is threefold. First, it is a constant reminder to think beyond binaries, and, rather, to see a constellation of overlapping geopolitically informed concepts, where some are older than others, but nonetheless coexist in the present. Second, the key concept that I trace is the place of political agency in time that informs different arguments over the notion of historicism in different historical periods – the image of layers of clusters jutting against one another here is more apt than to posit a linear succession of events that smoothens out the texture and effaces the frictions that arise from clustering.

The association of sovereignty with historical subjectivity takes place differently in different geopolitical contexts as Edward Said has lucidly demonstrated. This is to take both time and place into account, to add local color to the concepts at hand by historicizing them. Third, the differentiated idea of how political agency is implicated in the different historicisms being posited by different actors is crucial in historicizing the ways in which IR presupposes the state as agent-subject.

How these are necessarily tied to the question of whether one is a passive or active maker (agent-actor) of history that could be held responsible for "its" past (at the expense of contingency) invites one to re-view the international politics of history in a new light. This is to ask with Jean-Luc Nancy how to "do justice to identities – without giving in to their delusion, to the presumption that they are, substantially, identities ('subjects' in this sense)" (2003: 279).

To resist the delusion is to historicize. Here, I use the term historicize as Foucault defines it, as "insurrection of subjugated knowledges . . . because historical contents alone allow us to see the dividing lines in the confrontations and struggles that functional arrangements or systematic organizations are designed to mask" (2003: 7).

While this book is by no means a historiography of the history problem, what I sketch out is the historical contents that enable a re-viewing of what its persistence elucidates, to show the political architecture produced by the cluster of histories of geopolitically formed and informed struggles over how to talk about history and agency.

As the central thematic is to ask the place of state as an agent-actor, that is, the subject of history, I focus on the term historicism instead of History, or history, or historiography. The term historicism is by no means singular in meaning, either. Yet because a differentiated meaning of historicism is contingent upon how the place of political agency is theorized in time, as the main framework of the chapters which are to form the cluster, as a clearing caricature, I work with two ideal types of historicism: one which, in the name of the law of history, denies political agency for those considered backward, and second, one which asserts endogenous agency in the name of history against such a structurally determined thesis of history.

Chapter 1 elucidates the rationale for this move. The subsequent chapters show how these have come to interrelate, globally, in the specific geopolitical formation of Japan-West relationships and Japan-Asia relationships, over time. By presenting these as clusters, I then show in Chapter 4 how the impasse is constituted as debris. The central concern that constitutes the arc of this book is how the notion of the state as the sovereign subject of history is to be spoken of after the war.

This book is an intervention in the instrumentalization of history by the states in the postcolonial and postimperial present. But to find out how it got here, we must reexamine a longer duration of history than the postwar period. We must also sustain a nuanced account of the international politics of history that acknowledges that there are multiple meanings associated and remembered with regard to the use of history that are clustered, layered, sedimented and, at times, in conflict with one another.

Multiple actors have, toward divergent ends, spoken of history differently. The common term history conveys the impression of a scene where all the actors are speaking of the same event. Yet some invoke it to endow timeless authority, as in the way medieval religious authorities did, some to discredit the claims of others in the name of irrefutable truth, and yet others to predict the future by excavating timeless laws from history. The irreducibility of what history means by one standard definition is reflected in the plethora of names given to the "history problem" in postimperial Japan: as *shukan* (subjective view), *ninshiki* (recognition), education, revisionism, responsibility, and politics.

I, therefore, take my definition of history from J.D. Salinger:

> Among other things, you'll find that you're not the first person who was ever confused and frightened and even sickened by human behavior. You're by no means alone on that score, you'll be excited and *stimulated* to know. Many, many men have been just as troubled morally and spiritually as you are right now. Happily, some of them kept records of their troubles. You'll learn from them, if you want to. Just as someday, if you have something to offer, someone will learn something from you. It's a beautiful reciprocal arrangement. And it isn't education. It's history.
>
> (1979: 208–209)

What I have to offer is what I learned from select records of troubles kept, records which continue to grow in number every day. Many, many women and men have been sickened with history, and this is not limited to Japan. Many are sickened, yet we talk past one another, sometimes on purpose, but oftentimes not.

A brief note on scope(s)

In terms of the scope of reference, oftentimes, the history problem is compartmentalized into a question of what happened during wartime. In Japan's case, this would refer to the First Sino-Japanese War (1894–1895), Japan's invasion of

Taiwan (1895), the Russo-Japanese War (1904–1905), the Japanese invasion of China beginning in 1937 with the Marco Polo Bridge Incident in 1931, and World War II (1941–1945). Yet as Lisa Yoneyama elucidates, such modes of punctuation effaces violence legitimated in the name of history outside of the context of warfare (2016).

Commenting on the plethora of terminologies that have been in use in Japan since the end of war in 1945, philosopher Tetsuya Takahashi observes that most terms pertained to wartime responsibility or education or as cognitive dissonance. Yet he considers the term "history problem" useful since one is able to cast the scope to also include the interwar and colonial period as well as Japan's modernity at large, when the Ainu indigenous group and the people of Liu'qiu (present-day Okinawa) face internal colonialism (2002).

In other words, it pertains not only to wartime events but also to Japanese modernity/Westernization (which are intertwined) and its evaluation of how this had implications for Asia as well as Japan at large. Japanese Sinologist Yoshimi Takeuchi continued to grapple with the meaning of modernity and its implications for Japan and Asia or, rather, what the "advent" of modernity in Asia bequeaths upon those who are named by the West as being part of the East (Takeuchi et al., 2006). This book also takes the history problem in the spirit of Takeuchi, who refused to stop thinking about Asia in postimperial Japan.

This inclusion of the meaning of modernity as a backdrop also differentiates this book from other works whose main thrust has been to compare postwar Japan with Germany, as this comparative approach has restricted the scope to questions of war memory and history. Numerous studies that contrast postwar Japan with Germany have upheld the German model of atonement as the ideal standard. Franziska Seraphim characterizes this tendency to compare Japan with Germany within academic and U.S. media representation of Japan's history problem as nothing less than a new form of Orientalism.

This is because Germany and the rest of the West here are cast once again as civilized figures who deal with history rationally, whereas Japan is backward, irrational, and uncivilized. This is evinced in Seraphim's quote from the *Economist*: "Japan is still a nationalistic nation despite its great international economic ties, and is trying to hold its culture in place without influence from western nations" (2008: 205–206).

Such a cultural explanation, which echoes the stadial view of history and civilization, while appearing respectful of a multicultural approach to the use of history, reduces the persistence of the history problem in Japan as an anomaly to be corrected by following, once again, the West. Instead of asking what the persistence of the history problem in East Asia might tell us about the potential and limits of decolonizing history – that is, making history inclusive and open – the persistence is explained as a consequence of a Japanese cultural trait (Seraphim, 2008).

The pairing of Germany with Japan seems like a natural choice. Both were part of the axis powers, both were defeated, and both committed abhorrent war crimes. Yet such a comparison discounts the different historical trajectories that Germany and Japan followed, in part for geopolitical reasons, but also in part by American strategists' presupposition about the non-viability of a multilateral framework in East Asia as opposed to its viability in Europe. Those in Asia were not deemed mature enough to participate in a multilateral framework in contrast to the "civilized" brothers in Europe (Hemmer and Katzenstein, 2002).

But what if one were to comparatively study the politics of history among former empires and, as a question of decolonizing history, place it in conversation with Guha and Said? In a recent edited volume, which examines the politics of memory in France, Japan, Portugal, Italy, and other former imperial powers, different authors have asked how former empires deal with how to remember its imperial past.

This is a shift from a war-centric framing of the history problem to one in which the colonial period and imperial pasts come into the fold. If one were to consider the issue of "comfort women" – also known as military sex slave victims – it is true that these women were forced to serve the Japanese military during wartime.

Yet to restrict the scope to wartime is to neglect the underlying effect of the transformation of the Korean political economy under Japanese colonial rule. The majority of the "comfort women" came from impoverished classes, and less so from the educated elites. While this is not to dismiss the violence committed during war, nonetheless, there is a stake in framing the scope of the history problem beyond the question of how to talk about war.

It has been pointed out that the comparison of Germany and Japan that focuses on the act of war, and thereby the category of wartime and postwar, occludes the ways in which the advent of U.S. hegemony in East Asia has produced the "dominance of the 'good war, bad war' binary focusing on the Second World War . . . [disabling] a more rigorous critique of the inter-imperial cooperation that continues today" (Fujitani, 2015: 163). The Tokyo War Crimes Trial, led by the Allied powers, centered on war, and by doing so, left the longer term exploitative relations of all the advanced capitalist nations with their colonies and their other imperial victims beyond the scope of reach (Fujitani, 2015: 154).

The issue of colonialism and imperialism was left out because the Allied powers themselves were colonial powers. The rehabilitation of Japan under U.S. hegemony, therefore, meant that while the de-warring of history may have effectively taken place – especially as symbolized in the blotting out of any militaristic passages in school textbooks – the decolonization of history did not take place.[8] This is why the study of the politics of history prior to war and imperial formation is also of import for the purpose of understanding the contemporary condition.

The scale of the collectivity in question has varied widely in the span of two centuries in East Asia as the Sinocentric tributary system became dismantled,[9] and various modes of solidarity and anti-colonial, as well as anti-Western, regionalism were attempted and disavowed. This layered complexity also calls for historicizing the nation-state as a political category in relation to empire and colonialism as a frame of reference to think of the past and the present. We cannot comprehend the persistence of the history problem solely on the basis of the nation-state.

Thus far, I have argued for a broader take on the history problem that goes beyond the war/nonwar binary by attending to imperial formation and history before World

War II. Let us step back and map out the even broader contour of the vexed relation between Japan, history, and colonialism so as to make sense of why the persistence of the history problem could be understood through the lens of the de-colonial project of international history. In philosophical terms, this underscores the issue of the continuity principle in theorizing state responsibility on the one hand, and more importantly, in the context of international relations, the extent to which the state could be theorized as the agent-subject in history. The two points are conjoined.

The continuity principle in theorizing political responsibility, simply put, is the question of whether I am the same as the I from yesterday. In the context of Japan, this culminates in the debate over whether there was a revolution in 1945 that gives credibility to the claim that the state prior to 1945 is different from that after 1945. Many point to continuity rather than discontinuity, mostly on the basis of the U.S. Occupation's decision to retain the emperor and not indict him in the Tokyo War Crimes Trial (Dower, 2000).

Because the state of history since 1945 has been heavily shaped by the U.S. presence in Japan, directly until 1952 and indirectly through the U.S.-Japan Security Treaty, much of the postwar debate on history writing cannot but address the United States. This focus on the United States, along with the stubborn impression that the war was lost to the United States, but not to the rest, in turn also efface the presence of the Asians.

Furthermore, the remnants of geopolitical tensions and Cold War divisions continue to shape and constrain each state's politics of history differently, as we see in the different approaches to Japanese colonial history by the Republic of China and the People's Republic of China. Economic wealth and the viability of state support for the victims also alter the responses.

Filipina survivors of the "comfort women" system accepted the Asian Women's Fund's reparation money, whereas the South Korean survivors rejected the monetary compensation and sought to go further. This was partially enabled by the South Korean government's support to these women. It is for these reasons that the history of the altering shape of states as the subject of history matters so much.

The other rationale for approaching the history problem at the crossroads of IR theory and the history of East Asian interstate and postcolonial relations is to elucidate the implied assumption of agency. The question of whether the state could be considered an agent-subject in global politics arises from the need to consider what it means to be historically responsible. Logically, those who do not act with volition cannot be held responsible for such acts.

On the basis of this point, I differentiate types of approaches to history in this book and take a layered and overlapping approach to re-view the ways in which the history problem is caught in an impasse. This also necessitates that the scope of the book extends even further back and away from the Far East into the Renaissance and Enlightenment periods of Western history, when the concept of political autonomy and agency become intertwined with the politicization of history (Ankersmit, 2002; Fasolt, 2004).

While the scope is vast and the run feels wild, it is a necessary exercise to see and feel the political architecture and its collapsed aftermath. The scale and span of the discourse covered is ambitious – for each and every point could easily have led to another chapter, another book. One might ask why not cover only what took place after 1945? In lieu of an answer to that, here I want to reflect on the contentions over how to periodize history.

The term "Greater East Asia War" was introduced on December 12, 1941, a few days after Japan's attack on Pearl Harbor (Narita, 2010: 42). Prior to that, for practical purposes, what went on between Japan and China was deliberately called "incident" and not "war". This was because if it were declared a war, embargo would ensue. It was also after the attack on Pearl Harbor that the war as a righteous campaign was openly announced. Prior to that, Japan's colonization and invasion of Asia was difficult to legitimate let alone theorize.

Media reports on Asia mostly took the form of fragmented documentary, but after Pearl Harbor, the films viewed in Japan came to emphasize the event, in relation to larger narratives, as history (Narita, 2010: 59). With the attack on Anglo-Saxon power (Japan attacked both Hawai'i and British Malaya – therefore, also spelling the end of the British influence in Asia), the atmosphere at that time, according to Naoko Itagaki, a scholar of Japanese wartime literature, was that of the beginning of a "new world picture that includes Japan as part of the East" (Narita, 2010: 43).

After December 15, 1945, on the orders of General Headquarters, the term "Greater East Asia War" was banned from use in public statements. The term introduced instead was "History of War in the Pacific", which periodizes the span from the Manchurian incident in 1931 to surrender in 1945, covering the "Manchurian Incident", "Sino-Japan Incident", and "War in the Pacific" (Narita, 2010: 66).

Despite the inclusion of Asia in such historiography, the main emphasis was on the war in the Pacific after 1941, which means that the war in Asia is occluded, and so is the fact of Japan's colonization of Taiwan and Korea, which began much earlier. In this sense, even the inclusion of Asia, by calling the war the "fifteen year war in the Asia-Pacific", fails to address the larger intertwinement of discourse on enlightenment and colonization in the name of the "civilizing mission".

Specifically, for Asia, the progressive history associated with the Enlightenment entails a peculiar predicament: here history begins from the stagnant "Orient" and culminates in the mobile "Occident". Geography becomes tied to temporal hierarchy, thereby giving the East-West relation a political significance. The publication of "Theory Affirming the Greater East Asia War" by Fusao Hayashi in 1964–1965 takes the scale of history under consideration far beyond the fifteen years to a "hundred years war" (Narita, 2010: 171).

In this schema, the beginning of war dates to when the Western powers forcibly opened Japan with gunboat diplomacy in the mid-nineteenth century, ending the centuries of "peace" sustained under Tokugawa rule (ibid). Depicting this hundred years as pure power politics between Japan and the West, and for escaping rule by the white powers, Hayashi takes a revisionist stance toward the interpretation of the Manchurian incident and the meaning of war (Narita, 2010: 172).

While I do not necessarily concur with Hayashi's thesis, I nonetheless deem this challenge of examining the politics of history beyond the fifteen years, to the hundred years before 1945, as a layered conundrum over how to contend with progressive history, the wovenness of geography to temporal hierarchy, and resistance entailing the assertion of an agentic sovereign subject to understand the impasse in the present, a necessary task.

A road map

Chapter 1, "On the Recursivity of the Politics of History", makes a case for differentiating between two versions of historicism: agency-denying historicism and agency-enabling historicism. Employing an abductive method, I critically engage with Chakrabarty and Guha's writings on history writing and show that their definition of historicism as being part and parcel of colonialist knowledge that denies non-European agency is indispensable, yet is also inadequate in understanding modern Japan's engagement with historicism.

To better understand the shift in the way in which historicism has been employed by Japanese thinkers in different periods of modernization I argue that instead of collapsing British liberal thought with German political thought, as Guha does, we should attend to the differences among different Western powers and contextualize historicism. By placing historicism in the European context, I show how the divergent meanings of historicism developed in late eighteenth- and nineteenth-century Europe pivot around the question of how to conceive of agency in time.

In Britain and France, the study of history was likened to the study of nature and the history of mankind was subject to objective rational study. In Germany, building on Kant's application of the organismic metaphor to the theorization of the body politic, an alternative conception of historical development, as the "unfolding" of individual culture, manifested in rebellion against the Enlightenment. Both kinds of historicism place the world in relation to historical development, but each does so to a different end.

The first kind of historicism presumes the comparability of different social groupings in different stages of development. The second kind of historicism rejects the existence of the implicit standard which makes the act of comparison possible in the first instance. By examining the discourse of historicism in German political thought I make the case that there is more than one meaning attributable to the term historicism.

The divergent meanings of historicism have political implications when they are used to understand a particular condition in world history. In Chapter 2, "On the Rise and Demise of Civilizational History in Meiji Japan", I examine how Japanese intellectuals initially were receptive to agency-denying British and French historicism that viewed world history as civilizational history and how this was inflected in the shift in Japan's relationship with China and Korea. In identifying the new center of civilization/*zhonghua*/中華 as Europe instead of Qing China, Japan decenters Qing China from the interstate political landscape.

This in part has to do with how in East Asia the question of who was civilized was only loosely associated with racial difference, in contrast to the discourse in Western civilizational history, which increasingly associated whiteness with civilization.

Because civilization was presumed to be open and inclusive and having little to do with racial identity, leading Japanese intellectuals, such as Yukichi Fukuzawa, Ukichi Taguchi, and Kunitake Kume, sought to engage with Guizot and Henry Buckle's progressive and scientific history and make world history more inclusive.

Yet, by the 1890s, civilizational history and the implicit standard of civilization are used by Western powers against "backward Asia", including Japan. As a consequence of this awareness of Eurocentrism in civilizational history, the Meiji state altered its relationship with historicism, toward a model closer to agency-enabling German historicism. This resulted in the politicization of history writing toward nationalist ends, bolstering the influence of emperor-centered historians.

Agency-denying historicism presented Japan with the dilemma of how to overcome its "backward" status within Eurocentric civilizational history at the beginning of twentieth century. The reconfiguration of history writing as agency-enabling historicism manifests in the 1930s and 1940s as a result of the convergence of three global currents: (1) a sense of crisis over the meaning of civilization, even within Europe, at the end of World War I. The atrocities and massive scale of death on European soil, instead of in faraway colonies, brought about in Europe a critical reflection on the meaning of civilization. (2) the search, outside Europe, for alternatives to civilization as the basis for envisioning a different kind of global order; and (3) the earlier emergence, within Germany, of the concept of *kultur* as a key term for envisioning and asserting historical agency, in response to French and British influence.

In Chapter 3, "The Assertion: Japan as the Subject of World History", I examine how, as a result of and response to the convergence of these global intellectual currents, Kiyoshi Miki, the head of the cultural division of Prime Minister Fumimaro Konoe's think tank Showa Research Association, provides a blueprint for legitimating Japanese imperialism. This was done in the name of the Greater East Asia Cooperative Body *(Toa kyodotai)* and in the name of asserting Japan as the subject/agent of history.

This Greater East Asia Cooperative Body theory later became a basis for Konoe's declaration of the Greater East Asia Co-Prosperity Sphere in the 1940s. Miki's treatise on historicism, which drew heavily on Kant's writings conceiving of culture as the site where freedom can be actualized, provided a systematic legitimation of Japanese imperialism in the 1930s and 1940s. Here, culture, as the site of resistance against civilizational historicism/agency-denying historicism and method with which to overcome the West, proved to be violent.

With the end of the Fifteen Years War in the Asia-Pacific[10] in 1945 and the advent of the U.S. Occupation, Japan as a subject of history becomes a palimpsest: the subject is both there and not there. In Chapter 4, "On the Postwar Palimpsest Subject of History", I show how this palimpsest history continues to haunt Japan's history problem in East Asia. With the thawing of Cold War tensions, Asian victims' demands for Japan to take responsibility surged in the 1990s, prompting a reexamination of the role of history writing role in international politics.

In this context, literary critic Norihiro Kato pointed out in (1995) that the absence of Japan as the subject of history since 1945 made it possible for postwar

Japan to evade being held responsible by Asian victims. Therefore, in *Haisen-goron [After Defeat]* he posits the thesis that, in order to apologize to Asia, Japan must constitute a subject of history which can be held response-able. This thesis provokes an allergic reaction within Japan because Kato's call to constitute the agent/subject of history eerily resembles the movement of the 1930s and 1940s, when Japan asserted itself as the subject of history and, in the process, subjugated Asia.

I suggest that in light of the more recent memory of the violence committed in the name of agency-asserting history in the 1930s and 1940s there is a reluctance to constitute Japan as a subject of history once again. Differentiating the two types of historicism and their effects on how Japan sees itself in relation to the world enables us to see that the dilemma posed by the history problem is not over "how to grapple with progressive history", but rather, "after historicism(s), what might one have to say about history".

In conclusion, I argue that the persistence of the history problem between Japan and Asia shows that both agency-denying historicism and agency-enabling historicism reshaped the East Asian international order in significant ways and the legacy of this engagement with the two versions of historicism continue to haunt the region. If both versions of historicism have proven to be violent, this also suggests that we must break out of a formulaic paradigm where we assert ourselves as the sovereign subject of history in response to being denied historical agency. We must consider why, after decolonization, we continue to equate and fetishize becoming sovereign to becoming a subject of history.

By this point, I hope to have elucidated (1) why a re-view of the persistence of the history problem entails tracing history's relation to agency, (2) why differentiating between kinds of historicisms enables us to understand the postimperial impasse over history and what the stakes of straddling different disciplinary approaches to the politics of history are, (3) on the basis of differentiating the two types of historicisms how the history of Japan's engagement with world history could be more fine-tuned, and why I chose these particular thinkers, and (4) how these moves can tackle the conundrum about history that often goes unnoticed, yet continues to fracture efforts to forge solidarity toward attaining historical justice.

While the segment on Japanese history of history is more or less in chronological order, the chapter plans are crafted with an eye to identifying the theoretical dilemma that is both particular and ubiquitous to those whose identities are historically constituted by being called "backward" or "less developed". This is a theoretical starting point toward rethinking what modernity means. As alluded to earlier, the familiarity between the discourse of 1930s Japan and Dipesh Chakrabarty's call to "provincialize Europe" renders this project of interest to those who may not necessarily be readers of Japanese international relations.

Instead of confining Japan's "history problem" to an issue peculiar to East Asian international politics, I place the persistence in the larger context of the global interconnection of ideas about how to assert agency in history. In a sense, I am working backward, as any discussion of war responsibility must logically engage with the state of history and its agency. While this unconventional approach is not to discount the objective view of the past altogether, I posit that a contextualized reconstruction of the conundrum regarding history at different periods can elucidate both the difference and the eerie familiarity of the troubles faced.

This book not only seeks to identify the ways in which history oppresses, dominates, and naturalizes existing inequality and injustice, but also considers the problem of subject formation that cannot be elucidated and thought apart from these structures of domination. This is to probe the tension of the moderns who politicized and depoliticized history toward divergent aims – aims which, nonetheless and by definition, must plot toward *a future*. It is in this sense that we moderns are trapped between the desire for and disavowal of a linear sense of time.

Notes

1 While there also is a history problem between China and Korea over the ownership of the land which Korea traces back to their dynasty, the issues garnering the most attention are the Nanjing Massacre and the Japanese imperial army's use of military sexual slavery – euphemistically known as "comfort women". Less acknowledged are the massacre of Koreans which took place after the Great Kanto Earthquake; the massacre of Okinawans by the Japanese imperial army, who suspected that Okinawans were American spies, thus forcing a group suicide in the last year of the war; the use of forced labor in Japanese factories, the most notorious case taking place in the Hanaoka region; and the military unit's use of vivisection to obtain data for biological weapon production. Cf. Tak Fujitani, Geoffrey M. White, and Lisa Yoneyama eds., *Perilous Memories: The Asia-Pacific War(s)* (Durham and London: Duke University Press, 2001); Joshua A. Fogel ed., *The Nanjing Massacre in History and Historiography* (Berkeley: University of California Press, 2000); Tessa Morris-Suzuki, Morris Low, Leonid Petrov, and Timothy Y. Tsu, *East Asia beyond the History Wars: Confronting the Ghosts of Violence* (New York: Routledge, 2013); Sheila Miyoshi Jager and Rana Mitter eds., *Ruptured Histories: War, Memory and the Post-Cold War in Asia* (Cambridge, MA and London: Harvard University Press, 2007); Gi-Wook Shin, Soon-Won Park, and Daqing Yang eds., *Rethinking Historical Injustice and Reconciliation in Northeast Asia: The Korean Experience* (London: Routledge, 2007); Thomas U. Berger, *War, Guilt, and World Politics after World War II* (Cambridge: Cambridge University Press, 2012). The number of textbooks that include mention of the "comfort women" have briefly increased in 1990s, yet under the current Prime Minister, Shinzo Abe, the Ministry of Education, Culture, Sports, Science and Technology – Japan's textbook evaluators – have increasingly asked textbook authors who seek to discuss the "comfort women" and Rape of Nanjing to alter the term "rape" or to retract the statement that "many of the 'comfort women' died en masse during war" from textbooks.

   Cf. Ministry of Education, Culture, Sports, Science and Technology-Japan, Comment on authorization system: www.mext.go.jp/a_menu/shotou/kyoukasho/kentei/03062201/14-75.htm (Accessed October 28, 2017).
2 *The New York Times*, "Japan and South Korea Settle Dispute over Wartime 'Comfort Women'", www.nytimes.com/2015/12/29/world/asia/comfort-women-south-korea-japan.html (Accessed November 29, 2017).
3 Walter Sim, "'Comfort Women' Issue Can't Be Swept under Rug", *The Straits Times*, www.straitstimes.com/asia/east-asia/comfort-women-issue-cant-be-swept-under-rug (Accessed December 25, 2017).
4 Asian Women's Fund, "Letter from Prime Minister to the Former Comfort Women", www.awf.or.jp/e6/statement-12.html (Accessed January 10, 2018).

5 Both statements were formulated by Yomiuri news agency, which conducted the opinion poll.

6 Signed by forty-eight delegates in September 8, 1951, the San Francisco Peace Treaty (SFPT) formally ended the state of war, recognized Japanese sovereignty, ceded control of Okinawa and Bonin islands to the United States, relinquished territories obtained under Japan's expansion, and the decisions of the International Military Tribunal for the Far East (IMTFE, otherwise known as the Tokyo Trial) were to be accepted. Geopolitically, the United States' decision to exclude the People's Republic of China, even against British insistence, has resulted in Japan signing a bilateral treaty with Taiwan in 1952, resulting in partial peace. Both Taiwan and China were not invited. India rejected the invitation in light of how the treaty was tied to the U.S.-Japan Security Alliance, an alliance formed under unequal relations between the two. Burma did not participate given the problematic reparation clause in the treaty. Both North and South Korea were excluded in light of U.S. concern over Korean communist agitation in Japan. As a result, Koreans remaining in Japan had no access to the benefits other Allied civilians were given. Vietnam, Laos, and Cambodia were still under French colonial rule. Indonesia signed a separate peace treaty in 1958, and the Philippines reserved ratification, leaving Ceylon (as Sri Lanka was then known) and Pakistan the two countries in Asia that straightforwardly supported SFPT.

7 Japan's relationship with other states in Asia are inflected with diverse geopolitical restraints as well as ironic appropriations. Take, for example, the 2007 visit made by Japanese Prime Minister Shinzo Abe to the descendant of Indian Judge Radhabinod Pal in India (Onishi, 2007). While Judge Pal wrote his dissenting opinion in the Tokyo Trial in order to contest the lack of justice shown by the Allied powers in Asia, a statue of him has been erected in the Yasukuni Shrine in 2005 with the objective of supporting the idea that Japan's war was a Holy War to save Asia from the West. Quite often Taiwan's stance toward Japan over history is deemed as less hostile in contrast to China, yet this is more about postcolonial Taiwan's "internal" tension between the population that arrived with Chiang Kai-shek after he lost the civil war and those Taiwanese who lived under Japanese colonial rule.

8 Nonetheless, this does not mean that demilitarization effectively took place, either, as the continued presence of the United States military in Japan attests, along with the existence of the Japanese Self-Defense Force, whose military expenditure has been on the rise under Prime Minister Shinzo Abe. Cf. Setsu Shigematsu and Keith L. Camacho eds., *Militarized Currents: Toward a Decolonized Future in Asia and the Pacific* (Minneapolis, MN: University of Minnesota Press, 2010).

9 The classic take on the Chinese World Order is given by John Fairbank (1968); a more recent account is by David C. Kang (2010). On anti-Westernism, Pan-Islamism, and Pan-Asianism, cf. Cemil Aydin (2007) and Eri Hotta (2007).

10 There are contentions over how to call this period – some refer to World War II, yet this would emphasize the European theater and Japan's war against Western powers at the expense of occluding Japan's invasion and colonization of states in Asia. Others who seek to hold a more balanced view call it the Fifteen Years War in the Asia-Pacific.

References

Anderson, Benedict. *Imagined Communities*. London and New York: Verso, 1991.

Ankersmit, Friedrich. *Historical Representation*. Stanford, CA: Stanford University Press, 2002.

Arendt, Hannah. *Between Past and Future: Eight Exercises in Political Thought*. New York: Penguin Books, 1968.

Asian Women's Fund. "Letter from Prime Minister to the Former Comfort Women." www.awf.or.jp/e6/statement-12.html (Accessed January 10, 2018).

Aydin, Cemil. *The Politics of Anti-Westernism in Asia: Visions of World Order in Pan-Islamic and Pan-Asian Thought*. New York: Columbia University Press, 2007.

Bartelson, Jens. *The Genealogy of Sovereignty*. New York: Cambridge University Press, 1995.

Berger, Thomas. *War, Guilt, and World Politics after World War II*. Cambridge: Cambridge University Press, 2012.

Billig, Michael. *Banal Nationalism*. London, Thousand Oaks, and New Delhi: Sage Publications, 1995.

Brown, Wendy. *States of Injury: Power and Freedom in Late Modernity*. Princeton, NJ: Princeton University Press, 1995.

Buruma, Ian. *Wages of Guilt: Memories of War in Germany and Japan*. London: Random House, 1994.

Cadava, Eduardo, Peter Connor, and Jean-Luc Nancy eds. *Who Comes after the Subject?* New York and London: Routledge, 1991.

Dower, John. *Embracing Defeat: Japan in the Aftermath of World War II*. Australia: Penguin Books, 2000.

Fairbank, John eds. *The Chinese World Order: Traditional China's Foreign Relations*. Cambridge, MA: Harvard University Press, 1968.

Fasolt, Constant. *The Limits of History*. Chicago and London: University of Chicago Press, 2004.

Fogel, Joshua ed. *The Nanjing Massacre in History and Historiography*. Berkeley and Los Angeles: University of California Press, 2000.

Foucault, Michel. *'Society Must Be Defended' Lectures at the College de France 1975–1976*. Translated by David Macey. New York: Picador, 2004.

Fujitani, Takashi. "Post-Imperial Japan in Transnational Perspective." In *Memories of Post-Imperial Nations: The Aftermath of Decolonization, 1945–2013*, edited by Dietmar Rothermund, 150–170. New Delhi: Cambridge University Press, 2015.

Gibney, Mark, Rhoda Howard-Hassmann, Jean-Marc Coicaud, and Niklaus Steiner eds. *The Age of Apology: Facing Up to the Past*. Philadelphia: University of Pennsylvania Press, 2009.

Guha, Ranajit. *History at the Limit of World-History*. New York: Columbia University Press, 2002.

Hemmer, Christopher and Peter J. Katzenstein. "Why Is There No NATO in Asia? Collective Identity, Regionalism, and the Origins of Multilateralism." *International Organization* 56, no. 3 (2002): 575–607.

Hobsbawm, Eric. *The Age of Empire 1875–1914*. New York: Vintage Books, 1989.

Hobson, John. *The State and International Relations*. New York: Cambridge University Press, 2000.

Hotta, Eri. *Pan-Asianism and Japan's War: 1931–1945*. New York: Palgrave Macmillan, 2007.

Howland, Douglas and Luise White eds. *The State of Sovereignty: Territories, Laws, Populations*. Bloomington and Indianapolis: Indiana University Press, 2009.

Ienaga, Saburo. *Ichi Rekishi Gakusha no Ayumi [Path Trodden by a Historian]*. Tokyo: Iwanami Gendai Bunko, 2003.

Inoue, Toshikazu. *Shusengoshi 1945–1955 [History of End of War 1945–1955]*. Tokyo: Kodansha Sensho Metier, 2015.

Kang, David. *East Asia before the West: Five Centuries of Trade and Tribute*. New York: Columbia University Press, 2010.

Kato, Norihiro. *Amerika no Kage [The American Shadow]*. Tokyo: Kodansha Gakujyutsubunko, 1995.

Kato, Norihiro. *Haisengoron [After Defeat]*. Tokyo: Chikuma Bunko, 2005.

Lind, Jennifer. *Sorry States: Apologies in International Politics*. Ithaca and London: Cornell University Press, 2010.

Maeda, Akira ed. *'Ianfu' Mondai no Genzai: 'Paku Yuha Gensho' to chishikijin ['Comfort Women' Issue's Present: 'Yu-ha Park Phenomenon' and the Intellectuals]*. Tokyo: Sanichi Shobo, 2016.

Morris-Suzuki, Tessa, Morris Low, Leonid Petrov, and Timothy Y. Tsu eds. *East Asia beyond the History Wars: Confronting the Ghosts of Violence*. New York: Routledge, 2013.

Nagahara, Keiji. *20 Seiki Nihon no Rekishigaku [The Japanese Discipline of History in Twentieth Century]*. Tokyo: Yoshikawa Kobunkan, 2003.

Nakanishi, Terumasa. "China Plays Its History Cards." *Japan Echo* 32, no. 4 (2005): 18–23.

Nancy, Jean-Luc. *A Finite Thinking*. Edited by Simon Sparks. Stanford, CA: Stanford University Press, 2003.

Narita, Ryuichi. *'Senso Keiken' no Sengoshi [Postwar History of 'War Experience']*. Tokyo: Iwanami Shoten, 2010.

Narita, Ryuichi. *Kingendai nihonshi to rekishigaku [Modern and Contemporary Japanese History and Historiography]*. Tokyo: Chuko Shinsho, 2012.

Oguma, Eiji. *A Genealogy of 'Japanese' Self-Images*. Translated by David Askew. Melbourne: Trans Pacific Press, 2002.

Onishi, Norimitsu. "Decades after War Trials Japan Still Honors a Dissenting Judge." *The New York Times*, August 31, 2007. www.nytimes.com/2007/08/31/world/asia/31memo.html (Accessed December 20, 2017).

Onuma, Yasuaki. *'Ianfu' mondai to wa nandattanoka [What Was the 'Comfort Women' Problem About?]*. Tokyo: Chuko Shinsho, 2007.

Osbourne, Peter. *The Politics of Time: Modernity and Avant-Garde*. London and New York: Verso, 1995.

Said, Edward. *Culture and Imperialism*. New York: Vintage Books, 1993.

Salinger, Jerome David. *The Catcher in the Rye*. New York: Little, Brown and Company, 1979.

Sang-Hun, Choe. "Japan and South Korea Settle Dispute over Wartime 'Comfort Women'." *The New York Times*, December 28, 2015. www.nytimes.com/2015/12/29/world/asia/comfort-women-south-korea-japan.html (Accessed November 15, 2017).

Schissler, Hanna and Yasemin Nuhoglu Soysal eds. *The Nation, Europe, and the World: Textbooks and Curricula in Transition*. New York: Berghahn Books, 2005.

Schroeder, Paul. *Systems, Stability, and Statecraft: Essays on the International History of Modern Europe*. New York: Palgrave Macmillan, 2004.

Seraphim, Franziska. "Negotiating War Legacies and Postwar Democracy in Japan." *Totalitarian Movements and Political Religions* 9, nos. 2–3 (2008): 203–224.

Shigematsu, Setsu and Keith L. Camacho. *Militarized Currents: Toward a Decolonized Future in Asia and the Pacific*. Minneapolis, MN: University of Minnesota Press, 2010.

Sim, Walter. "'Comfort Women' Issue Can't Be Swept under Rug." *The Straits Times*, December 15, 2017. www.straitstimes.com/asia/east-asia/comfort-women-issue-cant-be-swept-under-rug (Accessed December 25, 2017).

Soh, Chunghee Sarah. *The Comfort Women: Sexual Violence and Postcolonial Memory in Korea and Japan*. Chicago and London: University of Chicago Press, 2008.

Spruyt, Hendrik. *The Sovereign State and Its Competitors: An Analysis of Systems Change*. Princeton, NJ: Princeton University Press, 1996.

Stoler, Ann. *Duress: Imperial Durabilities in Our Times*. Durham and London: Duke University Press, 2016.

Takahashi, Tetsuya. *Rekishi/shuseishugi [History/Revisionism]*. Tokyo: Iwanami Shoten, 2001.

Takahashi, Tetsuya ed. *<Rekishininshiki> Ronso [<Historical Recognition> Debates]*. Tokyo: Sakuhinsha, 2002.

Takahashi, Tetsuya. "Japanese Neo-Nationalism: A Critique of Kato Norihiro's 'after the Defeat' Discourse." In *Contemporary Japanese Thought*, edited by Richard Calichman. New York: Columbia University Press, 2005.

Takeuchi, Yoshimi, Tetsushi Marukawa, and Masahisa Suzuki. *Takeuchi Yoshimi Serekushon II Ajia e no/kara no manazashi [Selection of Writings by Yoshimi Takeuchi II Gaze from/to Asia]*. Tokyo: Nihon Keizai Hyoronsha, 2006.

Tanaka, Yuki. *Japan's Comfort Women: Sexual Slavery and Prostitution during World War II*. New York: Routledge, 2002.

Wendt, Alexander. *Social Theory of International Politics*. New York: Cambridge University Press, 2004.

Wight, Colin. *Agents, Structures and International Relations: Politics as Ontology*. New York: Cambridge University Press, 2006.

Yomiuri Shinbunsha Yoron Chosabu. *Nihon no Yoron [Japanese Opinion Polls]*. Tokyo: Kobundo, 2002.

Yoneyama, Lisa. *Cold War Ruins: Transpacific Critique of American Justice and Japanese War Crimes*. Durham and London: Duke University Press, 2016.

Yoshimi, Shunya. *Posuto Sengo Shakai [Post-Postwar Society]*. Tokyo: Iwanami Shoten, 2010.

Yoshimi, Yoshiaki. *Jyugun Ianfu [Comfort Women]*. Tokyo: Iwanami Shoten, 1995.

Young, Robert. *White Mythologies: Writing History and the West*. New York: Routledge, 1990.

1 On the recursivity of the politics of history

Revisionism has been the adjective most commonly used by critics to characterize Japanese Prime Minister Shinzo Abe's exertion of political pressure on history textbook publishers about how Japan's past is to be written.[1] Denial of what happened, it is argued, is tantamount to distorting historical truths. We cannot reconcile with those in Asia so long as we let such a revisionist temperament run amok. One must pursue reconciliation, offer reparation, apologize, and curtail the revisionists. Such claims are compelling for many.[2]

The response to such moves has overwhelmingly been phrased in terms of the import of historical truths and facts. What distinguishes the historians' profession from that of politicians in relation to what had happened is the committed disavowal of anachronism (Fasolt, 2004: 6). Anachronism projects current political concerns upon the past, to alter the ways in which the past is narrated in light of the present. The refusal to let the present shape the past takes the form of a commitment to attend to evidence – which today is no longer limited to written words, but also could include monuments, oral history, and much more. Facts can be used not only to inform opinion but also to refute the validity of an opinion. The call to open the archives, to demand transparency in government, involves the assumption that informed opinions is crucial to healthy democratic rule.

Nonetheless, to frame the antidote to the state's manipulation of history as correction and restoration of factual truths risks neglecting the inherent tension between truths and politics. According to Andrew Schaap, there is a limit to the notion that historical reconciliation is possible by truth telling and offering of reparation because such depoliticization of history leads to the closure of politics. He writes, "while *the aspiration to reconcile is an enabling condition* of politics, politics must be invoked to resist the moment of closure that reconciliation might otherwise tend towards" (Schaap, 2005: 8, italics added).

The stance he takes navigates a slender road that could easily be interpreted as giving ammunition to the apologists and those who refuse to deal with the demands to confront history. Still, what I want to explore in this chapter is to simultaneously hold onto the aspiration while also taking the role of politics in the politics of history seriously. This is to ask what makes history political, to attend to the recursivity of the politics of history, instead of treating politics as a matter to be excised from and kept apart from history.

To take the politics in the politics of history seriously is not to succumb to the axiom that the victor writes history, that power is all that matters. To echo Schaap, the aspiration to reconcile is of import, and so is the pursuit of facts and truth. My reservation is rather pointed toward the notion that "truth has a despotic character", as Hannah Arendt puts it (1968: 236). In "Truth and Politics," an essay written in response to the overwhelming criticisms of her book, *Eichmann in Jerusalem*, Hannah Arendt asks why truth tellers historically have been subject to persecution. What danger did Socrates pose to the community? What makes philosophical truths so problematic for the realm of human affairs, the realm, in Plato's characterization, of men in caves watching illusions playing out on the walls?

The problem here is that the realm of thought is characterized by singularity whereas the realm of human affairs is conditioned by plurality: "[t]he trouble is that factual truth, like all other truth, peremptorily claims to be acknowledged and precludes debate, and debate constitutes the very essence of political life" (1968: 236–237). Historical factual truths can be a powerful weapon because it can stamp out politics. Yet this also illuminates how Plato's *Republic*, a rule by a philosopher-king, can also be tyrannical. What gives rise to the reluctance to bow before philosophical truth? How might we attend to this reluctance without equating all instances of reluctance to denial? To attend to the persistence of the politics of history is to shed light on the affective dimension of history writing before dismissing the resistance and reluctance to let truth rule as a sign of ignorance to be fixed.

This raises a question: how can we aspire to reconcile while also recalibrating the relationship between politics and history, without having one dominate the other? What this cursory sketch of the relationship between truth and politics evinces is the need to review the international politics of history not solely in terms of reinstating correct history against revisionist tendencies, but also to ask what animates this very turn to history. To this end, in this chapter, I offer a schematic history of historicism. Historicism is a notoriously contested term, but for this reason it is ideal for rethinking the politics of history, for politics

> involves the clash that emerges when appraisive concepts are shared widely but imperfectly, when mutual understanding and interpretation is possible but in a partial and limited way, when reasoned argument and coercive pressure commingle precariously in the endless process of defining and resolving issues.
>
> (Connolly, 1974: 40)

To ask what motivates the turn to divergent meanings of historicism among different actors at different geographical sites is to inch toward the

> realization that opposing uses might not be exclusively self-serving but have defensible reasons in their support could introduce into these contests a measure of tolerance and a receptivity . . . Politics would not be expunged, but its character would be enhanced.
>
> (Connolly, 1974: 40–41)

This is not to deny that there are self-serving uses of historicism. Yet as I argued in the Introduction, to reduce the contentions over history as being solely instrumental, to call it a history card, is to denude of the local color of the persistence into a black or white matter, its viscosity notwithstanding. How might we visualize the impasse more thickly? Instead of defining what historicism is, I ask how divergent and oppositional concepts of historicism emerge (not originate), and form a clustered impasse.

If historicism's status as a contentious term is the first reason to attend to the history of historicism, this is also anchored by another related second reason, that is, on the divergent relation between historicism and agency.

A particular phrase is repeated over and over in the film, *Judgment at Nuremberg* (1961): "I did not know it would come to this". The central figure is an idealistic American judge who arrives at Nuremberg at the end of World War II to judge the culpability of those who were in powerful positions during Hitler's reign. The phrase is uttered by German defendants, each pleading that there was no way to know, but only through hindsight, that the Holocaust would happen. The German defendants are themselves former judges, therefore rendering the film's overarching thematic as being the place of the state of/in judgment.

The repetition of the plea, "I did not know it would come to this", raises a question: what is the guarantee that individuals would act differently if they could go back in time without the hindsight that we now have? What is presupposed in judging the judges when handing out the indictment, "you should have known better"? The repetition implicitly underlines a paradoxical premise about free will, agency, and responsibility, namely, that responsibility arises where one is in a position to exercise agency – to act autonomously in time with knowledge, and to face the possibility that such action caused the suffering under question. Judith Butler writes that while telling a story and accounting for oneself are not the same, a response to an "allegation must, from the outset, accept the possibility that the self has causal agency, even if, in a given instance, the self may not have been the cause of suffering in question" (2005: 12).

While Butler writes in the context of social theory of the act of accounting for the self, in the realm of international politics, too, a similar question about the place of agency in time arises, especially as we imagine the figure of the sovereign as an agent-actor, simultaneously an actor and a unit within a society of states.[3] Yet actors are by definition partial and never omnipresent. The phrase "I did not know it would come to this" conveys the finitude of man and the limit of interweaving politics with history. But more needs to be said. While there are many ways in which history writing is problematized in global politics, quite often the issue focuses on omissions or distortion, on the politics of truth and facts, but less so on the presupposition of agency.

What I want to demonstrate in this book is that in order to see how the history problem persists in the form of a cluster, we need to delve further into what any discussion of responsibility for the past presupposes: of whether individuals have acted as autonomous agents in time, as sovereign subjects of history. It is over the state of the autonomous agent-subject – be it a sovereign, an empire, or an individual – that the concept of historicism produces dissonant definitions, thereby, in turn, implicating questions of responsibility. The tensions over history are shot through with questions of political agency, of subject and subjectivity, and this also calls for a consideration of the historical relationship between the sense of having agency and one's positionality in relation to a dominant power. To this end, we step away from contemporary Japan and to the contemporary postcolonial critique of historicism.

This turn to the postcolonial critique of historicism – put plainly that historicism served to naturalize European domination of the world – is an unexpected yet necessary move. This is because what is at stake in both instances is the question of how to respond when one's agency is denied by the other. This move is grounded in the observation that much of the discussion surrounding world history and its role in legitimating the unequal power relations that we find in the contemporary period, forcefully postulated by Dipesh Chakrabarty's *Provincializing Europe* (2000), can also be found at the turn of the twentieth century in Japan.

Engagement with postcolonial literature in postwar Japan remains marginal within the discipline of international relations. This mostly has to do with how Japan is understood as a postimperial state rather than a postcolonial state. Japan was an empire, not a colony, unless one wishes to extend the current subjugation under the U.S. alliance architecture in the Asia-Pacific in such a framework. This brief sketch shows the extent to which much of the analysis of the politics of history is based on the hindsight that we have in the present: that Japan was an empire and a colonial power. This application of what we know in the present to the past, I argue, renders the familiarity of the argument among postcolonial critics in early twentieth century Japan counterintuitive. The aim of this chapter, therefore, is to make the unexpectable expectable so as to identify what *moves* the politics of history, to envision the ingredients that constitute the debris in the present.

In this chapter, I contextualize how historicism has come to embody at least two potential meanings within the broader geopolitical tensions that inform its very oscillation: the Holy Roman Empire vs. the Sovereign, the Enlightenment progressive history vs. the German Romantic rebellion, and European imperialism vs. the non-Western resort to culture as the site of sovereignty. These layers of geopolitical formations are by no means linear or neat, but what legitimates such a schematic reconstruction are the moments when a starkly familiar argument about history can be found across different periods and across oceans.

As an expression of gratitude to the gift of hindsight and with the awareness of its limitations, the subsequent chapters are written chronologically but with an attempt at emphatic reconstruction of the historical context of the period the thinkers I engage with breathed in. The chapters are all oriented toward the aim of enabling my writing of Chapter 4 about Japanese literary critic Norihiro Kato and the postwar debate on the postwar subject of history that he stood at the center of in the 1990s.

Kato proposed in his essay, *"Haisengoron [After Defeat]"* that in order to respond to Japan's other/Asia, we must explore how to establish Japan as a subject who may respond. Before we get to read about Kato, we must read about the records of the troubles kept by many others before him, namely, the troubles over the idea of becoming the sovereign subject of history. And these records of troubles are rife outside Japan too. So Chapter 1 begins with a broader intellectual history of how history became political in the modern sense, with the birth of the subject in Renaissance Italy. This is an immanent critique of historicism rather than a neat total history. I show how the international politics of history finds its roots in the positing of human agency in the realm of history, a realm which used to belong to the whim of the gods, and how such a presupposition continues to hum in the present.

I. Explaining the unexpected: on how history becomes political in the global context

There are at least two versions of historicism that informed modern Japan's relationship to history writing, international relations, and imperialism: agency-denying historicism and agency-enabling historicism.[4] Chapters 2 and 3 will address the influence each version of historicism had in shaping Japanese foreign and colonial policies. Why it makes sense to do so is to be answered in this chapter.

In Part I, I provide the context of how historicism and colonialism have been associated in Ranajit Guha and Dipesh Chakrabarty's influential formulations on the role history writing has played in shaping international relations in modernity, in the name of the civilizing mission. I then briefly contrast this formulation to how the Japanese colonial regime has employed historicism since its Westernization in 1868 and how its use has varied over time. I do so to locate a tension between Guha's theory on history writing and the empirical evidence at hand. The tension is evidenced in the shift in terminologies used to define Japanese foreign and colonial policies from "civilization" to "culture". I make a case for differentiating between the two types of historicism: agency-denying historicism and agency-enabling historicism.[5]

In identifying the dissonance between Guha and Chakrabarty's charge against historicism and Japanese colonial theory and practice, I show that the charge leveled against the role that history writing played in legitimating colonialism in modernity needs to be modified. The relationship between history writing and colonialism is important to engage with because it affects the answer to the question of how we might undo that relationship in a manner that allows us to decolonize history. By identifying the dissonance between Guha and Chakrabarty's characterization of historicism and how historicism shaped Japanese colonial and imperial policies, I argue for the need to place historicism back in its European, and in particular German, political context to recover the alternative version of historicism – there is not one, but at least two versions of historicism.

How did the two versions of historicism come into being? To answer this, the term must be placed back in its political context. In Part II, I show that the question of how to identify history as a site of conceiving political agency and autonomy becomes a critical question in late eighteenth century Germany which, in contrast to Britain and France, was deemed "less developed". Perceived positionality in the schema of Enlightenment progressive history – in the German case, that of backwardness – matters in the sense that it shaped the efforts to conceive of the meaning of historicism differently.

Napoleon's occupation of Germany, which had yet to become a nation-state, and the failure of the revolution in Germany posed the question of how to assert autonomy against French and British hegemony. Historian Maurice Mandelbaum argues that the ambiguity of the meaning of historicism is a reflection of three interrelated yet distinct movements: the dominance of the Enlightenment view of history – which is progressive history, the subsequent Romantic rebellion against the Enlightenment in Germany, and the advent of the Darwinian concept of life. Political context matters and the stake in envisioning agency in time is inflected by the differentiation of two versions of historicism – of agency-denying historicism and agency-enabling historicism.

As a whole, my disagreement with Chakrabarty's charge against historicism is specific.[6] The critique of how the "West" employed history toward its colonialist ends fails to acknowledge that there is diversity within the "West". The limit of the binary framework becomes especially evident when any general claim about history travels to the Far East, which geopolitically is part and parcel of the "non-West", yet contain empires (Qing China, Japan, Choseon Korea in the case of East Asia), thereby productively refuting the related presupposition that "it is this sovereign self of Europe which is today being deconstructed, showing the extent to which Europe's other has been a narcissistic self-image through which it has constituted itself" (Young 2004: 49). It is not only Europe, but also elsewhere, where the positing of the self as the subject of history is being deconstructed and constructed, constituting the impasse over history.

The modification I argue for is one that acknowledges that historicism has at least two different versions, and therefore divergent implications. Acknowledging that the "West" is by no means monolithic or singular has implications for understanding how history writing became an integral part of colonial, imperial, *as well as* anti-colonial, and anti-Western discourses. This move is important to get past the blind spot that is inevitably created when questions of positionality become reified into identity politics, thereby constituting an ahistorical image of the "West" and the "non-West".

To say that history *is* Eurocentric is to occlude, in Arif Dirlik's words, "the incoherence of Eurocentrism as a historical phenomenon, because it is oblivious to the historicity of Eurocentrism, as well as to the contradictions that both dynamized its history and limited its claims" (1999: 4). For if history writing solely served colonialist modes of knowledge, why would non-Western thinkers find a stake in having their own history? Why not disavow history altogether? There is an ambiguity in the Enlightenment period's conception of historicism that appealed to non-Western subjects because historicism could also be used in the service of asserting political agency and autonomy, instead of denial.

II. Indictment of historicism: on the coloniality of knowledge

Let us examine the charge brought against historicism by Ranajit Guha. In discussing how history writing is part and parcel of colonialist knowledge, he first refers to how people in the new world were identified as "people without history" by the European conquistadors.[7] Shifting to the discussion of South Asia, he writes, "again the strategy was the same as the previous instance – that is, a joint operation of wars and words, modified only to the extent that the wars were to be British and the words German".[8] According to Guha, the war was fought by the British to subjugate the Indians, while the words came from Germany – and specifically, from the writings by Hegel on the concept of world history.

Guha refers to Hegel's *Philosophy of History*, where he connects geographical differences to temporal differences by claiming that history begins from the stagnant – here China is referred to as the "empire of stillness" – Orient and culminates in the West.[9] Such a rectilinear account of historical development presumes that there is only one path of historical movement. Different positions on the line are flattened into "before" or "after", "ahead" or "behind", "developing" or "developed", or, "the same". In this move of abstraction, "historicality as the true historical existence of man in the world is converted by the act of superseding into philosophy of history and the concreteness of the human past made to yield to the concept of World-history".[10]

World history refuses to acknowledge the complexity, richness, and historicality of India and instead defines India in terms of where it stands on this linear trajectory of historical development as mapped by Hegel. Historicism is colonialist in that the depiction of India as "backward" served to ease the conscience of liberal British authorities, for their expropriation and exploitation of the Indian people could be legitimated as the "white men's burden" to "bring up" and help "advance" the Indians so that over time, Indians can approximate the British.[11]

Likewise, Dipesh Chakrabarty has contended that Western progressive history, which for him is equivalent to historicism, has served a particular function in the reordering of the global order in modernity:

> Historicism enabled European domination of the world in the nineteenth century. Crudely, one might say that it was one important form that the ideology of progress or "development" took from the nineteenth century on. Historicism is what made modernity or capitalism look not simply global but rather as something that became global *over time*, by originating in one place (Europe) and then spreading outside it. This "first in Europe, then elsewhere" structure of global historical time was historicist . . . In the colonies, it legitimated the idea of civilization.[12]

According to Chakrabarty's characterization, historicism served to legitimate and naturalize European domination. The schema of "first in Europe, then n elsewhere" casts non-Europeans into the waiting room of history.[13] There were those who were more "civilized" than the other, and because "civilization" was deemed a good thing, those who are more "civilized" ought to help the lesser "civilized" to achieve this good. Such was the trick of historicism, which naturalized European domination.

Moreover, this trick of historicism extends well beyond the heyday of European colonialism. The language of "not yet" continues to exercise its power long after decolonization as modernization theory and developmental studies, legitimating neocolonial relations between "advanced" Western states and "developing" states elsewhere.[14] Historicism in this sense continues to frame differences, such as whether one is ahead of the other, and because the Western powers have self-appointed themselves as the epitome of what an end of history looks like, the resulting prescriptions always asks the same question: how can we make the rest look like the West? Seen this way, the charge against historicism, that it is complicit with colonialism and neocolonialism, makes sense.

In Guha and Chakrabarty's readings, historicism is part and parcel of colonialist knowledge, which continues to sustain and uphold Western hegemony. Thus, in Ann Laura Stoler's words, "students of colonialism located 'structure' with colonizers and the colonial state, and 'human agency' with subalterns, in small gestures of refusal and silence among the colonized".[15] For Guha, history writing is equated with the hegemonic structure that silences and denies the voice and agency of the colonized.[16] What one finds here is the schema that associates history with the structure that denies the agency of the subaltern.

This charge against historicism, that it is complicit with colonialist knowledge, has informed the study of Japanese history writing and colonialism by Stefan Tanaka and Alexis Dudden. Tanaka draws on Edward Said's *Orientalism* to elucidate how Japan employed on the historiography of China the same move that the French and British used on the Orient: "the French and British developed and defined a positional superiority; the Orient, as the past, was an object by which the progress of Europe could be measured".[17] According to Tanaka, modern Japanese historiography employed this cognitive framework to reconfigure the relationship between Japan and China: China became Japan's Orient.[18]

Dudden, in her study of Japan's colonization of Korea, identifies how the language of the civilizing mission served to legitimate and ease Japan's altering relationship with and domination of Korea.[19] Prior to Japan's Westernization and adoption and application of "international" law and "common" sense upon Korea, Japan and Korea were deemed "equals" who were both symbolically (and in the case of Korea, actually) vassals under Chinese suzerainty.[20] This suzerain-vassal relationship, which was characteristic of the Chinese tributary system, was recoded by the European and Japanese imposition of a new norm, which conceives of international relations as relations among independent and autonomous sovereign entities.[21]

The way in which the Japanese state legitimated its later domination and annexation of Korea in 1910 was to characterize and depict the Koreans as a "less civilized" population in need of Japanese "help". Here again, what is operational is this language of "less" or more "civilized", which posits and naturalizes unequal relations and legitimates domination. While Dudden's work examines the implication of the Japanese state's adoption of the language of international law, her work nonetheless serves to illuminate how the language of civilization served to mark Japan and Korea apart and subsequently legitimate, in Western eyes, Japan's "civilizing mission".

These two studies, and multiple others, which associate knowledge production with the discourse on power, appear to confirm the validity of Chakrabarty and Guha's charge.[22] Japan was a colonial power and the discipline of history was complicit in legitimating Japan's "civilizing mission". Such identification of history writing being complicit with Japanese imperialism has also been made by Japanese historians and socialists in postwar years as well – thereby setting the post-1945 agenda for intellectuals and historians as locating human agency among ordinary Japanese people and victims in Asia.[23]

Indeed, for theorists such as Osamu Nishitani, the idea of history is a modern import for Japan.[24] Before Westernization, there was historiography, but no "history *[rekishi]*". The term *rekishi* (in Chinese, *lishi*) was a term invented by Meiji Japanese who sought to translate Western history into Chinese characters, and this term was subsequently exported in turn to China, where, until then, there was *shi*, but no *lishi*.[25] "*Shi*" here in modern China is translated as historian, yet historically, *shi* in Zhou dynasty China is associated with the task of shamanic interpretation, as "*shi*"s responsibility was not exclusively historical. He was also a scribe and an astrologer (Iggers and Wang, 2008: 46). The early Meiji period, from 1868 to 1890, can be characterized as a period where Western knowledge was actively digested by Japanese thinkers. The state's motto of the period was *bunmei kaika* – enlightenment and civilization. This also included the idea of civilizational historicism.

For Peter Osbourne, this identification of the role historicism plays in politics shifts the stake from an epistemological matter to a political one about the affective dimension of history writing. At the same time, this attests to its "insolubility" because it also signals the tendency to reproduce the very same "structure of temporal distancing".[26] This tendency emanates from the desire to relate to historicism otherwise. Examining the longer span discourse on Japanese historicism since 1868 signals the limit to equating historicism solely with progressive history and the civilizing mission.

By 1890, critics such as Setsurei Miyake and Katsunan Kuga were arguing that this idea of civilizational history pertained only to Europe and offered no space for those in the East, the Orient. Likewise, historian Eri Hotta defines the discourse on Pan-Asianism and anti-Westernism in the 1930s and 1940s in a similar vein: that Asia is weak and something must be done about this.[27] As such, the shift of terminology associated with historicism also takes place after 1890 because Japan's relationship to and position in history had to be reconfigured, given that in the civilizational discourse, Japan, in Western eyes, was always part of the stagnant Orient. Subsequently, Japanese engagement in war and imperialism in the 1930s and 1940s was characterized as being of world historical significance, where Japan asserted itself as the subject of history.[28]

The discourse of the 1930s and 1940s, unlike that in the early Meiji era, associates cultural autonomy, rather than civilization, with historicism. The intellectual architect of this reconfiguration of history, Kiyoshi Miki, whose thesis on historicism begins with a reading of Immanuel Kant's *Third Critique*, was appointed as the head of the cultural section of Prime Minister Fumimaro Konoe's Showa Research Association. The fact that Miki was not the head of the civilizational but instead the cultural section also elucidates the need to revisit the association of history writing, civilizing mission and colonialism.

Additionally, around the same time, Japanese colonial policy toward Korea, Manchukuo, and Taiwan as well as in the Philippines was renamed "cultural" policy.[29] While the terms "civilization" and "culture" continue to be conflated in the discipline of international relations, the sudden prevalence of the term *culture* in Japanese colonial and imperial discourse poses a question: how do culture and colonialism and imperialism relate to historicism in contrast to civilization?

Placing these terminologies – civilization and culture – in their historical and political context of early twentieth-century Asia, Prasenjit Duara observes that European civilization, especially in the aftermath of World War I, came to be associated with machine civilization and materialism, and Asian civilization with culture and spirituality among Asian thinkers.[30] Likewise, Partha Chatterjee observes that for the colonized, the realm of culture and spirituality became sacred sites of contestation – especially where the colonized were dominated militarily and economically by the colonizer.[31] In Chatterjee's account, culture is associated with resistance.

Aijaz Ahmed argues that " 'culture' generally and the literary/aesthetic realm in particular are situated at great remove from the economy and are therefore, among all the superstructures, the most easily available for idealization and theoretical slippage".[32] There is a binary tendency of pitting culture against civilization in the period especially after World War I.[33] This suggests that while the term culture remains a slippery, contentious term, the shift from "civilization" to "culture" and its consistency of use across the Japanese empire, in both the realm of policy and the discourse on history, leaves the charge that historicism is part and parcel solely of civilizational and colonialist knowledge simultaneously both relevant and lacking in trying to understand how historicism became ubiquitous in the global political discourse.

In Guha's formulation of history writing's role in shaping international order, history writing is associated with the concept of civilization and as a hegemonic structure, which the colonized must rebel against. For him, this rebellion entails locating human agency among the colonized. Civilization and history writing form the structure by which the colonized is pitted against the colonizer. Yet in 1930s and 1940s Japan, culture and history writing, and not civilization, were used to legitimate Japanese imperialism and to assert Japanese agency in world history against the West and Asia. One might argue that a binary framework should never be triangulated, as it was never designed to be so. Yet given how the discourse of making new culture was employed to legitimate Japanese imperialism, Guha's strict formulation which associates history writing with the civilizing mission is wanting.

Guha's binary framework, which associates civilization, history writing, and hegemonic structure with the colonizer and the location of human agency in the colonized, attributes coherence and stability to the colonial and imperial "West". Yet this might be attributing cogency where it may not necessarily exist, constituting an ahistorical West. In her reading of the historical writings produced under the colonial administration in Dutch Indonesia, Ann Laura Stoler observes that colonial history writing is far from stable: it imbues "disquiet and anxieties . . . register[s] the febrile movements of persons off balance – of thoughts and feelings in and out of place".[34]

History writing could be read as a reflection of the exercise of hegemonic power, yet she cautions against projecting an overly coherent structure of power. For her, what is "not written" can be "distinguish[ed] between what was 'unwritten' because it could go without saying and 'everyone knew it', what was unwritten because it could not yet be articulated, and what was unwritten because it could not be said".[35] The strong association made between the European Enlightenment and imperialism also obfuscates how the Enlightenment project itself was contradictory in its intention as well as effects.[36] Stoler offers a more fine-grained approach to the study of the structure that Guha identifies as history writing, inviting one toward "the ethics of discomfort" that refuses reification (Stoler, 2016: 18).

The "West" is by no means singular in its effect, either.[37] While Britain and Germany were both colonial powers, to state that the war in India was fought by the British and the words came from Germany is to attribute undue coherence and singularity to "Western" colonial powers.[38] Earlier I alluded to how the distinction between structure and human agency was employed by Guha. Within Western political thought on historicism too this distinction could be made. The term historicism among Western powers by no means resonated across Europe in the same manner. The fact that historicism did not embody a singular meaning is underscored in historian Maurice Mandelbaum's study of late nineteenth-century European political thought from which Chakrabarty draws his definition of historicism.

According to Mandelbaum:

> *Historicism is the belief that an adequate understanding of the nature of any phenomenon and the adequate assessment of its value are to be gained through considering it in terms of the place which it occupied and the role which it played within a process of development* . . . Essential to historicism is the contention that a meaningful interpretation or adequate evaluation of any historical event involves seeing it as part of a stream of history.[39]

Chakrabarty takes this definition and connects the concept of historical development to progressive history, which is in association with a specific notion of civilization and history that he identifies with "the enlightenment".

Chakrabarty's appropriation of Mandelbaum's definition of historicism leaves out a critical caveat, which, if taken seriously, should warrant a modification of the charge against historicism. Mandelbaum acknowledges that the terms "development" and "progress" both have a directional property, yet the exact meaning of what *kind* of history one can conceive of from these terms remains open. He writes,

> There was no fundamental conflict between the views of those who conceived of history as subject to a law of Progress, and those who, on the analogy of the growth of living things, regarded development as an inherent tendency within cultures to unfold that which was implicit within them.[40]

Indeed, both images capture movement, of heading toward a place that is not here, but rather there. For political purposes, then, the actor becomes the one who acts, who is mobile, and those who are acted upon, as a site of stillness. Then, there arises a subtle difference in terms of how historical movement is envisioned on the one hand, and the question of "who" moves on the other, thereby binding geographical differences into temporal ones, albeit in not so over-deterministic a manner as Chakrabarty makes it out to be. There was no conflict, strictly in terms of ordinary language usage, between cultural development and progress as a movement. Chakrabarty, it appears, has taken Mandelbaum's definition of historicism slightly out of context.

Explaining why the term historicism is underspecified, Mandelbaum contextualizes the origin of the term in relation to two different yet related movements in late eighteenth-century Europe. What I do in the rest of this chapter is to offer a more detailed engagement with the origins of the term historicism in Europe to elucidate that (1) there are at least two versions of historicism, and that (2) the difference emerges from the question of how to conceive of political agency in time.

III. The tension within the "West": historicism and the place of human agency

As a caveat, this tracing of the ways in which the positing of political agency is intertwined with the distinction between the past (which is no more and which no one can change) and the present (which is not yet and, therefore, is in the realm of change and, therefore, of political action) constitutes the very categories that we use to periodize history and inclines substantially toward a more intellectual history of historical categories rather than a history that accounts for changes made by people.

Many of the historiographical categories that designate temporal spans and differentiate between them on one basis or another are informed by political inclinations, aspirations, and moods. For instance, the idea of modernity is constituted by its distinction from the medieval period which came before, which in turn will not have traction but for the distinction between the modern and premodern, with its implication of some distinctive rupture that neatly separates the one from the other.

Such artificial distinctions, conferred on historical kaleidoscope by a particular political, ideological, or aesthetic perspective, do not fully account for the actual flow of events that are part of histories lying outside the coherence implied by such temporal categories; histories made, unmade, and remade daily by human beings in the course of living under different circumstances and undertaking different activities, each according to their respective beliefs, rationales, and purposes. Nonetheless, I focus on this intellectual dimension of historiography because, irrespective of whether it reflects a historical reality, the categories generated by this historiographical enterprise were, and are, used by those with political dreams of making grand history, to justify their history-making actions, just as much as they are used by those who resist them.

Such is the political function of historicism. Its categories are drawn from politics in the sense that they are, to quote Frank Ankersmit, "invariably inspired by *political* idea(l)s". Even "apparently nonpolitical variants of historical writing are, in the end, no less a variant of political history than political history proper" (2001: 268). That is to say, we must attend to the political uses of history writing, including history writing that, perhaps with prejudice and perhaps inaccurately, reads and represents history making only schematically.

Further caveats are in order. The purpose of the discussion to follow is to trace the concept of agency and how it resonates among different historical actors. In doing so, we encounter many categories that assume or imply some apparently coherent and time-limited historical phenomenon, such as the "the Age of Enlightenment" or the European "Renaissance". Such categories do not do justice to the texture of time and the knotted strands of history. But within such illusory categories lie other categories, as products of those times, categories such as "will" and "freedom", which are celebrated for emancipating human history making from more theological and cosmological conceptions and hence providing the legitimation for more current political ambitions. I use these categories and these terms in order to explore the different meanings and interpretations that a subsequent politics extracted from them and not because I necessarily subscribe to their historiographical utility.

Frank Ankersmit argues that the modern origin of historical writing cannot be dissociated from its political context. For him, the point of rupture lies in the moment when Niccolò Machiavelli sought to reconfigure the study of history as a means by which to envision the potential to act differently in the future.[41] Until then Fortuna, who plays a major role in history, was symbolized by a wheel that could lift or drag men.[42]

In this reading, the Renaissance vision of history, man's relationship to history is passive: "man simply stands apart from the forces that are fighting over him; he is, in a sense, at their mercy. Though he experiences the conflict of these forces, he takes no active part in it".[43] It was this passive stance toward history which Machiavelli denounced: "the majority of those who read [history] take pleasure only in the variety of the events which history relates, without ever thinking of imitating the noble actions".[44]

What Ankersmit identifies is a shift in attitude toward history – from a realm governed by gods' whims or fortune into a realm of human affairs, where man might affect the course of history. For Ankersmit, the secularization of history translates into the politicization of history. In Vico's famous formulation, while god has nature, man has history. God has nature because he created nature and is, therefore, knowable to god but not to man. Man has history because man makes history.

By this analogy history is, therefore, knowable to man, and knowability implies predictability, or at least the potential thereof.[45] This act of laying claim to history and taking it away from god, according to Ernst Cassier, is reflective of Renaissance humanisms' confidence. Here, the image of history shifts decisively from a wheel, which lifts or drag men, to a sailboat, which man could steer though the ocean may be capricious.[46]

If during the time that is known as the Renaissance the realm of history become politicized without completely proclaiming victory over fortune, in the "Age of Enlightenment", this humility toward fortune and nature is increasingly polarized. On the one hand, there is the notion that the world in its entirety – which includes nature, in addition to history – is knowable, and, therefore, subject to manipulation and technological control. On the other, there is the increasing sense of alienation from nature, which in turn renders nature as an object of veneration and romanticization.

Alienation and disenchantment are not necessary prerequisites for a turn toward nature. Yet alienation and disenchantment did produce, especially among the European Romantics, nostalgia for a vanishing way of life and a fascination for folk simplicity and the natural state. With this polarization of opinion toward the phenomena of the world, the question, latent in the Renaissance, whose implications become accentuated in the "Age of Enlightenment" is one that concerns the autonomy of man in history.[47]

With the rise of the scientific outlook also arose the scientific study of *human nature*. There is a contradictory tendency in the European Enlightenment. On the one hand is faith in reason and rationality; the belief that "there was a universally valid standard for the assessment of human achievements, and that such a standard was accessible to reason, which was the same at *all times and in all places*".[48] On the other hand, if man is explainable by natural science, it would amount to a notion that mechanical law that governs the realm of nature is also equally applicable to human beings.

Here again, we see the complex interplay of man as the subject of history, and man as the object of historical study, which has increasingly come to be likened to the study of nature, as the three different yet related definitions of historicism hold. Therefore, in one of the many strands of historical thinking, reason knew of no boundary and, in this sense, was ahistorical. The image of nature at this point involves a disenchantment – nature comes to symbolize that which is "governed by fixed laws set up at the creation", nature is mechanical, repetitive, subject to causal regularities, and unchanging, yet first set in place by the almighty god.[49]

This ahistorical approach to the assessment of human achievement presumed that the natural scientific means of uncovering the laws governing natural phenomena could be used by social scientists to uncover historical laws that govern not only nature but also human nature.[50] Should this be the case, then humans have no volition or agency over history because they are governed by historical law not of their own making.

In his studies on the history of historicism in Europe, Mandelbaum writes that the notion of historical development emerges from two different yet related movements in late eighteenth-century Europe. The first is the extension of Enlightenment scientific thought to history, most notably in France and England. The other is the Romantic rebellion against Enlightenment history, which reimagined historical development in organicist and cultural terms, most notably in Germany. To identify how the differentiation of the two versions of historicism came into being, we will now place in context how the concept of history, culture, agency, and nature were reconfigured in Germany.

To be sure, the overview is partial and schematic because the dilemma over human agency and god and nature predates the period under discussion and, as Hannah Arendt notes, one must make a distinction between Christian theological debates on history and the secular conception of history. However, I focus less on the theological aspect of this debate in part because the main object and site of study is outside Europe in the non-Christian East, and because the intellectual debates around these issues centered on the European secular corpus and not the theological corpus.[51]

The conundrum of how to conceive of agency in history and nature in the Enlightenment period is reflected in Immanuel Kant's conflicting accounts of history and its relationship to nature. In the *Critique of Pure Reason* and the *Prolegomena*, the world is conceived of as a system of phenomena subject to necessary causal relations – the phenomena of the world are explainable and predictable and causally determined. Here, human action is as predictable as the cycles of the moon.[52] This treats the human as a biological being, part of the human species.

Yet in the *Critique of Practical Reason*, humans are beings that follow their moral obligations, which come from their own reason rather than that which is external to them. Kant marks an important break from other Enlightenment thinkers in his account of how human rational agency can be developed. Whereas other Enlightenment thinkers saw rational maturity as a process of overcoming superstition, for Kant, rational agency also hinged on questions of autonomy. Moral autonomy requires that the rational law that the rational agent is to follow emerges *endogenously* and thus autonomously, not exogenously.

For Kant, if the law is given exogenously this would negate human autonomy and human dignity. This necessitates a reconfiguration of the world outside: nature and history are objects to be legislated according to internally derived human reason: "Autonomy requires that one interrupt the natural flow of inclinations, replacing the object's effect on the will with the motive of reason".[53] In the *Foundations of the Metaphysics of Morals*, there is once again an emphasis on the human as a rational and autonomous being who legislates moral law through the use of practical reason.[54]

There is a contrast between the image of history as being dictated by the causal mechanism of nature on the one hand, and humans as moral beings who can legislate their own law and *give law to nature* on the other. The fact that the humans exist in both the sensible and rational world constitutes the abyss: how can one insist on the autonomy of one's reason when one also is part of the sensible natural world, which is dictated by a causal mechanism? The tension is as follows: do humans make history and exercise agency or are they devoid of any volition of their own, unknowingly dictated by the law of history? Who is the sovereign subject of history?

Von Krockow characterizes this abyss as a tension between structure and agent. Here, the law of history is likened to a structure, which dictates the agent's behavior, and the argument that the agent might exercise agency as an argument that affirms human volition and individuality.[55] The agent-structure dilemma translates to different levels of analysis, not limited to the individual. Does humankind shape history, or does history shape humankind? Moreover, how can one know that human agency can imprint itself in the phenomenal world? If humans make history, how can they confirm this? How can agency be affirmed and become cognizable?

Kant's answer to this question is culture:

> Man is indeed the only being on earth that has understanding and hence an ability to set himself purposes of his own choice, and in this respect he holds the title of lord of nature . . . It is a formal and subjective condition, namely, man's aptitude in general for setting himself purposes, and for using nature (independently of [the element of] nature in man's determination of purposes) as a means [for achieving them] in conformity with the maxims of his free purposes generally (hence [in a way that leaves] that being free) is *culture*. Hence only culture can be the ultimate purpose that we have cause to attribute to nature with respect to the human species.
>
> ("Critique of Teleological Judgment", [83] "On the Ultimate Purpose That Nature Has as a Teleological System", [431–432])

Unlike animals, which are presumed to merely follow their natural instinct, humans are capable of setting themselves purposes. Humans are the lords of nature because they use nature as a means of achieving ends – "he must have the understanding and the will to give both nature and himself reference to a purpose that can be independent of nature, self-sufficient, and a final purpose".[56]

Humans become the lords of nature by working on nature toward the purposes they set themselves. Still, for Kant, this culture is the culture of discipline, which "is negative and consists in the liberation of the will from the despotism of desires, a despotism that rivets us to certain natural things and renders us unable to do our own selecting".[57] It is discipline that frees humans from their natural disposition, and sets them apart from animals, and it is cultural discipline that "make[s] great headway against the tyranny of man's propensity to the senses, and so *prepares him for a sovereignty* in which reason alone is to dominate".[58]

For Kant, the way in which human autonomy over history is manifested can be discerned in the realm of culture. Here, culture is a site where humans can transcend their finitude because it is conceived of as human's working on nature, which reconfigures that which is given to them into something purposive. The existence of culture hints at the possibility of realizing humankind's progress.

It gives hope that there is a possibility of imprinting human work on nature that would last beyond the individual human's short life span.[59] Culture and the assertion of freedom and sovereignty are interlinked within Kant's *Critique of Judgment*.

Pheng Cheah offers a sociopolitical context of how culture and the organismic metaphor of the political body became an integral part of the late eighteenth-century German preoccupation with *bildung* and *kultur*, which "refer to processes of human cultivation as well as organic forms".[60] Cultivation is associated with organic forms because the term culture is a "metaphorical extension of cultivation as agrarian activity", and in the late eighteenth century, as a reaction to industrialization and atomization of social relations, culture became a critical link that connected the cultivation of inner spirituality to the phenomenal world.[61]

It is also around this time that the distinction between civilization and culture is made. Civilization is "mere civilization, which is concerned with external, sensuous, or material refinement", whereas culture – which is part of *bildung* – is an imprint of humankind's ability to rework nature toward purposive ends.[62] What Cheah's contextualization of German idealism's preoccupation with culture elucidates is how the meaning of culture is reconfigured against material civilization and as a site in which human spiritual sovereignty can be prepared within.

In addition, Cheah illuminates how the turn to and veneration of nature by German Romantics – which conceives of historical development as "unfolding" – is preceded by Kant's awkward application of the organismic metaphor to the political body. This has to do with the question of what to do with nature – which in the period of the Enlightenment was no longer divine but mechanical, blind, and antithetical to the assertion of freedom (in the sense that if human action is driven by natural instinct, then humans are no different from animals).

If humans are part of nature, then they are also dictated by mechanical causal relations, which reduce their existence to mere cogs in the grand scheme of nature. Yet Kant here is also unwilling to attribute to god the role of creator and, therefore, initiator of life. This leaves Kant with the problem of how to conceive of life in a way that is dynamic – allowing for the exercise of contingent freedom – yet also auto-causal, already containing a purposive direction.

Given this problematic, Kant turns to Johann Friedrich Blumenbach's theory of epigenesis, which conceived of organismic life as being capable of self-formation and as rational-purposive.[63] Blumenbach's concept of *Bildungstrieb* – formative force – theorized that all organisms had a force *within* their bodies that generated and shaped the body itself toward its final form.[64] His theory was significant because it also "liberated life process from divine preformation . . . [his] epigenesis is the organic counterpart of the declaration of human rights".[65]

Cheah makes this connection between human rights and epigenesis for their respective provenance in what is within, not without. As Mandelbaum observes, the dissociation of the development of mankind from divine preformation – the idea that the form of an organic being was already present at the germ cell level – allowed for imagining the development of bodies, both individual and social, as organismic. The notion of development as unfolding emerges from the attempt of human beings to theorize their freedom from external forces, divine or mechanical.[66]

Furthermore, the analogy of the political body to organismic being also was key to more egalitarian images of the political body. Prior to Kant the image of the political body was that of a machine in which the parts were subjugated to the whole. Within the image of an organismic body, the relationship of the parts to the whole was a mutually reciprocal and harmonious one, where the parts were both ends and means to one another, and to the whole.[67] This reconfiguration appealed to later German Romantics as well as Japanese thinkers in the 1930s, who envisioned society as a harmonious whole, not based on the subjugation of the part to the whole or on individualistic social-contractual relations which reduced parts into means.[68]

The organismic metaphor of the political body, therefore, represented an emancipatory hope. The metaphor serves as a fragile and tenuous link that sustains the image of the human being as an autonomous, moral being and humankind as part of nature. The turn to the organismic metaphor is an answer to the problematic of the mechanistic vision of the world, and of world politics, which seemed to threaten the possibility of spontaneity and creativity, and of envisioning agency in humans themselves.

Yet this organismic metaphor as a bridge over the abyss is tenuous because it hinges on receiving the gift of a hint from nature about human purposiveness, yet humans give themselves the credit for remaking nature through culture. Culture is now "a self-reflexive activity that brings forth in a rational creature this ability to set ends at all".[69] In this sense, this emancipatory streak in the organismic metaphor is a precarious hope.

Still, what this shows is how the later German Romantic appeal to nature and culture is underwritten by a desire to associate historicism with more agency-affirming ends amid these overlapping conundrums over how to relate agency to time and nature. The shift from German idealism to romanticism is, therefore, less of a rupture than what one might assume. And this interwovenness did not escape the eyes of those outside of the "West".

The subtle distinction between historical development as unfolding and as process is associated with the conundrum faced by Kant in trying to locate human dignity and autonomy in the organismic metaphor of unfolding. By the end of the eighteenth century, there were two ways of comprehending history according to Mandelbaum: first, historical development as process, which is history in the "superficial, outer mode" and, second, as a "mode by means of which man can penetrate to the inner springs of power-sympathetic understanding of culture".

The first looks at history as process, the second seeks to engage with history in an intimate manner where human autonomy and dignity can be discerned through the *bildung* of culture.[70] Therefore, different approaches to historicism are engendered from the interaction between Enlightenment progressive history, and the Romantic rebellion. The second kind of historicism, which conceives of historical development as unfolding, is what I call historicism informed by a culturalist approach. This cultural historicism is distinct from civilizational historicism in the sense that it revolts against the imposition of an external standard.

In this sense, the first kind of historicism is agency-denying, the second, agency-enabling. While this distinction is schematic, it serves to highlight the different place of agency in history and their respective conundrums that haunt it. For our everyday experience attests that we are seldom the masters of history, yet we are also endowed with the capacity to identify structure so as to resist it, that is, to politicize history toward the end of asserting agency.

Only by acknowledging that historicism has two versions can we identify the appeal of historicism in places where European imperialism provoked intellectuals in the non-West and colonized parts of the world to reconfigure the meaning of history for themselves. From the previous examination, what we see are two versions of historicism: agency-denying historicism, which can be related to civilizational progressive history, and agency-enabling historicism, which is associated with cultural unfolding.

As Kant's conundrum epitomizes, the turn to culture as the site of realizing human freedom is motivated by the search for autonomous ways of relating to history. The differentiation of these two versions of historicism arises from the implicit contention over how to locate agency: the thinking of history alternatively can, though it need not always, be constitutive in conceptualizing political agency.

This is the thread that knots the international politics of history. At the heart of it lies the question of the structure's relationship to the agent – what is more commonly known as the agent-structure problem, which in simple terms asks to what degree the structure determines the agent and vice versa. The dilemma that arises, as Robert Young analyzes Edward Said, is that if one were to attribute total domination by structure, as happens when Said characterizes Orientalism, then this gives rise to the question of where the critic with an Archimedean perspective could arrive *from*:

> Said wants to hang on to the individual as agent and instigator while retaining a certain notion of system and of historical determination. He must do the latter in order to argue for the existence of such a thing as "Orientalism" at all but on the other hand he must retain a notion of individual agency in order to retain the possibility of his own ability to criticize and change it.
>
> (1993: 134)

But such a move would reintroduce the agentic subject, thus leading to the recurrence of structuralist analysis committed to the developmental view (Harootunian, 2002: xv), or the opposite, analysis that romanticizes the power of the subaltern who commits what Ortner calls the "ethnographic refusal" (1995, cited in Seo, 2005: 147). What historicism stands for greatly depends upon where one identifies positionality within the given historical condition. This is to say that tracing the varying meaning of historicism says more about the politics that shapes it.

And this is the constellation of ideas that travels in unexpected places. To second Harootunian, the ways in which ideas resonate say more about the similarity of the shock experienced with the advent of modernity, regardless of geographical location, east or west (2002). It is Kant's *Third Critique* that Kiyoshi Miki picks up to reflect on the significance of the discourse on *kultur* in the Far East, Japan.

In his 1928 piece "Kagakuhihan no kadai" ["On the Task of the Critique of Science"], Miki identifies this hidden thematic of Western political thought that begins from the Greek notion of history as poetry, passes through the birth of individuality in Renaissance Italy after the fall of Rome, the rise of natural science and the secularization of the Christian concept of time, to Dilthey's existentialism, and oscillates between grounding history objectively and subjectively, alternating and grappling over the question: who is the sovereign subject of history?[71]

Conclusion

As we have seen, historicism, or historical development, has at least two versions: one is to conceive of development as process, and the other is to envision historicism as the unfolding of culture. Without acknowledging this other version of development as unfolding (and its emancipatory streak), it becomes difficult to explain why historicism became a prevalent mode of thinking world politics both with and against imperial and colonial projects. The adoption of historicism cannot be simply reduced to the slavish mimicking of the law of history or a doctrine of progress. The possibility of being independent of externally given law and the newfound appreciation of individual culture as an endogenous foundation that unites the community are critical components that might enable the envisioning of the world in an alternative manner.

Taken together, Guha's point that the words were German, and wars were fought by the British is partly right. Yet the German words he refers to are not the only kind that animated the turn toward the politics of history. Without an adequate acknowledgment of the rise of German historicism and its role in affecting non-European thinkers' attempts at envisioning alternative world order, one cannot understand how historicism became a pervasive and critical problem of international politics in the nineteenth and twentieth centuries.

Posing the question differently, if history were solely used to deny agency to the colonized, why did the colonized not simply disavow history altogether instead of seeking to become subjects of history? Why does becoming a subject of history become the prerequisite to envisioning political emancipation and agency? History becomes essential to Europe's others because developmental history in global politics has two versions: "process" and "unfolding".

Progressive process tends to be associated with linear history and causal relationships ruled by mechanical reason and law. Unfolding on the other hand is often associated with the organismic metaphor of societal development, of auto-causality and of agency free of a deterministic law of history – a promise of spontaneous agency. By showing the emancipatory dimension of historicism and the use of history, we can see why history writing appealed to anti-colonial and non-Western thinkers, instead of it becoming a matter to disavow altogether.

What the tracing of links between the organismic metaphor and historicism as unfolding in this chapter unveils is the emancipatory streak embodied in the very concept of historical development. The presupposition entailing the retrieval of this fragile hope illuminates both the appeal and danger of adopting historical thought within anti-Western and anti-colonial projects.

The kernel of hope to envision national liberation and autonomy can be discerned in anti-colonial thinkers' turn to national culture and privileging culture as the sole sovereign space that remains free of Western colonial domination.[72] The reading of historicism solely as progressive history has its limits. This misconception of historicism fails to acknowledge the struggle over how to theorize political agency and how historicism and development as unfolding were both concepts meant to contest the diminished sense of political agency in Germany and elsewhere, and, as we will see in the next chapter, in Japan.

Notes

1 Dudden, Alexis. "Standing with Historians of Japan." *American Historical Association*, 2005. www.historians.org/publications-and-directories/perspectives-on-history/march-2015/letter-to-the-editor-standing-with-historians-of-japan (Accessed January 1, 2018).

2 As will be discussed in Chapter 4, the political move by Prime Minister Shinzo Abe does have implications for history textbook content to a certain extent because the Minister of Education, Culture, Sports, Science and Technology (MEXT) is a political appointment. Nonetheless, the textbook evaluation system conducted by MEXT, on closer inspection, does not necessarily favor one textbook publisher over another. In fact, the demand for correction made of Fusosha Publisher, which has become notorious for playing down what Japan has done during wartime, is quite extensive in contrast to the correction demanded of other publishers.

   Cf. www.mext.go.jp/a_menu/shotou/kyoukasho/kentei/001.htm (Accessed December 4, 2017).

3 On this incessant conflation of state as an actor and as a unit, see Paul Schroeder (2004) and Alexander Wendt's, *Social Theory of International Politics* (New York: Cambridge University Press, 1999). For an overview of the ways in which the state is theorized within various schools of thought in contemporary international relations, John Hobson's *The State and International Relations* is useful. For a more historical account of the politics of representing the state, see Hanna Fenichel Pitkin, *The Concept of Representation* (Berkeley, Los Angeles, and London: University of California Press, 1967) and Francis William Coker, *Organismic Theories of the State* (New York: Columbia University Press, 1910).

4 Historians of the discipline of history identify three distinct definitions of what historicism is: (1) as historiographic concepts – here the method for the study of the historical kind and the natural kind are considered to be distinct and, therefore, requires a different method of interpretation; (2) as that which refers to historical laws and the assumption that there exist laws of history which would allow for predictions and explanation of historical events; and (3) as the argument that interpretation of history must be treated differently and independently from the aims of natural science which aims for prediction and explanation. This last is the definition used within historiography and not in political science and, therefore, is an implicit criticism of how political scientists use history to make predictions based on history and natural science model Cf. Robert D'Amico, "Historicism", in Aviezer Tucker ed., *A Companion to the Philosophy of History and Historiography* (Wiley-Blackwell, 2009); George H. Nadel, "The Philosophy of History before Historicism", *History and Theory*, Vol. 3, No. 3 (1964): 291–315; Georg G. Iggers, "Historicism: The History and Meaning of the Term", *Journal of the History of Ideas*, Vol. 56, No. 1 (January, 1995): 129–152; Friedrich R.

Ankersmit, "Historicism: An Attempt at Synthesis", *History and Theory*, Vol. 34, No. 3 (October, 1995): 143–161.

5 Interpretivism seeks "to understand what a thing 'is' by learning what it does, how particular people use it, in particular contexts . . . rather than seeking generalized meaning abstracted from the particular", Peregrine Schwartz-Sheah and Dvora Yanow, *Interpretive Research Design: Concepts and Processes* (New York and London: Routledge, 2012): 23.

6 I engage with Chakrabarty in particular because his work has become the canonical reference point for postcolonial approaches to the study of international relations every time history is discussed.

7 Ranajit Guha, *History at the Limit of World-History* (New York: Columbia University Press, 2002): 8.

8 Ibid.

9 Georg Hegel, "The Division of History", in *Introduction to the Philosophy of History*, trans. Leo Rauch (Indianapolis, IN: Hackett Publishing Company, 1988): 94.

10 Guha (2002: 3).

11 Uday Singh Mehta, *Liberalism and Empire: A Study in Nineteenth-Century British Liberal Thought* (Chicago: University of Chicago Press, 1999).

12 Dipesh Chakrabarty, *Provincializing Europe: Postcolonial Thought and Historical Difference* (Princeton, NJ: Princeton University Press, 2009): 7.

13 Ibid., 8–9.

14 Naeem Inayatullah and David Blaney, *International Relations and the Problem of Difference* (New York: Routledge, 2004).

15 Ann Laura Stoler, "The Pulse of the Archive", in *Along the Archival Grain: Epistemic Anxieties and Colonial Common Sense* (Princeton, NJ: Princeton University Press, 2009): 47.

16 Ranajit Guha, *Dominance without Hegemony: History and Power in Colonial India* (Cambridge: Harvard University Press, 1997).

17 Stefan Tanaka, *Japan's Orient: Rendering Pasts into History* (Berkeley, Los Angeles, and London: University of California Press, 1993): 21. I do not discuss Said in relation to Guha and Chakrabarty in part because Said modifies his stance on this cognitive framework he identifies in *Orientalism* in his subsequent work, *Culture and Imperialism*. In his later work Said notes how narratives of exclusion and inclusion cannot be easily dissociated from one another.

18 Tanaka, *Japan's Orient*.

19 Alexis Dudden, *Japan's Colonization of Korea: Discourse and Power* (Honolulu: University of Hawai'i Press, 2006).

20 Jun Yonaha, *Honyaku no Seijigaku: Kindai Higashi Ajia no Keisei to Nichiryu Kankei no henyo [Politics of Translation: Formation of Modern East Asia and Alteration of Japan-Liu'qiu Relations]* (Tokyo: Iwanami Shoten, 2009); on how Japan's relationship with Qing China was unlike that of Choseon Korea, see Ronald Toby, *State and Diplomacy in Early Modern Japan: Asia in the Development of the Tokugawa Bakufu* (Stanford, CA: Stanford University Press, 1991).

21 In fact, the language of sovereignty was so foreign in East Asia that American vessels that sought to trade with Japan ended up in Liu'qiu/Okinawa in search of a sovereign with which to enter into treaty.

22 Tak Fujitani, *Splendid Monarchy: Power and Pageantry in Modern Japan* (Berkeley: University of California Press, 1998); Carol Gluck, *Japan's Modern Myths: Ideology in the Late Meiji Period* (Princeton, NJ: Princeton University Press, 1987).

23 Victor Koschmann, *Revolution and Subjectivity in Postwar Japan* (London and Chicago: University of Chicago Press, 1996). This type of diagnosis of the "history problem" in post-1945 Japan has further contributed to the impasse over how to deal with history writing. This will be discussed in Chapter 4.

24 There is a divide on this matter between those who attend to history as philosophy, and history as historiography. For an account of history as historiography and how this is

implicated in imperial transition, see Lynn A. Struve ed., *Time, Temporality, and Imperial Transition: East Asia from Ming to Qing* (Honolulu: University of Hawai'i Press, 2005). For a more succinct account on the relation between Confucian historiography and evidential learning, see Georg Iggers and Edward Wang, *A Global History of Modern Historiography* (Great Britain: Pearson Education Limited, 2008): 46–58.

25 Osamu Nishitani, *Sekaishi no Rinkai [Limits of History]* (Tokyo: Iwanami Shoten, 2006): 62.

26 Peter Osbourne, *The Politics of Time: Modernity and Avant-Garde* (London and New York: Verso, 1995): 18.

27 Eri Hotta, *Pan-Asianism and Japan's War 1931–1945* (New York: Palgrave Macmillan, 2013).

28 Kiyoshi Miki, in Hiroshi Uchida ed., *Miki Kiyoshi Toa Kyodotai Ronshu [Collected Essay of Kiyoshi Miki's East Asian Cooperative Body]* (Tokyo: Kobushi Shobo, 2007).

29 On the cultural turn in Japanese historiography, see Louise Young, "Early-Twentieth Century Japan in a Global Context: Introduction to Japan's New International History", *American Historical Review* (October, 2014): 1117–1128; see also Ethan Mark, "The Perils of Co-Prosperity: Takeda Rintaro, Occupied Southeast Asia, and the Seductions of Postcolonial Empire", *American Historical Review* (October, 2014): 1184–1206.

30 Prasenjit Duara, "The Discourse of Civilization and Pan-Asianism", *Journal of World History*, Vol. 12, No. 1 (2001): 99–130.

31 Partha Chatterjee, *Nation and Its Fragments: Colonial and Postcolonial Histories* (Princeton, NJ: Princeton University Press, 1993): 24–26.

32 Aijaz Ahmed, *In Theory: Classes, Nations, Literatures* (London and New York: Verso, 1994): 8.

33 On the origin of how Asia came to be identified as spiritual see Rustom Bharucha, *Another Asia: Rabindranath Tagore & Okakura Tenshin* (New Delhi: Oxford University Press, 2010).

34 Stoler (2010: 1–2).

35 Ibid., 3.

36 This book treats the European Enlightenment, as a placeholder, as being artificially consistent. For an overview of the different strands of Enlightenment in Europe, see Jonathan Israel, *Radical Enlightenment: Philosophy and the Making of Modernity 1650–1750* (Oxford: Oxford University Press, 2002).

37 To be sure, the critics of the West make a distinction between the so-called real geographical West and the geopolitical West.

38 Said acknowledges that his charge in *Orientalism* is based on British and French Orientalism and does not take into account the difference between GermanOrientalism and British Orientalism.

39 Maurice Mandelbaum, *History, Man and Reason: A Study in Nineteenth-Century Thought* (Baltimore: Johns Hopkins University Press, 1977): 42–43.

40 Ibid., 44–45.

41 Friedrich R. Ankersmit, *Historical Representation* (Stanford, CA: Stanford University Press, 2001): Reinhart Kosselleck, *Futures Past: On the Semantics of Historical Time*, trans. Keith Tribe (New York: Columbia University Press, 2004); Claude Lefort, "Machiavelli: History, Politics, Discourse", in David Carroll ed., *The States of "Theory": History, Art, and Critical Discourse* (New York and Oxford: Columbia University Press, 1990).

42 Ankersmit, *Historical Representation*, 266.

43 Ernst Cassirer, *The Individual and the Cosmos in Renaissance Philosophy*, trans. Mario Domandi (Chicago: University of Chicago Press, 1963): 76–77.

44 Niccolò Machiavelli, *The Discourses* (New York: The Modern Library, 1950): 104.

45 Hannah Arendt, "The Concept of History", in *Between Past and Future: Eight Exercises in Political Thought* (New York: Penguin Classics, 2006): 77.

46 Cassirer (1963: 76–77).

47 Christian Graf von Krockow, *Die Entscheidung [Ketsudan: Yunga, Shumitto, Haidegga]*, trans. Tamaki Takada (Tokyo: Kashiwa Shobo, 1999): 20.
48 Mandelbaum (1971: 52). Italics mine.
49 Stephen Toulmin, *Cosmopolis: The Hidden Agenda of Modernity* (Chicago: University of Chicago Press, 1992): 110.
50 Manuel quotes French philosopher Claude Helvetius "that morals should be treated like all other sciences, and that one should arrive at a moral principle as one proceeds with an experiment in physics. The moral laws thus scientifically derived would be useful to society. Just as the physical laws of science had led to technological inventions and progress in the mechanical arts, so the formation of moral laws would result in greater social progress for humanity." Frank E. Manuel, *The Age of Reason* (Paper Book Press, 1993): 38–39. Also see J.W. Burrow, "The Stuff of the World and the Promises of Science", in *The Crisis of Reason: European Thought, 1848–1914* (New Delhi: Yale University Press, 2000): 33.
51 For a thorough Western history of theology, sovereignty, and god, see Jean Bethke Elshtain, *Sovereignty: God, State, and Self* (New York: Basic Books, 2008); Karl Lowith, *Meaning in History: The Theological Implications of the Philosophy of History* (1957).
52 Immanuel Kant, *Critique of Judgment Including the First Introduction*, trans. with an introduction by Werner S. Pluhar (Indianapolis and Cambridge: Hackett Publishing Company, 1987); Lewis White Beck, "Editor's Introduction", in Lewis White Beck ed., *On History* (Indianapolis: The Library of Liberal Arts, 1981): xvi.
53 Lewis Hinchman, "Autonomy, Individuality, and Self-Determination", in James Schmidt ed., *What Is Enlightenment? Eighteenth-Century Answers and Twentieth-Century Questions* (Berkeley, Los Angeles, and London: University of California Press, 1996): 490–495.
54 Hannah Arendt, *Lectures on Kant's Political Philosophy*, ed. Ronald Beiner (Chicago: University of Chicago Press, 1992): 26–27.
55 Von Krockow (1999: 20, 25).
56 Kant (1987: 431).
57 Ibid., 432.
58 Ibid., 434). Italics mine.
59 Pheng Cheah, *Spectral Nationality: Passages of Freedom from Kant to Postcolonial Literatures of Liberation* (New York: Columbia University Press, 2003): 96.
60 Ibid., 38. Jennifer Mensch defines organicism as a "view of nature as something that cannot be reduced to a set of mechanical operations. The stage for organicism was historically set by investigations into the connected concerns of natural history and embryogenesis, investigations leading to inevitable conclusions regarding nature's vitality and power." *Kant's Organicism: Epigenesis and the Development of Critical Philosophy* (Chicago and London: University of Chicago Press, 2013): 1.
61 Cheah (2003: 39).
62 Ibid., 44.
63 Ibid., 25, 54–55.
64 Ibid., 87.
65 Ibid., 54–55.
66 Mandelbaum (1971: 57).
67 Cheah (2003: 74); An "organism's autonomous constitution and political freedom elucidates the sociopolitical values of liberty and equality in terms of the organism's three moments. The reciprocal causal relationship between an organism's parts implies equality amongst citizens. That the parts produce each other and whole at the same time that the whole produces the parts implies the liberty of the citizens vis-à-vis the polity. The reciprocity of the parts and whole clearly contradicts the myth that the organismic metaphor justifies a despotic and instrumentalist relation between the political body and its citizenry". 90–91.
68 Cheah (2003: 31); also Frederick C. Beiser ed., *The Early Political Writings of the German Romantics* (Cambridge: Cambridge University Press, 1996): xii–xiii. On the

Japanese conception of organismic whole, see Harry Harootunian, *Overcome by Modernity: History, Culture, and Community in Interwar Japan* (Princeton, NJ: Princeton University Press, 2000).
69   Cheah (2003: 97).
70   Mandelbaum (1971: 59).
71   Kiyoshi Miki, "Kagakuhihan no kadai [On the Task of the Critique of Science]", in *Gendai Nihon Shiso Taikei 33 [Contemporary Japanese Political Thought 33]* (Tokyo: Chikuma Shobo, 1975). See Michael Allen Gillespie, *Hegel, Heidegger, and the Ground of History* (Chicago and London: University of Chicago Press, 1984) for a lucid sketch of this arc. Also, Azade Seyhan, *Representation and Its Discontents: The Critical Legacy of German Romanticism* (Berkeley, Los Angeles, and Oxford: University of California Press, 1992).
72   Chatterjee, *Nation and Its Fragments*; on the European use of technological supremacy to justify its civilizing mission cf. Michael Adas, *Machines as the Measure of Men: Science, Technology, and Ideologies of Western Dominance* (Ithaca, NY: Cornell University Press, 1990).

References

Adas, Michael. *Machines as the Measure of Men: Science, Technology, and Ideologies of Western Dominance*. Ithaca, NY: Cornell University Press, 1990.

Ahmed, Aijaz. *In Theory; Classes, Nations, Literatures*. London and New York: Verso, 1994.

Ankersmit, Frank R. "Historicism: An Attempt at Synthesis." *History and Theory* 34, no. 3 (1995): 143–161.

Ankersmit, Frank R. *Historical Representation*. Stanford, CA: Stanford University Press, 2001.

Arendt, Hannah. *Between Past and Future: Eight Exercises in Political Thought*. New York: Viking Press, 1968.

Arendt, Hannah. *Lectures on Kant's Political Philosophy*. Chicago: University of Chicago Press, 1989.

Barucha, Rustom. *Another Asia: Rabindranath Tagore & Okakura Tenshin*. New Delhi: Oxford University Press, 2010.

Beiser, Frederick ed. *The Early Political Writings of the German Romantics*. Cambridge: Cambridge University Press, 1996.

Burrow, J.W. *The Crisis of Reason: European Thought, 1848–1914*. New Delhi: Yale University Press, 2000.

Butler, Judith. *Giving an Account of Oneself*. New York: Fordham University Press, 2005.

Cassirer, Ernst. *The Individual and the Cosmos in Renaissance Philosophy*. Translated by Mario Domandi. Chicago: University of Chicago Press, 1963.

Chakrabarty, Dipesh. *Provincializing Europe: Postcolonial Thought and Historical Difference*. Princeton, NJ: Princeton University Press, 2000.

Chatterjee, Partha. *Nation and Its Fragments: Colonial and Postcolonial Histories*. Princeton, NJ: Princeton University Press, 1993.

Cheah, Pheng. *Spectral Nationality: Passages of Freedom from Kant to Postcolonial Literatures of Liberation*. New York: Columbia University Press, 2003.

Coker, Francis William. *Organismic Theories of the State*. New York: Columbia University Press, 1910.

Connolly, William. *Terms of Political Discourse*. Princeton, NJ: Princeton University Press, 1974.

D'Amico, Robert. "Historicism." In *A Companion to the Philosophy of History and Historiography*, edited by Aviezer Tucker. Malden, MA: Wiley-Blackwell, 2009.

Dirlik, Arif. "Is There History after Eurocentrism?: Globalism, Postcolonialism, and the Disavowal of History." *Cultural Critique* no. 42 (Spring 1999): 1–34.

Duara, Prasenjit. "The Discourse of Civilization and Pan-Asianism." *Journal of World History* 12, no. 1 (2001): 99–130.

Dudden, Alexis. *Japan's Colonization of Korea: Discourse and Power*. Honolulu: University of Hawai'i Press, 2006.

Dudden, Alexis. "Standing with Historians of Japan." *American Historical Association*, 2005. www.historians.org/publications-and-directories/perspectives-on-history/march-2015/letter-to-the-editor-standing-with-historians-of-japan (Accessed January 1, 2018).

Elshtain, Jean Bethke. *Sovereignty: God, State, and Self*. New York: Basic Books, 2008.

Fasolt, Constant. *The Limits of History*. Chicago and London: University of Chicago Press, 2004.

Fujitani, Takashi. *Splendid Monarchy: Power and Pageantry in Modern Japan*. Berkeley: University of California Press, 1998.

Gillespie, Michael. *Hegel, Heidegger, and the Ground of History*. Chicago and London: University of Chicago Press, 1984.

Gluck, Carol. *Japan's Modern Myths: Ideology in the Late Meiji Period*. Princeton, NJ: Princeton University Press, 1987.

Guha, Ranajit. *Dominance without Hegemony: History and Power in Colonial India*. Cambridge: Harvard University Press, 1997.

Guha, Ranajit. *History at the Limit of World-History*. New York: Columbia University Press, 2002.

Harootunian, Harry. *Overcome by Modernity: History, Culture, and Community in Interwar Japan*. Princeton, NJ: Princeton University Press, 2002.

Hegel, Georg. *Introduction to the Philosophy of History*. Translated by Leo Rauch. Indianapolis, IN: Hackett Publishing Company, 1988.

Hinchman, Lewis. "Autonomy, Individuality, and Self-Determination." In *What Is Enlightenment? Eighteenth-Century Answers and Twentieth-Century Questions*, edited by James Schmidt. Berkeley, Los Angeles, and London: University of California Press, 1996.

Hobson, John. *The State and International Relations*. New York: Cambridge University Press, 2000.

Hotta, Eri. *Pan-Asianism and Japan's War: 1931–1945*. New York: Palgrave Macmillan, 2007.

Iggers, Georg. "Historicism: The History and Meaning of the Term." *Journal of the History of Ideas* 56, no. 1 (1995): 129–152.

Iggers, Georg and Edward Wang. *A Global History of Modern Historiography*. Great Britain: Pearson Education Limited, 2008.

Inayatullah, Naeem and David Blaney. *International Relations and the Problem of Difference*. New York: Routledge, 2004.

Israel, Jonathan. *Radical Enlightenment: Philosophy and the Making of Modernity 1650–1750*. Oxford: Oxford University Press, 2002.

Kant, Immanuel. *Critique of Judgment Including the First Introduction*. Translated with an introduction by Werner S. Pluhar. Indianapolis and Cambridge: Hackett Publishing Company, 1987.

Koschmann, Victor. *Revolution and Subjectivity in Postwar Japan*. London and Chicago: University of Chicago Press, 1996.

Kosselleck, Reinhart. *Futures Past: On the Semantics of Historical Time*. Translated by Keith Tribe. New York: Columbia University Press, 2004.

Kramer, Stanley, Abby Mann, Spencer Tracy, Burt Lancaster, Marlene Dietrich, Judy Garland, Maximilian Schell, Montgomery Clift, and Abby Mann. 1996. *Judgment at Nuremberg*. Santa Monica, CA: Distributed by MGM/UA Home Video.

Krockow, Christian. *Die Entscheidung [Decisionism: Junger, Schmitt, Heidegger]*. Translated by Tamaki Takada. Tokyo: Kashiwa Shobo, 1999.

Lefort, Claude. "Machiavelli: History, Politics, Discourse." In *The States of 'Theory': History, Art, and Critical Discourse*, edited by David Carroll. New York and Oxford: Columbia University Press, 1990.

Lowith, Karl. *Meaning in History: The Theological Implications of the Philosophy of History*. Chicago: University of Chicago Press, 1949.

Machiavelli, Niccolò. *The Prince and the Discourses*. New York: The Modern Library, 1950.

Mandelbaum, Maurice. *History, Man, & Reason: A Study in Nineteenth-Century Thought*. Baltimore: The Johns Hopkins University Press, 1971.

Manuel, Frank. *The Age of Reason*. New York: Cornell University Press, 1951.

Mark, Ethan. "The Perils of Co-Prosperity: Takeda Rintaro, Occupied Southeast Asia, and the Seductions of Postcolonial Empire." *American Historical Review* 119, no. 4 (2014): 1184–1206.

Mehta, Uday Singh. *Liberalism and Empire: A Study in Nineteenth-Century British Liberal Thought*. Chicago: University of Chicago Press, 1999.

Mensch, Jennifer. *Kant's Organicism: Epigenesis and the Development of Critical Philosophy*. Chicago and London: University of Chicago Press, 2013.

Miki, Kiyoshi. "Kagakuhihan no Kadai [On the Task of Critique of Science]." In *Gendai Nihon Shiso Taikei 33 [Contemporary Japanese Political Thought 33]*. Tokyo: Chikuma Shobo, 1975.

Miki, Kiyoshi. *Miki Kiyoshi Toa Kyodotai Ronshu [Collected Essay of Kiyoshi Miki's East Asian Cooperative Body]*. Edited by Hiroshi Uchida. Tokyo: Kobushi Shobo, 2007.

Nadel, George. "The Philosophy of History before Historicism." *History and Theory* 3, no. 3 (1964): 291–315.

Nishitani, Osamu. *Sekaishi no Rinkai [Limits of History]*. Tokyo: Iwanami Shoten, 2006.

Osbourne, Peter. *The Politics of Time: Modernity and Avant-Garde*. London and New York: Verso, 1995.

Pitkin, Hanna. *The Concept of Representation*. Berkeley, Los Angeles, and London: University of California Press, 1967.

Said, Edward. *Culture and Imperialism*. New York: Vintage Books, 1993.

Seo, Jungmin. "Nationalism and the Problem of Political Legitimacy in China," in Lynn White ed., *Legitimacy: Ambiguities of Political Success or Failure in East and Southeast Asia*. River Edge, NJ: World Scientific Publishing Co, 2005: 141–182.

Schaap, Andrew. *Political Reconciliation*. London and New York: Routledge, 2005.

Schroeder, Paul. *Systems, Stability, and Statecraft: Essays on the International History of Modern Europe*. New York: Palgrave Macmillan, 2004.

Schwartz-Sheah, Peregrine and Dvora Yanow. *Interpretive Research Design: Concepts and Processes*. New York and London: Routledge, 2012.

Seyhan, Azade. *Representation and Its Discontents: The Critical Legacy of German Romanticism*. Berkeley, Los Angeles, and Oxford: University of California Press, 1992.

Stoler, Ann. *Along the Archival Grain: Epistemic Anxieties and Colonial Common Sense*. Princeton, NJ: Princeton University Press, 2010.

Stoler, Ann. *Duress: Imperial Durabilities in Our Times*. Durham, NC: Duke University Press, 2016.

Struve, Lynn A. ed. *Time, Temporality, and Imperial Transition: East Asia from Ming to Qing.* Honolulu: University of Hawai'i Press, 2005.

Tanaka, Stefan. *Japan's Orient: Rendering Pasts into History.* Berkeley: University of California Press, 1993.

Toby, Ronald. *State and Diplomacy in Early Modern Japan: Asia in the Development of the Tokugawa Bakufu.* Stanford, CA: Stanford University Press, 1991.

Toulmin, Stephen. *Cosmopolis: The Hidden Agenda of Modernity.* Chicago: University of Chicago Press, 1992.

Wendt, Alexander. *Social Theory of International Politics.* New York: Cambridge University Press, 1999.

Yonaha, Jun. *Honyaku no Seijigaku: Kindai Higashi Ajia no Keisei to Nichiryu Kankei no Henyo [Politics of Translation: Formation of Modern East Asia and Alteration of Japan-Liu'qiu Relations].* Tokyo: Iwanami Shoten, 2009.

Young, Louise. "Introduction: Japan's New International History." *American Historical Review* (2014): 1117–1128.

Young, Robert. *White Mythologies: Writing History and the West.* 2nd ed. New York: Routledge, 2004.

2　On the rise and demise of civilizational history in Meiji Japan

The study of the past is often deemed as off-limits to politicization so long as one takes proper precaution to separate ideology and questions of morality from the objective study of the past. But the separation is seldom clean. In the case of Japan, the inception of the independent discipline of Japanese history had to reconfigure the political meaning of knowledge production which had long been derived from *kangaku akademizumu* – based on Chinese learning, and that of the influx of *bunmeishi* – Enlightenment history from the West.[1] The Enlightenment view of history is reflective of the rise of science and the rational view of the world. Speaking from the hindsight we have today, that wartime Japanese history was nationalistic and mired in myths, this raises a question: if Enlightenment history was influential in Japan, how did such commitment to critical study of evidence lose to the state propagation of such unscientific myths? To answer this question, we must place it in relation to how the political agency of the emergent Japanese state became associated with discussions of methods and objectivity. To this we turn to the dual meaning of historicism.

There are at least two versions of historicism: that which denies agency and that which enables agency. In this chapter, I argue that the version of historicism embraced is informed by one's shifting awareness and understanding of how one's positionality in Western historical time is intrinsically related to how inter-"national" politics is conducted. This chapter shows how in Meiji Japan, there is a shift from embracing agency-denying historicism to yearning for agency-enabling historicism as Meiji intellectuals become aware of how civilizational history and sustenance of Eurocentric international order go hand in hand. History writing is a political matter, as it is tied to one's projection of a sense of having agency in time.

Frank Ankersmit writes that the birth of modern historical writing takes place in sixteenth century Renaissance Italy when man does what the god of evolution hates: acts independently.[2] History prior to that moment belonged to the realm of god and was meant to be beyond man's comprehension. Machiavelli rebelled against such a view of history. He writes in the beginning of the *Discourses* that against "the lack of real knowledge of history" he is introducing a new kind of possibility: the possibility of imitating noble actions.[3] While Machiavelli concedes that Fortuna exercises great power over the outcome of political action, he nonetheless argues that "our free-will may not be altogether extinguished".[4] For him, the exercise of free will is akin to building dykes to channel the river named fortune. The study of history is what would enable the prince to build such dykes against Fortuna. Here, the gradual secularization of history is intertwined with objective study of the past toward a political end.

From that point on, much ink and blood have been spilled over acceptable modes of history. In the Age of Reason, advancement in science and technology led many to believe that not only in the realm of nature but also in history could one discern a governing principle and law behind historical phenomenon. Myths were to be eradicated and replaced with causal explanations of historical change. Such was the trend in England and France. But not all in Europe embraced this idea, especially not in Germany, a state which was considered "backward" in contrast to Britain and France.[5] Amid this reservation toward a scientific understanding of history, German historicism was born.[6] The previous chapter covered this German Romantic rebellion against Enlightenment history. Contra Chakrabarty, we found in nineteenth-century Europe two kinds of theories about historical development: one that considers historical development as "progressive", and the other that considers historical development as "unfolding".[7]

In the nineteenth century, history writing and global politics become inextricably linked. In European colonies, the European right to rule was in part justified by the colonized's "lack of history".[8] Here, Chakrabarty's characterization is apt: progressive history, or historicism, arrived to the non-West as Europe's way of telling the rest "not yet".[9] Progressive history provided a hierarchical scale to rank and order who was more civilized. The degree of one's civilization was measured according to how scientific one's approach to the study of the past was. What figures like James Mill found unscientific in existing Indian historical writing was the absence of a principle of cause and effect.[10] Hegel similarly dismisses historical writings in India and China because he claimed they lacked development. He writes that there are two kinds of states, the unhistorical and historical: "on the one side we see duration, stability; we see empires of *space*, as it were – an unhistorical history [i.e., a history without development in time] – as, for example, in China". On the other side, "spatial durability is countered by the form of *time*: the states, without changing in themselves or in principle, undergo endless change".[11] Because it lacks development, China is an empire of stillness.[12]

Importantly, Europe did not always depict Asian civilizations as undeveloped and without history. Up until the turn of eighteenth century, both Europe and China were considered civilizations. Yet by the second half of eighteenth century, the European image of Chinese civilization became a civilization that had already attained its height and now it was with this sense of Western triumph that the region of "Asia" becomes implicated in Western world history. To begin to speak of Asia, it must be first noted that Asia refers to both a geographical position and a theoretical position. As a geographical term, Asia means to an area east of Europe, which was first called "Asia" by Europeans.[13] Thus, the awareness of being Asian arises from an external naming and calling. As a theoretical position, Asia designates a site of stillness against which the West is the ever-changing subject of world history.

For example, in what might be considered to be one of the more problematic passages in Hegel's *Introduction to the Philosophy of History*, he explicitly designates Asia as being not only relatively, but also absolutely, east of Europe:

> World history goes from East to West: as Asia is the beginning of world history, so Europe is simply its end. In world history there is an absolute East, *par excellence* (whereas the geographical term "east" is in itself entirely relative); for although the earth is a sphere, history makes no circle around that sphere. On the contrary, it has a definite East which is Asia.[14]

The concept of Asia here becomes marked as a region which is always at the beginning of history. The concept of the absolute east provides Europe with both origin and direction. Asia is where the sun rises, achieving ever "higher brilliance" as it moves toward the west.[15] One might object to such characterization, because in most parts of the world, our orientation to the sun is always relative. Yet for Hegel, world history is unidirectional, as "history makes no circle around [the earth's] sphere".[16] In world history, Asia can never catch a hold of the West. From the east, one might wait for the west in the morning, noon, and night as the sun rises, soaking the land with its ray and gradually retreating into the silence of the horizon, only to be told that her positionality is not relative but absolute. The west will never come back to the east, as it has unilaterally reconfigured how time is to pass: time is neither no longer about the eternal oscillation between countless days and nights, nor about cyclical patterns where dynasties fall and rise, but directional. World history "goes from East to West", there is no replacing of the east with the west because the terms are no longer relational and relative but relational and absolute. And it is in the moment when a relative category is reified as an absolute identity that the politics of imagining Asia as civilizational or otherwise begins.

In the late eighteenth century, this conflation of historical underdevelopment or stagnation with particular geographical regions became fixed in Eurocentric historical narratives. This leaves thinkers in Asia with a peculiar condition: to affirm the idea of historical development is to deny one's agency, because Europe depicts Asia as a calcified backward site without historical movement. Yet to adopt a modern approach to history, this very act of denial seems unavoidable. The problem of how to think of historical development in Asia has, therefore, revolved around the question of how to conceive of political agency. This conundrum is initiated with the arrival of Western gunboats and unequal treaties at the shores of East Asia.

This chapter provides the context of this conundrum in order to elucidate the political stakes of rethinking Eurocentric histories and "Asia" for those living in a geographical space designated as backward. The writing of history is not solely about methodological accuracy. There is much more at stake. Contentions over how to write history are underwritten by one's desire to conceive of her agency in historical writing against those who would deny her agency. I elucidate this point by showing how one kind of theory of historical development, in this case civilizational history and a scientific approach to the study of the past, is embraced and then rejected by various segments of Japanese society in the early Meiji period. Civilizational history was one form of understanding historical development which was imported from Britain and France, and championed by leading thinkers such as Yukichi Fukuzawa and Ukichi Taguchi. Similarly, within the establishment of the academic study of history, figures such as Kunitake Kume and Yasutsugu Shigeno advocated for a scientific approach to history. While the shift from *hua-yi*, or Sinocentric order, arrived in a violent manner, the desirability of becoming civilized was a common premise held among both Westerners and the Japanese. This eased the adoption of the civilizational discourse in Japan. The idea of civilization and science resonated with the Meiji slogan of *bunmei kaika* (civilization and opening), and Fukuzawa and Shigeno are representative figures of this period. Yet by the 1890s there was a disillusionment with the racialized nature by which the concept of historical development had been employed by Western powers to deny equality to the non-Western Other.[17] In civilizational history, historical development takes place in a linear movement, whereby the West is ahead of the rest and Asia is posited as the stagnant Other. The French and British approach to historical development is found wanting because in their accounts, climate or race determined civilizational history, denying agency to Japan and to Asia at large. In this chapter, I trace the rise and wane of civilizational history in "Asia".

I. From hua-yi to civilization and enlightenment

Interstate order in East Asia before the mid-nineteenth century was governed by the principle of *hua-yi*, *hua* meaning the flowering of civilization and *yi* meaning the lesser civilized. The center of civilization was China, and its emperor and the other states were deemed as vassal kings. The kings were to pay tribute to the emperor periodically, and the tributary mission was accompanied by trade in goods.[18] The tributary system was not enforced uniformly across the region. Choseon Korea was closer and more thoroughly integrated into the hua-yi order, whereas Tokugawa Japan, unwilling to submit to the Chinese emperor, created its own miniature hua-yi order by 1630, claiming to be the center of the region while knowing all too well that their system of governance was an imitation of China's.[19] Korea and Liu'qiu – present-day Okinawa – sent tributes to both China and Japan while demonstrating which was deemed more important by the frequency of the missions.[20] Historian Jun Yonaha would characterize the order as "loose", hinging on the mutual agreement among parties to not take the hua-yi hierarchy too literally.[21] As for relations with the West, all four states banned the entry of Christian missionaries and permitted trade with states which respected this refusal. Therefore, while the French and the British were refused, the Portuguese and Dutch merchants were granted trading rights in the port of Nagasaki.

U.S., British, Russian, and French ships began to dot the shores in the nineteenth century. Korea and Japan refused the entry of these ships and when deemed necessary, shot at them. In 1837, an American ship was shot by the Japanese. In

1866, Korea shot another American ship. In the same year, the French waged an attack on Korea on grounds that it prohibited its missionary goal. While Korea and Japan sought to sustain their isolation from Western powers by defensive military means, Qing China took different measures vis-à-vis the West. Qing China permitted trade with Britain, writing in its own account that this was a way of giving pity to and appeasing the barbaric British in order to ultimately shoo them away. The British found themselves losing silver to the Chinese and resorted to selling addictive opium to resolve its trade deficit. In 1839, Qing bureaucrat Zexu Lin, in the interest of protecting the health of Qing empire's own population, apprehended a British merchant and dumped the opium. In Britain, the incident was transformed from a question of whether it was ethical to export a pernicious item which was banned within Britain into a self-righteous demand for the right to free trade.[22] In the name of promoting free trade, the Opium War was waged in 1840. The Opium War was a watershed moment in the history of East Asian interstate relations. Qing China, the long-standing center of civilization in the hua-yi order, was defeated by the British, which was considered as "yi", a lesser civilized entity. Thus, military defeat of Qing signaled an end to the era of hua-yi order and the beginning of a tumultuous period characterized by unequal treaties, intense structural transformation of the region, and incessant wars. Seeing the defeat of Qing, Japan repealed its orders to shoot any encroaching foreign ships in 1842.

In the immediate aftermath of the Opium War, there was a subtle shift in the way civilization was assessed within Japan. Although the initial news of the British defeat of Qing was received with much empathy, the moral of the story quickly altered into a lesson about humility. It was explained that Qing China was defeated for its arrogance and unwillingness to change.[23] The greatness of China was history. The actual China in front of Japan was hapless and hopelessly outmoded and stagnant. The image of stagnant China became further reinforced in Japanese Meiji-era intellectual Yukichi Fukuzawa's writings. For Fukuzawa, Confucian thought was impractical and useless. Real learning, which Fukuzawa sought to encourage, lay in the study of Western civilization.[24] The Opium War's outcome came to symbolize that Qing had lost its ability to lead and relate to the world. *Zhongguo*, the Middle Kingdom, was thus decentered in the Japanese eyes.

Among the four states of Qing, Choseon Korea, Japan, and Vietnam, which belonged to the tributary system, Japan was the first to initiate Westernization. With regard to the timing of Westernization, historians such as Shinichi Kitaoka attribute this to Japan's traditionally peripheral status in relation to the hua-yi order. In his formulation, China was long accustomed to considering itself the civilizational center of the world. This in turn made it difficult to recognize the potential superiority of other civilizations. Korea reacted similarly to Qing China, because it, too, considered itself as the true center of the civilized universe since the Ming-Qing transition.[25] In contrast, even before Westernization thinkers in Japan were accustomed to evaluating Japan in relative terms it had always been peripheral to neighboring China.[26] In Kitaoka's formulation, Westernization for Japan was less debilitating to its sense of centeredness because it was never truly a center of the region to begin with.

In addition, among the four states, Japan was the only one which was ruled by the military class and not the Confucian bureaucrats. Kitaoka claims that this enabled Japan to quickly make a realistic assessment of its prospects based on military power disparity instead of denouncing the British use of force as barbaric and against a Confucian ethical mode of conduct.[27] Indeed, the Opium War was a watershed moment for figures such as Shozan Sakuma, who was trained in Confucian political thought, to reevaluate the very values which used to give meaning to the world. Confucian ethics and values appeared to be of little use in front of Western military technology and guns. In the news of British defeat of Qing China, Sakuma sensed an arrival of a new era where practicality and military might would speak more than right.[28]

These factors may explain the turn to practical *(jissenteki)* politics, yet it does not explain why a Western approach to history, in this case, civilizational history, rapidly spread in early Meiji political discourse. After all, updating one's military capability would have practical consequences, whereas adopting Western civilizational history would seem to do little in helping Japan avoid subjugation by the Western powers.

Historian Hiroshi Watanabe poses an explanation for Japan's early Westernization in the study of history. Watanabe argues that what facilitated the engagement with Westernization and Western civilizational history was the ambiguity of the term civilization and its historical movement in Japanese political thought. Because history oscillated between the rise and fall of dynasties in Asia, the tentative rise of standards of living resonated with the notion of progress – the tentative uplift experienced between the cycles of rise and fall was not unfamiliar; therefore, the notion of progress and its sense of rise did not appear unfamiliar to the masses. In this regard, the notions of opening and progress came to be accepted and were often treated as two interchangeable terms. Yet just because the terms "*Bunmei*/Civilization" and "*Kaika*/Opening" were used did not mean that there was faith in human improvement or agency. The term "opening" is not spelled as an active verb in the Japanese language – one does not say that "I am opening history".[29] Rather, the closer translation of the attitude toward *bunmei kaika* would be more akin to "history is opening", where the subject of the sentence is wholly unclear and absent. The notion of progressive history and opening of civilization, therefore, appear similar on its surface, yet the assumption about the role of human agency is starkly different. This is to say that the notion of opening and progress have overlapped in the Japanese people's understanding of history, yet each retained a different sense in relation to agency.

In addition, in the discourse of hua-yi, the question of who was and could become civilized was not directly determined by racial difference as it came to be in the West.[30] In Chinese writing, China is spelled as *zhong-guo*. The term "*zhong*" means center, "*guo*" is roughly equivalent to a kingdom. This is separate from the ways in which the neighboring states referred to China. The traditional custom was to refer to the name of the dynasty such as the Qing, Tang, Sung, Zhou and Ming. The term China/Middle Kingdom/Zhongguo is, therefore, a more abstract term that designated the center of civilization which often coincided with the specific regional dynastic hegemon, yet retained an ambiguity as to its place. Among scholars in Edo-era Japan, there were debates as to whether the Middle Kingdom was a geographically specific matter, and whether, by following good custom, a kingdom geographically located outside of Ming or Qing could also become China by the exercise of virtue.[31] This is because the extent to which one was considered civilized in the region was dependent upon whether the leader followed the sagely Way. Put another way, whether one could become civilized was not racially determined. Especially in light of how Western powers cast their versions of international law as universal "standards of 'civilization' " states such as Japan had reason to believe that Westernization and reform efforts would eventually result in membership among the civilized powers.[32]

II. Rethinking civilization and the scientific approach to history in the Asian periphery

With the Meiji Restoration of 1868, Japan was to pursue the path of Westernization. The catch phrase of the government was *fukoku kyohei* (rich nation strong army) and *bunmei kaika* (civilization and opening). The most influential writings on civilizational history to be translated and circulated were Henry Thomas Buckle's *History of Civilization in England* (orig. 1857, trans. 1875) and Francois Guizot's *General History of Civilization in Europe* (orig. *Histoire de la civilisation en Europe* 1828, trans. 1877) (Hill, 2008). These writings were avidly read and subtly contested by various figures in early Meiji. According to Tanaka, the two dominant historical schools of thought which became influential at the beginning of Meiji period were that of Enlightenment history *(bunmeishi)*, led by figures such as Yukichi Fukuzawa (1834–1901) and Ukichi Taguchi (1855–1905) on the one hand, and the "national" school of textual analysis *(koshogaku)*, led by Yasutsugu Shigeno (1824–1910) and Kunitake Kume (1839–1931), on the other.[33] The key idea in the initial Meiji period was that of civilizational history and science. Scientific and positivist approach to study of the past was in vogue. In what follows, I offer a brief account of the two dominant schools of history in early Meiji Japan.

a. Contesting the law of history: pluralizing civilization and progress

Texts by Buckle and Guizot were popular among the masses for their potential to unveil the secret to Western power. The Western imposition of unequal treaties on Japan and the British defeat of Qing China weighed heavily in the minds of many, and histories accounting for the rise of the Western powers were hoped to provide a model for development. Buckle's claim that there exists a law of progress and development in society resonated with the readership in Japan. What was in demand among the masses was a book of "how-to", not a book about objectively studying a particular country's history.

While translations of Buckle and Guizot were influential, these civilizational histories nonetheless permitted little space for non-European states to tread the path of civilizational progress. In the case of Buckle, the explanation as to why England attained civilization was attributed to climate.[34] This meant that those who reside outside of such climate had little hope in attaining civilization. While this is different from other versions of civilizational history, which increasingly became racialized toward the end of nineteenth century, the problem it posed for those in Asia nonetheless remained the same.[35] Unless one became European one could not be civilized. In response to this damning law of history, the early Meiji *bunmeishi* can be seen as attempting to pluralize history.

Yukichi Fukuzawa theorized *bunmeishi*/civilizational history as an endeavor to capture the positionality of the subject against the universal law of development. What was necessary for Japan to keep its independence was a shift from "useless" Confucian studies to practical Western learning.[36] Fukuzawa's *Outline of a Theory of Civilization*, published in 1875, begins with a promise to unveil the Western secret to attaining civilization. Following Guizot and Buckle, Fukuzawa writes that by now, an understanding of different stages of civilization was "accepted by people all over the globe".[37] These stages consisted of three:

> The nations of Europe and the United States of America are the most highly civilized, while the Asian countries, such as Turkey, China, and Japan may be called semi-developed countries, and Africa and Australia are to be counted as still primitive lands.[38]

Here, Japan is positioned as a semi-developed country. He follows this diagnosis of the present with a warning that if men remained content with the current stage semi-development, the loss of independence may be inevitable.

How are the three stages of development differentiated in Fukuzawa's outline? In the primitive stage, men live under a precarious state where food and shelter are not reliably available. Here, "man is still unable to be master of his own situation; he cowers before the forces of nature and is dependent on the favors of others, or on the chance vagaries of nature".[39] What characterizes the primitive stage for Fukuzawa is the helplessness of man. The second stage consists of a more stable supply of basic necessities and institutions which "create an outward semblance of a state".[40] Pursuit of book learning becomes more feasible, but it is not "yet civilization", for it lacks devotion to "practical learning *(jitsugaku)*" and the "courage to raise doubts".[41] Men in the semi-developed stage remain "slaves of custom", as one can follow rules but cannot yet create them. Man is "adept at imitative craftsmanship", yet this craft remains at the level of mimesis.[42] Man in the civilized stage, where Europe and America stand, identifies the general structure which governs the universe, yet is unbound by the structure itself. Instead of slavish imitation, fully developed man demonstrates his capacity for free play of thought. Learning is no longer imitative but creative and inventive. Man is no longer a slave of custom; he actively plans the future and commits to its realization as a creator of the world.[43] Fukuzawa specifically identifies inventiveness as a character which differentiates Japan and China from Europe and America. He characterizes China as a country bound by old customs and habits, and identifies the reign of Confucianism as a period in which freedom of thought is suppressed, leaving man's thinking "simple" and "not complex".[44] Without a free play of ideas, a country becomes stagnant. In Fukuzawa's eyes, the Opium War and its outcome made sense as a battle between inventive British and custom-bound Qing. The battle symbolized the danger of hubris. Qing was punished for its arrogance in believing that it was the supreme ruler of the world, and for remaining content with the civilization it developed long ago.[45]

Although Fukuzawa draws repeatedly from Buckle and Guizot, he makes no mention of climate and instead attributes the development of civilization to inventiveness and practical learning. What Fukuzawa seeks to promote is the courage to raise questions and to promote free play of thought. Furthermore, while he does designate Europe and America as being the most civilized countries, he nonetheless qualifies this state as a relative matter[46] China is more civilized in contrast to Africa, he writes, and Europe is civilized in contrast to China. Yet if someone were to look back at the present from the future, the present state of Europe would "surely seem a pitifully primitive stage".[47] Here, Fukuzawa renders the notion of civilizational history as an open-ended process and in doing so sustains the possibility and necessity for Japan to pursue practical learning and inventive craftsmanship. By leaving the developmental process as an open-ended one, instead of a process where the end coincides as an apex in Europe and America, Fukuzawa reconfigures civilizational history as a study which identifies a universal pattern of social development while also offering a possibility of exercising control over this process by understanding this "general structure" and applying it to education and governance.[48]

Equally notable for introducing civilizational history was Ukichi Taguchi, who wrote *Nihon Kaika Shoshi (Short History of Japanese Civilization)* in 1877. Taguchi's history of civilization is focused on material progress and resembles Adam Smith's depiction of societal development from nomadic society to commercial, urban society.[49] Taguchi is similar to Fukuzawa in his commitment to find the universal principles which lie behind civilizational history. Taguchi differentiated historical writings which merely chronologically compiled data from those that identified the underlying causal relation between events. Real history for Taguchi was the latter.[50] Like Buckle's premise for the study of English civilizational history, the objective of historical study for Taguchi is to reveal an underlying law that governs social phenomenon. While Fukuzawa's writings were conjectural and not strictly objective, Taguchi sought to apply this search for universal law into the actual study of history.

While both Fukuzawa and Taguchi are considered as major proponents of a European civilizational history that posits Europe as being ahead of Asia, Taguchi, too, did not simply imitate Buckle and Smith. In his 1895 speech entitled "Rekishi wa Kagaku ni Arazu (The Study of History is not equivalent to the study of Science)", Taguchi directly refutes Buckle's thesis that the study of history can be conducted in the same way as the study of nature. Here, Taguchi first begins by asking what scientific study means. For him, scientific study is that which seeks to identify a law governing the universe.[51] Among scientific studies there are two kinds. The first kind documents data and facts, such as the study of human anatomy, which takes record of the human body's parts. The second kind explains nature's causal relations. In the second category belong physics, astronomy, chemistry, economics, sociology and psychology.[52] He asks whether the study of history fits either of these two categories, and argues that it does not. The study of history is not scientific because, unlike physical science, one can neither apply and test the law of history as one can with gravity, nor universalize its findings. What took place in the past can be documented but not tested the way a scientific hypothesis can be.[53] Further, the path of historical development for each country is unique in its own right, and therefore not subject to universalization. For Taguchi, the application of consistent method does not necessarily render the study of history as a scientific endeavor. In de-linking the method of historical study from universality, Taguchi subtly opens up a space to affirm a plural process of becoming civilized. In arguing so, Taguchi forecloses the possibility of comparatively contrasting and ranking different states in relation to the civilizational discourse. Development does take place, but each case is unique and escapes generalization.

For Fukuzawa and Taguchi, historical progress was identifiable through the application of universal law, yet for Fukuzawa, history was an "open-ended process", and for Taguchi, each state's progressive histories were incomparable, at least not in any scientific manner. Both adopt the notion of universal law, yet leave out geographical determinism, such as the effect of climate on civilizational temper. Both are identified as figures who introduced the concept of civilizational history, yet the writings of Fukuzawa and Taguchi attest that European civilizational histories were never left intact. Instead, the concept of civilizational history was reconfigured to give space to envision a place for non-Western history to move and potentially exercise agency among other civilizations.

Despite Fukuzawa and Taguchi's efforts, the *bunmeishi* (civilizational history) school of history eventually lost its appeal. This was because what Fukuzawa and Taguchi valorized, inventiveness and economic wealth, were also the means by which Western powers could dominate and subjugate others. In addition, news about the 1886 Normanton Incident, where a British captain was acquitted of the charge of letting all thirty-seven non-Western members of his crew (Japanese, Chinese, and Indians) drown to death when his ship was sinking, while rescuing every British and German crewmember, caused a resurgence in outrage at the unequal treaties.[54] The news of the period indicated that regardless of how civilized one attempts to become, in the end, civilizational status was determined by one's skin color.

If standards of civilization were being used to justify the domination of the uncivilized, the idea of civilizational standards itself seemed barbaric. Surely under the order of hua-yi the degree of one's civilization was measured by the extent to which one practiced the moral way of life, and this did constitute a differentiation between the civilized and the barbaric. The Confucians at the turn of Meiji identified the difference between the civilized and barbaric but did not use this difference as a prescription to change the way of life of the uncivilized Other. Consequently, cultivation of morality was encouraged yet never turned into a civilizing mission.[55] In contrast, the standards of civilization were used by Western powers to actively change practices which were deemed less than civilized. For example, the French began a war in Vietnam in 1858 and turned it into its protectorate in 1883. In 1877, Queen Victoria of England proclaimed herself as the empress of India. The Western domination over South Asia was a radical departure from how interstate relations were sustained under the hua-yi order.[56] While the notion of progressive history and the cyclical rise of history in older Sinitic notions of history resonated in the initial stage of the Meiji period, the implications of what it meant to become civilized became questionable.

There was a gap between the civilized image of the West and its actual predatory behavior. What made sense out of this gap was Herbert Spencer's writings on social Darwinism, which were avidly consumed starting in the 1880s.[57] If the actual law of history is the survival of the fittest, then one must do everything at his disposal to ensure this survival. This sense of insecurity was to also shape the academic discipline of history.

b. Against the scientific approach to the study of history: the ousting of positivist historians

On another front, within the establishment of academic history, both Shigeno and Kume took to the task of applying the scientific approach to writing the history of Japan. While Fukuzawa and Taguchi put emphasis on the notions of civilization, progress, and the universal law of history, the first generation of officially appointed academic historians focused on the idea of the scientific approach to the study of the past. They preoccupied themselves with methodology and the compilation of evidence.

The emphasis on a critical approach to text was not entirely an import from the West, as this was a tradition that existed in Chinese learning as well.[58] Both Shigeno and Kume were renowned scholars of Chinese learning before being appointed for the national history compilation project.[59]

Shigeno first came across Western political thought as a translator of Henry Wheaton's treatise on international law. The state appointed Shigeno to translate the Chinese text into Japanese, and this was published in 1870. He was then employed by the Ministry of Education to revive and continue the imperial custom of compiling Japan's dynastic historical records. Kume encountered Western civilization by accompanying the Iwakura Mission. Headed by Tomomi Iwakura, this delegates' tour through America and Europe had the purpose of testing the waters as to how feasible revising the unequal treaties would be and to observe and document Western civilization. Kume was appointed to accompany the delegate as a recorder of the mission, and his record was published in 1878. Having successfully served for the state as a record keeper, he then was appointed to the Ministry of Education's project of reviving official national history of Japan in 1879, joining Shigeno.

The project of compiling historical records was initially commissioned by the Ministry of Education and the Great Council of State, and later stationed in

University of Tokyo. With this, both Shigeno and Kume were appointed as professors of the department of history in 1888. The department of national history was established in 1889, making Shigeno and Kume some of the first professors of this discipline.[60]

In their approach to the study of the past, both Shigeno and Kume subscribed to careful study of texts *(kosho)*, a continuation of one branch of Chinese historical method, and a Rankean commitment to the objective study of the past. The characterization of history as an objective study of the past led Shigeno to proclaim that Japan had no history of its own. Shigeno critiqued preexisting historical writings on two grounds. In his speech on methods of studying national history given in 1879, Shigeno proclaimed that up until now, Japan had no official history *(seishi)*. The *Rikkokushi*, written in the ancient period, was considered as a mere listing of events in chronological order failing to grasp any narrative in its depiction of events. On the other hand, the *Gunki Monogatari*, written in the medieval age, also failed to qualify as a proper official historiography because there was too much emphasis on storytelling and narrative and little commitment to factual truths. Real history, Shigeno argues, lies in between the two. He points to Western historiography as the ideal model – Western historiography uses a chronological account while retaining a sense of causal relations among events. It offers the author's subjective point of view and also prompts the readers to push their thinking.[61] Shigeno's commitment to the objective study of the past made him a staunch critic of those who believed in historical myths and heroes, and he became known as the slayer of such heroes. On the basis of objective, careful analysis of classical texts, he argued that certain mythical heroes often celebrated in Shinto shrines were in fact mere fiction.[62] Kume was no different. Given that a critical approach to texts meant the rejection of myths, Kume, too, had no reservations about rejecting national myths if the facts did not fit the claim.

Enlightenment historian Taguchi was supportive of Shigeno and Kume. This is because for both the *bunmeishi* historians and the *koshogaku-ha* scientific approach to history, in theory, the objective approach to the study of history was to contribute to the common goal of achieving human progress. Destroying myths for Taguchi was a step toward progress, and he wanted to popularize this destruction and critical approach to history. He did that by printing an article by Kume arguing that Shinto was merely a primitive custom that did not even amount to religion in *Shikai* [Sea of History], a popular journal Taguchi oversaw.[63] This ironically led to the eventual dismissal of Kume from the university and the closing of the compilation project. Kume's commentaries were interpreted as being disloyal to the emperor and unpatriotic. Kume and Taguchi did not appear to recognize that strict objectivity would contradict the state's need to assert national history and employ history to a political end.

Hiroyuki Kato was the president of Tokyo Imperial University when the controversy over Kume's comments about Shinto erupted. Kato was an advocate of social Darwinism, and his stance on the proper role of education was shown by his earlier critique of Fukuzawa's *An Encouragement of Learning*, in which Fukuzawa advocated enlightenment and civilization for all and called for intellectuals to side with the masses to further their activism.[64] In his response, Kato identifies Fukuzawa's argument as a liberal one whose model is based on European states, who augment and help one another out to further the progress of civilization. European liberalism's success indicates that this path toward enlightenment is not an impossibility, yet Kato points out that both liberals and communists have in common the problematic of how to theorize state power. While the liberals and communists are of different political orientations, they are both mistaken, as the liberals advocate the weakening of the state and enlargement of people's rights, and therefore lead to the neglect of institutions of basic public and common goods. On the other hand, the communists expand the role of the state and reduce the rights of the people, extending state reach into even the production of agriculture and arts. Both parties have a rigid stance on the role of the state and its people. Fukuzawa, according to Kato, claims that the intellectuals must side with the people and vehemently against the state. Instead, Kato argues that the positioning of the role of intellectuals must depend on the individual circumstance and condition of the state. In the case of Japan, what is necessary is the state-led development of its people and, therefore, the intellectuals need not necessarily solely side with the people but, when appropriate, serve the state.[65] Kato's critique of Fukuzawa in essence argues for a stronger role of the state in discerning how education is to be managed. Kato inserts the role of a strong centralized state in matters of education by advocating for an "orchestrated 'struggle for survival' that maintains domestic calm and international peace".[66]

Therefore, for Kato the role of intellectuals was to work with and for the state when necessary and appropriate. Given this stance on education and intellectuals, and the prevalent sense that Japan is behind Europe, under Kato's leadership, the mission of Tokyo Imperial University was to be in service of the state's needs.[67]

As noted earlier, social Darwinism became a prominent framework with which to understand international politics for the masses as well as the elites in 1880s. Kato's stance on the role of intellectuals in supporting state struggle for survival was, therefore, reflective of the general ambivalence toward history writing which remained oblivious to Japanese state's need. It is of little surprise that when Kume came under criticism from Shintoists and Kokugaku scholars, Kato dismissed Kume.[68]

Kume's dismissal served as a litmus test that challenged the role a scientific approach to the study of the past was to have in nation-building. The scientific approach to the study of the past was deemed incompatible with the emergent understanding about how history should be used for political ends by the state because it was incompatible with Kato's understanding of social Darwinism. Verifying facts about the history of Japanese imperial line was less important than glorifying the myth surrounding the imperial household. In 1891, the Imperial Rescript on Education was issued. The identity of the Japanese state and nation was increasingly mediated by the figure of the emperor as the symbolic unity of the Japanese people.[69] Strict adherence to verifiable evidence led Shigeno and Kume to dismiss mythical figures' existence, and their colleague, Hoshino, had been publishing studies that indicated that the imperial line's ancestors came from Korea.[70] They did not clearly see the political influence history writing could have because they were obsessed with methods. The discussion related to the history of the imperial line became a treacherous topic.

III. The search for alternative to civilizational history

In this chapter, we examined the brief rise and wane of civilizational history from the period of 1868 toward the turn of the century. The emergence in Japan of the *bunmeishi* writers and the *koshogaku* scholars appears unrelated. Yet they are. In short, what we see in the first half of the Meiji period is an engagement with French and British civilizational histories and their approach to history as science, as well as the eventual realization that, for Japan, the study of history requires a different approach – one that is opposed to civilizational history altogether. To be sure, civilizational history, which conceives of Asia as backward, does not die out in the 1890s. As Stefan Tanaka shows, for example, this Western idea of Asia as being backward is replicated in Japanese universities' establishment of Oriental Studies programs.[71] In claiming that Japan is more civilized than other Asian states, Japan also replicates the civilizing mission program of the West in Korea, leading to Japan's colonization of Korea in 1910.[72] Yet these accounts of a Westernizing Japan do not capture the alternative approaches to history which were spawned after the 1890s as a reaction against the limits of civilizational history. The rise and wane of civilizational history in Meiji Japan up to the end of nineteenth century indirectly sketches out the limits of French and British linear civilizational histories and offers more pluralistic visions of international existence. It is this sensitivity to the limits of scientific history that later Japanese historians find in the German notion of *kultur* and approach to historical development as "unfolding", which become resources for an alternative approach to thinking Asia's relation to history – historicism as agency-enabling. From the 1890s on, there is a rise of nationalist historicism and a revaluation of Asia in cultural terms. The cultural turn renders Asia not as a static and backward empire, but as a site of resistance.

Notes

1 Margaret Mehl, *History and the State in Nineteenth-Century Japan* (London: Palgrave Macmillan, 1998).
2 Friedrich R. Ankersmit, *Historical Representation* (Stanford, CA: Stanford University Press, 2001).
3 Niccolò Machiavelli, "Discourses on the First Ten Books of Titus Livius", in *The Prince and the Discourses* (New York: The Modern Library, 1950): 104–105.
4 Niccolò Machiavelli, "The Prince", in *The Prince and the Discourses* (New York: The Modern Library, 1950): 91.
5 Pheng Cheah, *Spectral Nationality: Passages of Freedom from Kant to Postcolonial Literatures of Liberation* (New York: Columbia University Press, 2003). Cheah argues that this sense of backwardness was a critical component in the formulation of German theory on *bildung*, culture, and the use of organismic metaphors to depict the nation.
6 Maurice Mandelbaum, *History, Man, & Reason: A Study in Nineteenth-Century Thought* (Baltimore: The Johns Hopkins University Press, 1971).

7 Cf. Dipesh Chakrabarty, *Provincializing Europe: Postcolonial Thought and Historical Difference* (Princeton, NJ: Princeton University Press, 2000): 23; Mandelbaum, *History, Man, & Reason*; Frederick C. Beiser, *The German Historicist Tradition* (Oxford: Oxford University Press, 2011). Although Mandelbaum, whom Chakrabarty cites to offer his definition of historicism identifies two concepts of development, Chakrabarty characterizes historicism as a mode of thought which "seeks to find the general in the particular."

8 Vinay Lal, *The History of History: Politics and Scholarship in Modern India* (New Delhi: Oxford University Press, 2003); Ranajit Guha, *History at the Limit of World-History* (New York: Columbia University Press, 2003).

9 Dipesh Chakrabarty, *Provincializing Europe: Postcolonial Thought and Historical Difference* (Princeton, NJ: Princeton University Press, 2000): 8.

10 Lal, 29–41.

11 Georg Wilhelm Friedrich Hegel, *Introduction to the Philosophy of History*, trans. Leo Rauch (Indianapolis, IN: Hackett Publishing Company, 1988): 94–95.

12 Ibid.

13 Sannosuke Matsumoto, *Kindai Nihon no Chugoku Ninshiki [How the Japanese Recognized China in the Modern World: From Tokugawa Era Confucian Studies to Theory of Greater East Asia Co-Prosperity Sphere]* (Tokyo: Ibunsha, 2011): 4–10. The term Asia arrived to China by way of translation of Matteo Ricci's map of the world, and then on to Japan.

14 Georg Hegel, "The Division of History", in *Introduction to the Philosophy of History*, trans. Leo Rauch (Indianapolis, IN: Hackett Publishing Company, 1988): 92.

15 Ibid.

16 Ibid.

17 Thomas McCarthy, *Race, Empire, and the Idea of Human Development* (Cambridge: Cambridge University Press, 2009); Robert Young, *White Mythologies: Writing History and the West* (London and New York: Routledge, 1990).

18 Toshio Motegi, *Henyo Suru Kindai Higashi Ajia no Kokusai Chitsujo [Genealogy of East Asian Modern Conception of Interstate Order]* (Tokyo: Yamakawa Shuppansha, 2007).

19 Ronald P. Toby, *State and Diplomacy in Early Modern Japan: Asia in the Development of the Tokugawa Bakufu* (Stanford, CA: Stanford University Press, 1991); Urs Matthias Zachmann, *China and Japan in the Late Meiji Period: China Policy and the Japanese Discourse on National Identity, 1895–1904* (Abingdon, UK: Routledge, 2009).

20 Zachmann, 9; Gregory Smits, *Visions of Ryukyu: Identity and Ideology in Early-Modern Thought and Politics* (Hawai'i: University of Hawai'i Press, 1999).

21 Jun Yonaha, *Honyaku no Seijigaku: Kindai Higashi Ajia Sekai no Keisei to Nichi-Ryu Kankei no Henyo [Translation and Politics: Formation of Modern East Asian World Order and Alteration of Japan-Liu'qiu Relations]* (Tokyo: Iwanami Shoten, 2010).

22 Lydia H. Liu, *The Clash of Empires: The Invention of China in Modern World Making* (Cambridge, MA: Harvard University Press, 2004).

23 Matsumoto, *Kindai Nihon no Chugoku Ninshiki*, 17.

24 Yukichi Fukuzawa, *An Outline of a Theory of Civilization*, trans. David A. Dilworth and G. Cameron Hurst III (New York: Columbia University Press, 2009).

25 Those who established the Qing dynasty came from northern Manchu region which under Ming dynasty, dominated by Han, were deemed as less civilized. The end of Ming and its takeover by Qing, therefore, was considered a theoretical scandal by neighboring states, known as the flip of "hua" and "yi". It was in this light that Choseon Korea deemed itself as the true inheritor of Chinese civilization.

26 Shinichi Kitaoka, *Nihon Seijishi: Gaiko to Kenryoku [A Political History of Modern Japan: Foreign Relations and Domestic Politics]* (Tokyo: Yuhikaku, 2011): 16–17. For a detailed account of the ideological role China played in Japanese political thought see Zachmann.

27 Kitaoka, 17.
28 Sannosuke Matsumoto, *Meiji Shisoshi: Kindai Kokka no Sosetsu kara ko no kakusei made [History of Meiji Political Thought: From Establishment of Modern Nation-State to Advent of Individualism]* (Tokyo: Shinyosha, 2002): 5–7.
29 This point is made by Hiroshi Watanabe, *Higashi Ajia no Oken To Shiso [Confucianism and After: Political Thoughts in Early Modern East Asia]* (Tokyo: University of Tokyo Press, 1997): 247.
30 The idea of race enters Chinese political discourse much later, on the importation of race into China see Sung-chiao Shen and Sechin Y.S. Chien, "Turning Slaves into Citizens: Discourses of *Guomin* and the Construction of Chinese National Identity in the Late Qing Period", in Sechin Y.S. Chien and John Fitzgerald eds., *The Dignity of Nations: Equality, Competition, and Honor in East Asia Nationalism* (Hong Kong: Hong Kong University Press, 2006): 49–70. European concept of civilization was not always racially determined; on the diversity within Western political thought on civilization see Sankar Muthu, *Enlightenment against Empire* (Princeton, NJ: Princeton University Press, 2003).
31 Collected Arguments On the Concept of The Middle Kingdom (Chugoku Ronshu), compiled by Sato Naokata's disciple, Ono Nobunari and published in 1706. Compiled by Wm. Theodore de Bary, Carol Gluck, and Arthur E. Tiedermann, *Sources of Japanese Tradition, Volume Two: 1600 to 2000* (New York: Columbia University Press, 2005): 96–98.
32 See Cemil Aydin, "The Universal West: Europe beyond Its Christian and White Race Identity (1840–1882)", in *The Politics of Anti-Westernism in Asia: Visions of World Order in Pan-Islamic and Pan-Asian Thought* (New York: Columbia University Press, 2007): 15–38; on civilization and international law see Gerrit W. Gong, *The Standard of Civilization in International Society* (Oxford: Oxford University Press, 1984).
33 Keiji Nagahara, *20 Seiki Nihon no Rekishigaku [The Japanese Discipline of History in Twentieth Century]* (Tokyo: Yoshikawa Kobunkan, 2003): 8–9. While there were two other schools, one which subscribed to Confucian political thought led by Nagazane Motoda (1818–1891), which is later to exert its influence in authoring the Imperial Rescript on Education *(kyoiku chokugo)* on the one hand, and of another which advocated Shintoist religion's revival as national religion, on the other, these two were minor in contrast to the two dominant schools.
34 Henry Thomas Buckle, "Chapter II: Influence Exercised by Physical Laws over the Organization of Society and over the Character of Individuals", in *History of Civilization in England* (London: Longmans, Green, and Co., 1873): 39–151.
35 On race and history, see McCarthy.
36 Yukichi Fukuzawa, *An Encouragement of Learning*, 2.
37 Fukuzawa, *An Outline of a Theory*, 17–18.
38 Ibid., 17.
39 Ibid., 18.
40 Ibid.
41 Ibid.
42 Ibid.
43 Ibid., 18–19.
44 Ibid., 26–27.
45 Yukichi Fukuzawa, "Sekai Kunizukushi [The World Filled with States]", in *Fukuzawa Yukichi Chosaku Shu [Collection of Writings by Yukichi Fukuzawa]*, Vol. 2 (Tokyo: Keio Gijyuku Daigaku Shuppankai, 2002): 76–77.
46 Fukuzawa, *An Outline of a Theory*, 20.
47 Ibid.
48 Ibid., 18–19.
49 John S. Brownlee, *Japanese Historians and the National Myths, 1600–1945: The Age of the Gods and Emperor Jimmu* (Tokyo: University of Tokyo Press, 1997): 83.

50 Tatsuo Morito, "Bunmeishika narabi 'Shakai Kairyo' Ronja to shiteno Taguchi Teiken [Teiken Taguchi as Civilizational Historian and Social Reformist]", in *Taguchi Teiken Shu [Collection of Writings by Teiken Taguchi]* (Tokyo: Chikuma Shobo, 1977): 432.

51 Teiken Taguchi, "Rekishi wa Kagaku ni Arazu [History Is Not Science]", in *Taguchi Teiken Shu*, 98.

52 Ibid., 100.

53 Ibid., 102.

54 Masahiro Tanaka, "Normanton Incident", in *The Comprehensive National History Reference*, Vol. 11 (Tokyo: Yoshikawa Kobunkan, 1990).

55 Koichiro Matsumoto, "'Bunmei' 'Jyugaku' 'Daawinizumu' ['Civilization,' 'Confucianism,' 'Darwinism']", in *Edo no Chishiki kara Meiji no Seiji e [From Knowledge in Edo Period to Meiji Political Thought]* (Tokyo: Perikansha, 2010): 215–247.

56 On the comparative study of tributary relations in South Asia and its clash with British understanding of territory as property, see Thongchai Winichakul, *Siam Mapped: A History of the Geo-Body of a Nation* (Hawai'i: University of Hawai'i Press, 1997).

57 On the changing image of nature in Japanese political discourse, see Julia Adeney Thomas, *Reconfiguring Modernity: Concepts of Nature in Japanese Political Ideology* (Berkeley, Los Angeles, and London: University of California Press, 2001); Masao Maruyama, *Nihon Seiji Shisoshi Kenkyu [Study on Japanese Political Thought]* (Tokyo: Tokyo Daigaku Shuppankai, 1999).

58 Margaret Mehl, *History and the State in Nineteenth-Century Japan* (New York: St. Martin's Press, Inc., 1998): 91.

59 The term *kosho* is derived from the Chinese learning's critical approach to text. This is the reason why Shigeno and Kume are called the *koshogaku-ha*.

60 Mehl, 87–97.

61 Yusaku Matsuzawa, *Shigeno Yasutsugu to Kume Kunitake – Seishi wo Yumemita Rekishika [Yasutsugu Shigeno and Kunitake Kume: Historians Who Dreamt of Official History]* (Tokyo: Yamakawa Shuppansha, 2012): 48.

62 Mehl, 108.

63 Ibid., 126–133.

64 To be sure, Fukuzawa's usage of the term "nature" is far from consistent, it has been used to support and corporealize the national body at the cost of excluding the mass on some occasions, and on others, alternatively insisting on people's natural rights to empower the mass. Cf. Thomas, 68–71.

65 Hiroyuki Kato, "Fukuzawa sensei no ron ni kotau [My Response to Mr. Fukuzawa]", in Shinichi Yamamuro and Toru Nakanome eds., *Meiroku Zasshi (Jyo) [Meiroku Journal (Upper Volume)]* (Tokyo: Iwanami Shoten, 2010): 66–68.

66 Ibid., 106.

67 Tanaka, "Normanton Incident," 41.

68 Mehl, 130; Nahagara, 36–37.

69 Tak Fujitani, *Splendid Monarchy: Power and Pageantry in Modern Japan* (Berkeley, Los Angeles, and London: University of California Press, 1998). The Japanese imperial line mostly existed as a ceremonial figure for centuries while actual political power was in the hands of the shogunate – the warrior class. With Meiji Restoration there was a symbolic "return" of power to the righteous ruler of Japan, which the Meiji oligarchs claimed rests in the emperor. Theoretically the oligarchs planned the emperor to serve the role of Christ for Christians, eclectically mixing Confucian value of loyalty to the elder and father with the deification of the imperial line.

70 Matsuzawa, 70.

71 Masahiro Tanaka, *Japan's Orient: Rendering Pasts into History* (Berkeley: University of California Press, 1993).

72 Alexis Dudden, *Japan's Colonization of Korea: Discourse and Power* (Hawai'i: University of Hawai'i Press, 2006).

References

Ankersmit, Frank R. *Historical Representation*. Stanford, CA: Stanford University Press, 2001.

Aydin, Cemil. *The Politics of Anti-Westernism in Asia: Visions of World Order in Pan-Islamic and Pan-Asian Thought*. New York: Columbia University Press, 2007.

Beiser, Frederick. *The German Historicist Tradition*. Oxford: Oxford University Press, 2011.

Brownlee, John. *Japanese Historians and the National Myths, 1600–1945: The Age of Gods and Emperor Jimmu*. Tokyo: University of Tokyo Press, 1997.

Buckle, Thomas. *History of Civilization in England*. London: Longmans, Green, and Co., 1875.

Chakrabarty, Dipesh. *Provincializing Europe: Postcolonial Thought and Historical Difference*. Princeton, NJ: Princeton University Press, 2000.

Cheah, Pheng. *Spectral Nationality: Passages of Freedom from Kant to Postcolonial Literatures of Liberation*. New York: Columbia University Press, 2003.

Dudden, Alexis. *Japan's Colonization of Korea: Discourse and Power*. Honolulu: University of Hawai'i Press, 2006.

Fujitani, Takashi. *Splendid Monarchy: Power and Pageantry in Modern Japan*. Berkeley: University of California Press, 1998.

Fukuzawa, Yukichi. *Fukuzawa Yukichi Chosaku Shu [Collection of Writings by Yukichi Fukuzawa]*. Tokyo: Keio Gijyuku Daigaku Shuppankai, 2002.

Fukuzawa, Yukichi. *An Encouragement of Learning*. Translated by David Dilworth. Tokyo: Sophia University, 1969.

Fukuzawa, Yukichi. *An Outline of a Theory of Civilization*. Translated by David Dilworth and G. Cameron Hurst III. New York: Columbia University Press, 2009.

Gong, Gerrit. *The Standard of 'Civilization' in International Society*. Oxford: Oxford University Press, 1984.

Guha, Ranajit. *History at the Limit of World-History*. New York: Columbia University Press, 2002.

Hegel, Georg. *Introduction to the Philosophy of History*. Translated by Leo Rauch. Indianapolis, IN: Hackett Publishing Company, 1988.

Hill, Christopher. *National History and the World of Nations: Capital, State, and the Rhetoric of History in Japan, France, and the United States*. Durham, NC: Duke University Press, 2008.

Kitaoka, Shinichi. *Nihon Seijishi: Gaiko to Kenryoku [A Political History of Modern Japan: Foreign Relations and Domestic Politics]*. Tokyo: Yuhikaku, 2011.

Kuga, Katsunan. *Kokusairon [Theory of the International]*. Nihon no Meicho [Japanese Classics] 37. Edited by Masanao Shikano. Tokyo: Chuo Koronsha, 1971.

Lal, Vinay. *The History of History: Politics and Scholarship in Modern India*. New York: Oxford University Press, 2005.

Liu, Lydia. *The Clash of Empires: The Invention of China in Modern World Making*. Cambridge: Harvard University Press, 2004.

Machiavelli, Niccolò. *The Prince and the Discourses*. New York: The Modern Library, 1950.

Mandelbaum, Maurice. *History, Man, & Reason: A Study in Nineteenth-Century Thought*. Baltimore: The Johns Hopkins University Press, 1971.

Maruyama, Masao. *Nihon Seiji Shisoshi Kenkyu [Study on Japanese Political Thought]*. Tokyo: Tokyo Daigaku Shuppankai, 1999.

Matsumoto, Koichiro. *Edo no Chishiki kara Meiji no Seiji e [From Knowledge in Edo Period to Meiji Political Thought]*. Tokyo: Perikansha, 2010.

Matsumoto, Sannosuke. *Meiji Shisoshi: Kindai Kokka no Sosetsu kara ko no kakusei made [History of Meiji Political Thought: From Establishment of Modern Nation-State to Advent of Individualism]*. Tokyo: Shinyosha, 2002.

Matsumoto, Sannosuke. *Kindai Nihon no Chugoku ninshiki [How the Japanese Recognized China in the Modern World]*. Tokyo: Ibunsha, 2011.

Matsuzawa, Yusaku. *Shigeno Yasutsugu to Kume Kunitake – Seishi wo Yumemita Rekishika [Yasutsugu Shigeno and Kunitake Kume: Historians Who Dreamt of Official History]*. Tokyo: Yamakawa Shuppansha, 2012.

McCarthy, Thomas. *Race, Empire, and the Idea of Human Development*. Cambridge: Cambridge University Press, 2009.

Mehl, Margaret. *History and the State in Nineteenth-Century Japan*. New York: St. Martin's Press, 1998.

Morito, Tatsuo. "Bunmeishika narabi 'shakai kairyo' ronja to shiteno Taguchi Teiken [Teiken Taguchi as Civilizational Historian and Social Reformist]." In *Taguchi Teiken Shu [Collection of Writings by Teiken Taguchi]*. Tokyo: Chikuma Shobo, 1977.

Motegi, Toshio. *Henyo Suru Kindai Higashi Ajia no Kokusai Chitsujo [Genealogy of East Asian Modern Conception of Interstate Order]*. Tokyo: Yamakawa Shuppansha, 2007.

Muthu, Sankar. *Enlightenment against Empire*. Princeton, NJ: Princeton University Press, 2003.

Nagahara, Keiji. *20 Seiki Nihon no Rekishigaku [The Japanese Discipline of History in Twentieth Century]*. Tokyo: Yoshikawa Kobunkan, 2003.

Shen, Sung-chiao and Sechin Y.S. Chien. "Turning Slaves into Citizens: Discourse of *Guomin* and the Construction of Chinese National Identity in the Late Qing Period." In *The Dignity of Nations: Equality, Competition, and Honor in East Asia Nationalism*, edited by Sechin Y.S. Chien and John Fitzgerald, 49–70. Hong Kong: Hong Kong University Press, 2006.

Smits, Gregory. *Visions of Ryukyu: Identity and Ideology in Early-Modern Thought and Politics*. Honolulu: University of Hawai'i Press, 1999.

Taguchi, Teiken. *Taguchi Teiken Shu [Collection of Writings by Teiken Taguchi]*. Tokyo: Chikuma Shobo, 1977.

Tanaka, Masahiro. "Normanton Incident." In *The Comprehensive National History Reference*. Vol. 11. Tokyo: Yoshikawa Kobunkan, 1990.

Tanaka, Stefan. *Japan's Orient: Rendering Pasts into History*. Berkeley: University of California Press, 1993.

Theodore de Bary, William, Carol Gluck, and Arthur Tiedermann eds. *Sources of Japanese Tradition, Volume 2: 1600 to 2000*. New York: Columbia University Press, 2010.

Thomas, Julia. *Reconfiguring Modernity: Concepts of Nature in Japanese Political Ideology*. Berkeley: University of California Press, 2001.

Toby, Ronald. *State and Diplomacy in Early Modern Japan: Asia in the Development of the Tokugawa Bakufu*. Stanford, CA: Stanford University Press, 1991.

Watanabe, Hiroshi. *Higashi Ajia no Oken to Shiso [Suzerainty and Political Thought in East Asia]*. Tokyo: Tokyo Daigaku Shuppankai, 1997.

Winichakul, Thongchai. *Siam Mapped: A History of the Geo-Body of a Nation*. Honolulu: University of Hawai'i Press, 1997.

Yamamuro, Shin'ichi and Toru Nakanome eds. *Meiroku Zasshi [Meiroku Journal]*. Tokyo: Iwanami Shoten, 2010.

Yonaha, Jun. *Honyaku no Seijigaku: Kindai Higashi Ajia no Keisei to Nichiryu Kankei no Henyo [Politics of Translation: Formation of Modern East Asia and Alteration of Japan-Liu'qiu Relations]*. Tokyo: Iwanami Shoten, 2009.

Young, Robert. *White Mythologies: Writing History and the West*. New York: Routledge, 1990.

Zachmann, Urs Matthias. *China and Japan in the Late Meiji Period: China Policy and the Japanese Discourse on National Identity, 1895–1904*. Abingdon, UK: Routledge, 2009.

3 The assertion

Japan as the subject of world history

The late eighteenth-century German discourse on *kultur* allows one to see historical development as an unfolding of an autonomous entity against hegemonic structure. Kant theorized that culture is a realm where mankind's agency can manifest
and imprint itself in the phenomenal world. Such theorization which connects culture to agency-affirming emancipatory ends appealed to those outside of Europe.
Japan at the beginning of twentieth century was deemed as "backward" in relation
to Eurocentric civilizational historicism. Such predicament fostered a search for
alternative ways of engaging with history. Placing this appeal of agency-enabling
historicism in the context of interwar Japan, this chapter shows the interconnection and the precarious relation between German Idealism of Kant's and legitimation of Japanese imperialism and colonialism in the 1930s and 1940s. The
Japanese discourse on historicism and world history in the 1930s and 1940s is
underwritten by this quest for autonomy against agency-denying civilizational
historicism. Simultaneously, this quest also manifests in legitimation of Japanese
imperialism in Asia, thereby elucidating the precarious nature of pursuing agency
in the name of history. To clarify, this is not to attribute any agency to history writing. Rather, what this chapter does is to trace how a particular memory of how
history served to legitimate state action becomes sediment and continues to hum
in the intellectual atmosphere of post-1945 Japan. While agency-denying historicism is unacceptable for the non-West, responding to agency-denying historicism
with agency-enabling historicism also accompanied its weight of legitimating
violence.

In the previous chapter, we examined how agency-denying historicism or civilizational history briefly dominated the approach to the study of the past, only
to lose its appeal by the 1890s. In Japan, the period after the 1890s is characterized by what Kevin Doak calls "historicist nationalism", which values culture,
particularity, and the emergence of Asianism in the periphery.[1] By the end of
the nineteenth century, intellectuals such as Setsurei Miyake, arguing that Japan
belongs to Asia, called for opposition to Western imperialism and the appreciation
of Asian culture. He participated in the 1888 publication of *Nihonjin (Japanese)*, a
magazine which claimed that, in the realms of religion, morality, art, politics, and
production, one must preserve the country's Japaneseness. Katsunan Kuga also
claimed that the real danger in international politics lay in cultural absorption by

the West and that the Japanese people must be on guard against Western cultural imperialism.[2]

By the beginning of twentieth century, there was an increasing awareness of the ways in which the concept of civilization and culture alters how international existence and coexistence could be thought. Kuga's treatise on international relations is significant for his keen awareness of the ways in which Eurocentric norms become perpetuated in the name of objectivity. He distinguishes between material and nonmaterial ways of exercising power, arguing that what is more dangerous for Japan is the effect of unknowingly internalizing particular Western norms as universal. Beliefs and ideas are potent. Culture is acknowledged as a site of contestation of civilizational history among intellectuals.

Such identification of Eurocentric nature of international order was followed by a response. In 1938, philosopher Kiyoshi Miki wrote that political theory capable of uniting the East lay in the defeat of world history as the history of white people; that is, Eurocentrism.[3] The issue identified by Miki is the question of how to pluralize the ways in which we consider historical development. Miki by then was the leader of cultural division of Showa Research Association (SRA), a predecessor to the modern think thank that advised Prime Minister Fumimaro Konoe on his Asia policy. Miki's treatise on history was written amid convergence of several transnational intellectual movements: (1) the Pan-Asianist movement, which sought to redefine what "Asia" symbolized in history which worked in tandem with (2) the rise of dichotomous view of *kultur* – a German concept whose etymological origin lies in agriculture and cultivation – as an antidote to civilization which increasingly came to be seen as superficial refinement of external forms which in combination enabled (3) "Asia" to be reconfigured as a spiritual giant no longer perpetually "backward" as defined by the West. The intertwinement and manifestation of these trends are reflected in the treatise on international politics authored by SRA under the leadership of Miki, *Principles of Thought for a New Japan*. This treatise is considered as a most through systematic response to Eurocentrism in history written during the wartime era.[4]

At the same time, as we know today, Prince Konoe became the Prime Minister of Japan three times during the war period, and it was he who declared the New Order in the East in the name of Greater East Asia Co-Prosperity Sphere *(Daitoa Kyoeiken)*. Such theory of New Order served to give an appearance of legitimacy to Japanese imperialism.[5] Prime Minister Konoe's policy reflected Miki's writing on history. The Miki-Konoe connection raises a question: how did the response to Eurocentric history come to serve as an alibi to Japanese imperialism in Asia? If World War II, as philosopher Osamu Nishitani characterizes, is a war which sought to make Japan an agent of history, the history of the 1930s and 1940s suggests two things: Eurocentric linear history's denial of Asian agency is problematic, but so too is the response to this denial, which in the case of wartime Japan manifested itself as the politics of becoming a historical subject.[6]

To show this, in the first part of this chapter, I examine how different images of Asia – Asia as a civilizationally backward site, and Asia as a region which is culturally separate and superior to the West – have been posited by Japanese thinkers from 1890 on, and how this culturalist discourse is underwritten and incited by the problem of how to overcome Eurocentric linear history and envision political agency. In the second part, I focus on a particular theorist's, Kiyoshi Miki, writing and critique of Eurocentric history to elucidate how the rethinking of history is intertwined with the rethinking of international order in the 1930s and 1940s. Miki studied history under Seiichi Hatano and Hajime Tanabe at Kyoto Imperial University in 1916 and 1918, and then under Heinrich John Rickert and Martin Heidegger in Germany in 1922 and 1923, respectively. He then published his *Rekishi Tetsugaku (Philosophy of History)* in 1932 and joined and led Fumimaro Konoe's policy think tank, *Showa Kenkyukai* (Showa Research Association) in 1938. Konoe became the Prime Minister of Japan during the war period, and his declaration of a plan for the Greater East Asia Co-Prosperity Sphere in 1940 strongly reflects his attempt at theorizing historical existence and agency otherwise.

I. *Kultur* as site of resistance against civilization

The first half of Meiji witnessed a brief engagement with civilizational histories: histories which conceived of historical development in a linear manner which posited the West as being ahead of the rest with different degrees of agency attributed to a region named "Asia". This was also a period in which China as the regional center was decentered and reconfigured as a site of stillness among Japanese intellectuals who, therefore, partially internalized the Western assumption that Asia is "backward" and that a "civilized" Japan would be superior to China. Fukuzawa's short essay "*Datsua-Ron*" ("Leaving Asia") was penned in 1885, in the immediate aftermath of a failed Gapsin Coup in Choseon Korea and the assassination of Korean reformer Gim Okgyun in Shanghai. In his essay, Fukuzawa speaks of the need to leave the bad neighborhood, which metaphorically refers to Asia, and that the time to wait for the neighbors to modernize and reform has run out.[7] Fukuzawa's essay is marked with a sense of frustration at the pace with which Choseon Korea was reconfiguring its international stance and remodeling itself as a sovereign independent nation. Fukuzawa writes that Japan must leave Korea behind. This assumption that Korea was unable to reform itself later fed into Japan's justification for sending advisors to Korea, and ultimately colonizing it. In Fukuzawa's formulation, civilization lies in the West: what Japan must do is to internalize this view of civilization and history, to strive toward becoming like the West.

The Japanese state's adoption of Western civilization and its attendant norms altered the landscape of East Asian international relations. This notion of civilizational hierarchy first arrived in the form of the unequal treaty, imposed on the East by the Western powers. The standard of civilization was first used against non-Western states to justify colonial subjugation and the imposition of unequal treaties. "Civilization" presented itself as a neutral objective standard but it became a tool to perpetuate and force a particular model of political and economic organization upon other states.[8] The Japanese state continued to adopt the language of Western New Imperialism to justify its colonization of Korea, and to condemn Qing China's denial of responsibility for the Taiwanese massacre of Japanese citizens as an abdication of its sovereignty. In so doing, the Japanese state effectively rewrote East Asian international order.[9] In reconfiguring its relation vis-à-vis other Asian states Japan reproduced the Western language of civilization. This language justified the respective unequal treaties it negotiated in Asia. In order to subjugate other states in Asia, civilizational history was incorporated selectively, positioning Japan as more "civilized" than the rest.

Yet "leaving Asia" and remodeling Japan's political system after the West did not equate to equal treatment of Japan by the Western powers. As historian Kevin Doak writes, intellectuals' overriding concern in the first half of Meiji was about "civilization, universal development, [and] participation in the international system"; however, these aspirations were met with setbacks internationally.[10] Kaoru Inoue's failure to revise the unequal treaty vis-à-vis Western powers in 1887 reinforced the sense of resentment against the West. The Triple Intervention (by Germany, Russia, and France over the fate of the Liaodong Peninsula) further underscored the Eurocentric nature of international politics of the period. By the 1890s, there was a wide consensus that civilizational history was Western history, and international law was law that made European subjects as subjects and non-Europeans as objects. This produced a sense that reforming Japan along the Western – here, mostly British – "civilizational" model was of limited feasibility. It was against this background that another different notion of Asia emphasizing cultural difference became resurgent. Doak writes that the turn to culture, and the concept of *minzoku* (ethnic nationalism), and a heightened appreciation of the uniqueness of Japan gradually overtook the discourse focusing on civilization in the second half of Meiji. From 1888 on, "a romantic, historicist nationalism that asserted the particularity of the Japanese ethnic nation" became prominent.[11]

This concern with the effect of Westernization was also shared by the popular masses. Wariness toward Western imperialism and the Japanese state's pursuit of Westernization manifested as mass protest against Japan's negotiation of unequal treaties with Western powers, as well as criticism of Japan's increasingly imperialist stance toward its neighboring states. By the 1890s, there was a visible divide between the state policy of pursuing civilization and enlightenment and the general public and intellectuals' critiques of the feasibility and desirability of such a project. The contours of this division were discernible in how one viewed Asia. Those critical of the Japanese state's Western stance were also the ones who protected other Asian independence activists in India, Philippines, Vietnam, and China – the very movements from which the Japanese state explicitly distanced itself in order to work with other Western powers and win acceptance. In opposition to Western powers, transnational networks sought to envision an alternative international order and began to project cultural affinity and commonality among fellow Asians.[12] This led to diversification in how one sought to know and relate to Asia.

Even within the Japanese state establishment, by the end of the nineteenth century, there was an attempt to form cooperative ties between the state and China based on the argument that the two shared the same culture. Prime Minister Shigenobu Okuma was the first Japanese Prime Minister who sought an amicable relation with Qing China, and he set up a cultural organization called *Toa Dobun Shoin* – whose Chinese character naming "same letter" emphasizes the common usage of Chinese character as lingua franca – in 1898. This became a prestigious institute which trained future bureaucrats emphasizing actual fieldwork and knowledge of Chinese culture.[13] This emphasis on fieldwork challenged the hierarchical self-other relations which the study of history was adopting in Tokyo and Kyoto. By 1904, Tokyo Imperial University set up a program of Chinese History which was renamed an Oriental Studies Program in 1910, constituting what Stefan Tanaka calls "Japan's Orient". Thus, at the turn of the century, both within and outside the state, Asia is seen in both culturalist and civilizational terms.[14]

Outside of Japan, there is a reevaluation of Asia as an ideal form in contrast to the West. Art critic Tenshin Okakura traveled to India in 1901. Inspired by conversations with Rabindranath Tagore and Bengali spiritual leader Swami Vivekananda, he authored the books *The Ideals of the East* in 1903 and *The Book of Tea* in 1906, both of which characterized the East as a peaceful, spiritual giant in contrast to Western civilization, which was perceived as impersonal, mechanical, and violent.[15] By the turn of the century, the characterization of the West as a machine civilization was common, and technological and scientific advancement was used as proof of Western civilization's superiority over others.[16] Western hegemony was sustained by military and technological prowess, which facilitated its flouting of international law. In the case of Japan, the unequal treaty between Japan and America was negotiated in the presence of American gunboats. Thus, characterizing the West as a machine civilization was not a far stretch for Okakura. His contact with Tagore and Vivekananda, however, was significant because opposing Western machine civilization to Asia as a spiritual civilization was inspired by Vivekananda's philosophy.[17] Framing of Asia as a spiritual civilization reconfigured the image of Asia as materially and technologically backward; instead Asia was an ideal.

Indeed, the turn to culture as a counter to narratives of civilizational domination is a common trait in Asian and African anti-colonial thought, as well as German political thought. Partha Chatterjee writes that in the context of India under British colonial rule, the turn to culture takes place where one is subordinated materially: the battle begins in the domain of spirituality long before it erupts in the political domain.[18] This battle begins by dividing the world into two kinds of realms: the material realm, of "the economy and of statecraft, of science and technology", where the West dominates, and the spiritual realm of culture.[19] In doing so, the colonized locates its site of sovereignty within the spiritual realm, converting differences between into a positive affirmation.[20] Culture becomes a site in which to imagine worldviews.

Okakura's travel to India was one instance in which anti-colonial and anti-Western movements intertwined with the rewriting of the meaning of Asia. Asian independence activists formed transnational networks that used Japan as an intellectual hub and sanctuary and the rearticulation of Asia's meaning became part of a dialogue among non-state actors within Japan. Japan became a haven for Asian independence activists in the 1910s and 1920s; following its 1911 revision of the unequal treaty, Western powers could not pursue activists within Japanese sovereign territory. Indian independence activist Rashbehari Bose escaped to Japan and took refuge there from British forces. Sun Yat-sen also spent years in Japan as an exile, raising funds to support his revolutionary movement. In this context, there was an increasing polarization between state and non-state actors' stances with respect to Asia. Those who decentered China in the new discourse of civilizational standards distanced themselves from the emergent Pan-Asianist networks forming among independence activists throughout Asia, whereas those who considered that "Asia is One", and that Asian countries shared a fate vis-à-vis the "West" characterized Asians as sharing cultural commonality.

The gradual alteration of what Asia means dovetailed with the introduction of the concept of culture, *bunka* in the mid-1910s, into Japanese political discourse. According to historian Shin'ichi Yamamuro, the first use derives from the German philosophy of *kultur*. Distinguished from civilization, which is material, culture is based in the realm of the immaterial: art, spirituality, religion, and morality.[21]

This affinity is of no coincidence. The source of this resonance is Germany's position as the "peripheral" West. Germany is part of the West, yet in contrast to Britain and France, the timing of its industrialization and transformation into a nation-state, Germany is a "late developer". Both Japan and Germany – and, as Pheng Cheah underscores, every non-Western/peripheral subject – found themselves as "backward" in the linear, progressive, and mechanistic schema of British and French civilizational history.[22]

Being "backward" prompted the question in both Germany and Japan of how to think of history and agency otherwise. According to Pheng Cheah, it was Kant who provided grounds to relate culture to autonomy. Extending the identification of a common dilemma faced by German and anti-colonial thinkers, Cheah locates in German Idealism the rationale of "a philosophical history that sees organic life qua organized matter as an analogue of freedom and, therefore, as the paradigmatic metaphor for social organization and political life".[23] In his exposition of Kant's *Third Critique*, where political organization is depicted as a living entity, Cheah writes that Kant resorted to the organismic metaphor as a way to bridge a paradox: while man is an autonomous figure who can give himself law, he nonetheless lives in the natural world where he is constrained by mechanical processes. Especially in the Age of Reason where even nature was secularized and depicted as subject to mechanical reason and causal law, man's relation to nature and his moral autonomy appeared precarious.[24] Kant's solution to this paradox drew from Blumenbach's theory of epigenesis, which argued that life formation was spontaneous, developmental, *and* auto-causal.[25] Against mechanical reason and the law of causality, the theory of epigenesis enabled Kant to conceive of life as autonomous from externally dictated law and initiate its own development from within. This was in contrast to preformationist theory which presumed that the model for development and the end of a life form was already set by the time life came into being.

Yet the life span of a single human being is finite. Here, Kant finds in mankind's collective development of culture, which is cultivated for generations, a site where finite man transcends his finitude as a collective historical being.[26] Kant subtly shifts attention from man as an individual to man as part of a collective, thereby politicizing the meaning and significance of history and culture.[27] By seeking the manifestation of freedom in the realm of culture, Kant also attributes a new meaning to historicism. For Kant, the assurance that man's moral freedom can make a difference in the sensible world is found in the historical development of culture.[28] Culture becomes a site then in which mankind as community can realize its autonomy.[29]

Likewise in his critique of Edward Said's *Orientalism*, Robert Young also notes how the conundrum of locating exogenous agency haunts postcolonial scholarship. He writes that while much of the criticism on violence of history targets Hegel, less attention is paid to Kant and the issue of autonomy of philosophical reason in history. Said's critique suffers in part because he parts way from Foucault, who attended to the legacy of Kant and joins Habermas, who problematizes Hegel, but as an antidote, invokes the completion of the Enlightenment project.[30]

II. In search for alternative vision of Asia and history

There is an affinity between culture, history, and agency. Kiyoshi Miki begins his critique of the philosophy of history by attending to Kant's role in opening the way to German Romanticism and acknowledging the importance of culture as site for conceiving agency.[31] While this is an academic work, Miki's emphasis on the role of culture in affirming agency later is reflected on his theorization of Japanese international relations, as the *Toa Kyodotai* [East Asia Cooperative Body]. As the head of cultural division of prince and later Prime Minister Fumimaro Konoe's Showa Research Association (SRA), Miki serves as a conduit between German Idealism and Japanese imperial policy of the 1930s and 1940s. Given the role Miki served in imperial policy reformulation, his treatise on history should be examined and placed in the political context of the period. In doing so, I elucidate the precarious relation between asserting agency in the name of new cultural order and Japanese imperial violence.

In the period immediately after World War I, Japanese foreign policy experimented with cooperation and internationalism; both meant heeding to U.S.-led liberal order. Japan joined the League of Nations, accepted the arms reduction treaty despite its unequal terms, and joined a multilateral regime. At the same time, domestically, Japan established a two-party democracy. In 1930, one year after the Great Depression, the Showa Depression reached Japan. The Showa Depression altered Japanese views of what the ideal political and international framework ought to be. If the Great Depression was caused by U.S. economic liberalism and laissez-faire, the antidote was state intervention and regulation of the economy, and elimination of corruption instigated by the wedding of political parties and capitalists. The civilian government was also under attack for agreeing to unequal arms reduction treaty by the military. Militarism was on the rise, terror plots and assassination of prominent government leaders became frequent, and free speech was no longer. Once the ills of economic depression were traced to Anglo-Saxon-led liberal order, the solution was to turn to regional order independent of American influence. This led to exploration of alternative vision of regionalism which would be independent of Anglo-Saxon control. Even within the West there were discussions of the decline of the Occident, which in Japan came to be interpreted as the moment of relational reversal in history.

Discussions of regionalism among Japanese intellectuals surfaced in the 1930s, partially inspired by the writings of Hans Morgenthau and E.H. Carr. In the context of wartime Japan, the two figures were interpreted to support mobilization toward the end of realizing regionalism as means to transform domestic politics and achieve socialist ends.[32] Yet the shift to regionalism independent of American influence was difficult. There was a dissonance between the Japanese state's attempts to reorient itself domestically and the possibilities for regionalism made available by the international environment. In this period, historian Inoue identifies a sense of opportunity felt by the socialists and communists within Japan: in the name of total mobilization, the state could regulate and tame the capitalists, redistribute economic wealth to achieve more socialist ends, and include the poor into the system who had thus far been alienated.[33] Rather than characterizing Japan's total mobilization as top-down, Inoue writes that the people participated willingly in pushing the regime toward these utopic ends. While it is tempting to attribute Japan's shift from internationalism to regionalism as a symptom of the rise of militarism, leftists were also participating in debates on the new regional order, resulting in leftist collaboration with Japan's imperial expansion.

Geopolitically, the military most feared Soviet expansion. Preparation for future conflict with the Soviets took priority over any dealing with China, and expansion into China was deemed a bad idea by both the military and the civilian government. The expansion of war was not desired by anybody or planned. When the Marco Polo Bridge Incident triggered war between Japan and China, the initial government response was to localize the conflict and to end the fighting as soon as possible.[34] The conflict was settled between Japan and China four days after the incident, on July 11, in the form of truce. Yet Prime Minister Konoe also decided to send military reinforcements, presuming that this would serve as a show of resolve and consolidate the truce. The move backfired, as it was interpreted as a move not to enforce the truce but to overturn it and continue Japanese expansion. The Chinese resisted. This opened the way to full-scale war between Japan and China. The war expanded in the absence of intent to do so, leaving the theorization of significance of war up for grabs. It was this absence of planning which appeared as an opportunity for leftists such as Miki to steer the course of history.

In this context of war, diverse visions of an East Asian international order were conceived. In characterizing the dominant strands of thought in the 1930s, Wataru Hiromatsu identifies the existence of *minkan uyoku* (domestic right wing), the militarists, and the leftists. The right wing and militarists sought an emperor-led regional order. In opposition, the leftists called for the defeat of the emperor system. Yet following a March 15, 1937, incident, where the majority of leftist sympathizers were arrested, jailed, and tortured, the leftists' position shifted. Shortly after, movement leaders published letters renouncing the Japanese Communist Party's agenda of defeating the emperor system.[35] The letter argued for pursuing socialism under the leadership of the emperor, leading the Communist Party's position precariously close to that of the right-wing activists.[36]

By 1935, leftist dissent was no longer tolerated even within academia. There was little to no freedom of speech or thought. In his diary from 1937, Miki wrote, "We might be in a time where unless one were to imitate a madman, one cannot say what is right". The limits of free speech motivated Miki to join the Showa Research Association in 1938. The Showa Research Association (SRA), which began in 1933 as Konoe's brain trust, was an informal study group which sought to provide alternative policy options for Konoe. In 1937, the war between Japan and China challenged the remaining Japanese leftist intellectuals. In the most basic sense, it was a war in which Chinese nationalism was pitted against Japanese imperialism. For leftists critical of Japanese imperialism yet sought to formulate a way to signal an alternative direction, the interpretation of the meaning of what was happening in China had to avoid direct criticism of Japanese state policy.

Miki took up this project in his commentary on the Marco Polo Bridge Incident, "Nihon no Genjitsu" (The Reality of Japan), published in a journal, *Chuo Koron*, in November 1937. He begins his essay by declaring that the Marco Polo Bridge Incident brings about a new task for Japan. Miki argues that the war points to the need for a new political theory, one which speaks not only to the Japanese but is also agreeable to the Chinese and the European states. The preexisting Pan-Asianist argument, which hinged on the idea that Japan and China are of the same race, was insufficient and factually untrue. The war called for a theory of Asia that would acknowledge the vacuousness of the term "Asia", a term assigned to the region by the West. Within so-called Asia there is little homogeneity, for example, between the Indians and the Chinese. What Japan needs, then, is a *new* worldly theory of a united East, a theory wedded to a scientific approach to culture.[37] Given the limits of any idea of racial and cultural unity among Asians, Miki's proposal of a theory which did not need to base itself on this form of unity was welcomed by policymakers. His project was well received and led to an invitation to speak at the SRA. What made his work appealing for the members of SRA was its lack of reference to a mythical status for the emperor and his clarity about the limitations of preexisting theories for understanding the present.

However, the piece, "Nihon no Genjitsu," published in the journal *Chuo Koron* was heavily censored. There was a limit to how much influence Miki could exert through publishing his commentaries under military censorship. The way out was to join the government-sanctioned think tank, where Miki became a leading thinker.

Miki's decision to join the SRA inspired other leftist intellectuals to follow suit. In June 1938, Miki published "Chishiki Kaikyu ni Atau" ("To the Intellectuals"), which called on Japanese intellectuals to actively participate in shaping the future of Japan. He argued that, given that war was already taking place, what was important was to shape the direction of this war. Miki identified the role of the intellectuals as one of identifying and clarifying the historical meaning of the war.[38] Responding to this call, leftist intellectuals joined the Showa Research Association en masse in mid-1938. Given the restrictions on speech and freedom of thought and the motives of leftist intellectuals who joined the research association, the reading of SRA's pamphlet, *Shin Nihon no Shiso Genri (Principles of Thought for a New Japan –* from here on *Principles I)* calls for a reading which takes into account its historical context. Significantly, the treatise was written during a short window of opportunity leftist intellectuals had to exert influence on the discourse of rethinking Asia, thereby affecting how international relations could be theorized. In the following sections, we examine the framework of the *Principles I*, which delineates the stake of envisioning alternative order in Asia, and of the pamphlet which followed, *Principles II*, which seeks to spell out *how* to overcome the limits of Eurocentric order delineated in the first.

a. Principles of Thought for a New Japan

As Tetsuya Sakai writes, international relations theorists in the period after World War I – that is, the interwar years – signaled a sense of a worldwide crisis of order.[39] In light of this crises, both the members of SRA and the members of the later conference, "Overcoming Modernity", identified the Marco Polo Bridge Incident as evidence that world history was witnessing a decline of the West and emergence of a new kind of history in the East. World history up until then, according to the *Principles I*, was merely a history of the West, whose essence was Eurocentrism.[40] The *Principles* interpreted the significance of the Sino-Japanese War as the realization of a move toward an "actual" world history.

The *Principles I* begins with the identification of the world historical significance of the war as war and argues for the impossibility of finding a solution to the present conflict without pursuing domestic reform.[41] Spatially, the significance of the war lies in the unification of East Asia, and temporally in its overcoming capitalism and the capitalist stage of development. The unification of East Asia accords with world movement toward the formation of regional blocs, which is itself a movement toward the spatio-temporal unification of world history.[42] To facilitate this world historical movement, the *Principles I* argues that Japan ought to help China achieve modernization, which requires expelling Western imperialist influence from China. At the same time, if China is to join the united East it must avoid both falling back into its feudal past and being captured by modern capitalism. The *Principles I* also dismissed the government of Chiang Kai-shek as too Westernized and capitalistic.[43] Concomitantly, Japan must reform itself to overcome its capitalist-dominated system.

According to the *Principles I*, preexisting theories of world politics are inadequate for interpreting events like the Sino-Japanese War because of their abstraction: the "rise of individualism, liberalism, rationalism led to the abstraction of the world, and the rise of ethnic nationalism of the present is a critique of the abstraction, the limit of abstract universalism to comprehend the present".[44] In this vein the *Principles I* acknowledges the importance of nationalism and ethnonationalism. Yet, despite the tentative acknowledgment of nationalism as a valid critique of universalism and abstraction, in the name of the worldwide trend toward the formation of regional blocs, the *Principles* argues that Chinese nationalism must be recognized but overcome in order to realize the unification of the East Asian bloc.[45] In the same vein, the *Principles I* also argues that to realize the unity of the East, and to limit its own nationalism Japan itself must overcome its Japanism (Nihonshugi) and pursue a path toward cooperativism (kyodoshugi).[46]

The *Principles* constructs a dichotomous characterization of the East and the West. The East is based on the culture of the kingly way of rule (wangdao), the fusing of man and nature, the thought of heaven (tian) and the communitarian way of thought whereas the West is characterized by individualism, humanism, rationalism, liberalism, and the principle of atomistic self-interest.[47] Since the East, unlike the West, does not share a common preexisting culture, the creation of a new culture of the East that would overcome the limits of Western abstraction while avoiding a return to the East's own feudalistic ways must be pursued: "thus, with regards to Eastern culture, the task is to open the untapped trove of tradition and to acknowledge its worldly value and at the same time exit the Asian stagnation; simultaneously given that the crisis of the world is caused by the limitation of Western-led capitalistic order the new culture must also seek to overcome the limit of both".[48]

Liberalism, rationalism, atomism, and individualism on the one hand, and communism on the other, are thus all rejected based on their abstraction.[49] Liberalism considers the world as a collection of self-sufficient autonomous individual entities. Yet this ignores the fact that an individual cannot exist without society, and the same logic applies to individual states within international society. As there is no state without the world, according to *Principles I* states in must pursue unity of the East without relying on atomistic thinking or traditionalism. Likewise, because its understanding of history as warfare is an instance of abstract universalism, communism's understanding of history is unhistorical. Communism adheres to a linear history which understands movements in historical stages. Consequently, it cannot acknowledge the individuality and endogenous sources of change and difference in the world. As a result, communism is also not appropriate for understanding the present crisis.[50]

To the end of creating a new Asian order, rooted in concrete historical conditions, the *Principles* calls for recognizing the uniqueness of Japanese culture's ability to "subjectively unite what appears incompatible" under the name of praxis.[51] The uniqueness of Japanese culture is credited with giving Japan the ability to quickly incorporate Western technology especially in contrast to others. Based on this, the *Principles I* argue that Japan should take a leadership role in East Asia, while also overcoming its own domestic Japanism and nationalism. The final article adds that these arguments are not to justify Japanese invasion and rule over others in East Asia.[52]

As a whole, the *Principles I* outlines the limitations of preexisting concepts, explains the Sino-Japanese War is making a new East Asian culture that departs from preexisting traditions, and justifies Japanese leadership according to Japanese culture's unique ability to incorporate seemingly incompatible ideas. Yet this piece, published in January of 1939, lacked any outline of the means to overcome the limitations it critiques. In a sense the *Principles I* can be considered as a treatise on "why" the war must be fought. As Hiromatsu identifies, the mass conversion away from Marxism even among leftists shows how abstract concepts derived from particular Western experiences were found wanting. The *Principles I* articulated the limitations of Eurocentric means of conceiving of and acting in the world, but also registered the futility of believing, as right-wing thinkers did, in a forged cultural unity of the East. It made sense of the world. Yet the question of what the Japanese were to do after having made sense remained unclear. That question was pursued in a subsequent piece published in September of the same year: *Shin Nihon no Shiso Genri Zokuhen Kyodoshugi no Tetsugakuteki Kiso (New Principles of Japan Continued: The Philosophical Basis for Cooperativism* – henceforth *Principles II*). This piece shifted the emphasis toward the philosophy of praxis.

b. *Asia as a work of art*

Principles II, which was published in January, navigates a precarious line – it critiques capitalism, liberalism, communism, totalitarianism, Japanism, militarism, abstraction, and imperialism. It should be noted here that the critique of liberalism and capitalism were also made by right-wing thinkers, and their antidotes to Western excess were Japanism and militarism. The *Principles I* differentiates itself from the militarists and right-wing ideologues by also including Japanism, militarism, and imperialism as targets of critique. To put it crudely, this rejection of Japanism also meant that the romantic return to the past was also not a viable option in Miki's view. If one were to reject current Western order but also disavow romanticization of the Japanese past, what could then one turn to? The answer to this was found in the notion of poiesis, a form of artistic production which distinguished itself from mimesis. This is the reason why the method with which to overcome the present crisis was identified as poiesis in the *Principles II*.

Miki was still the head of the cultural division of SRA when the continued *Principles II* was authored in September of 1939. Long before 1939, in 1933, Miki had already begun to write on the relationship between the faculty of imagination and the constitution of the global worldview. In the journal *Shiso*, Miki began publishing a series of essays on the *Kosoryoku no Genri (Logic of Imagination)* in May 1937. He most likely joined the SRA a month after he began this series, which he continued in 1944, and completed the series in July of that year. Thus, it appears that the *Principles I* and *Principles II* were written in parallel with Miki's single-authored project on the *Logic of Imagination*. Given this chronological parallel of the two projects ongoing under Miki, it makes sense to read *Principles II* as a project which seeks to envision alternative Asian order by means of artistic metaphor, to think of Asia as a work of art.

The *Principles II* begins by identifying the Sino-Japanese War as a Holy War, a war executed in the name of building a new order in East Asia.[53] The premise of the war is that it is being fought in order to overcome the exclusionary practices of Sun Yat-sen's *Three Principles* (sanmin zhyuyi) as well as the mechanical abstract worldview being imposed by the West. The basis of this New Principle of thought is cooperativism, a practice whose basis lies in the act of making.[54] This practice is productive and poietic. Poiesis pertains to the unification of the objective law of nature with the subjective human will. The theory of this practice is a theory of historical production and historical creativity: "we are made by history and conversely, makers of history".[55]

The historical meaning of the war hinges on the act of making, that is, of creating a new order. This act of making is to overcome the debates on whether history determines, or development of history is determined by, an agent. The *Principles II* is based on the philosophy of form *(katachi no shiso)*, in particular a form which is historical and historically developing.[56] The *Principles II* rejects the organicism which had dominated discussions of regionalism because it presumed an unfolding of according to a preexisting form. To posit a preexisting form is to identify an endogenous cause of historical development, which forecloses the possibility of making something new. The *Principles II* also rejects dialectics for being merely critical, never productive and formative.

The notion of the form and the maker of the form is likened to artistic production. The *Principles II* denies that artistic production is merely mimetic. The artist might be copying the object before his eyes, yet the copying is possible only with the active engagement of the copier. Because this engagement is active and selective, what is being copied is not the same as the copy. The *Principles II*, The New Principle of East Asia, is about this formative production it copies but is different from the expansion or scaling up of the west. The *Principles II* envisions the making of new principles that will overcome the existing limits of the way in which international relations is thought. The significance of the formative moment of these principles is likened to the moment of the birth of individualism in Renaissance Italy in the West, when the idea of individualism gradually eroded the old theological cosmopolitan world order. The birth of the historical agent-subject in the Renaissance is both particular to the West because it occurred in a particular place, and universal because it reformulated the way in which the universe was conceived. The *Principles II* likens the impact of the creation of New Asian Order to the impact of the Renaissance, as the creation of the New Asian Order will have both particular and universal impacts.

The *Principles II* was a systematic clarification of the New East Asian Order proclaimed by Prime Minister Konoe in 1938, one year after the Marco Polo Bridge Incident. It redefined the war aim as making of a new culture. This war aim legitimated not only the theorists in the metropole, but also the soldiers on the ground in China. Ishida called the soldiers "cultural soldiers", recalling words by Tenshin Okakura, that "Asia is One".[57] The soldiers in the occupied territories saw their efforts as part of making a new East Asian culture, form, and order. As the first preamble of the *Principles I* stated, the war was about the cultural transformation of *both* Japanese domestic political order and of Greater East Asia, after all.

Because the *Principles I* cautioned against mere expansion or imposition of Japanism, the clarification of the war aim spoke to those who remained critical of Japanese imperialism. In this sense, the *Principles I* and *II* were more potent in endowing legitimacy to the war than the ideology of Japanism. The making of new culture sought to envision Sino-Japanese relations as cooperative making of a new culture. The reformers considered the model of cooperativism established in Manchuria as the ideal model to implement within Japan.[58] The plan to reform the existing corrupt order attracted a diversity of supporters, including theorists as well as militarists, farmers, factory workers, and others seeking reform in Japan. The linking of total war as a means to constitute a new kind of utopic regional order brought in support from all strata of society. This idea leads the socialist party to become the total nationalist party.

Having provided a blueprint to reorganize and legitimate the war as a means to reform both Japanese and Asian political order, the SRA was disbanded and then in 1940 absorbed into *taisei yokusankai*, the Imperial Rule Assistance Association. In the 1940s, the reconfiguration of meaning of the Marco Polo Bridge Incident as the beginning of New Order was reflected in narration of history in school textbooks as well. In the context of the SRA's influence on education policy, the understanding of history reluctantly converged the leftist intellectuals who joined the Showa Research Association and those who held the emperor-centered view of history, the *Kokokushikan*. While the two differed on the view of Japanism and whether making the concept of unique Japanese spirit as an absolute ideal was desirable, both turned to the realm of culture as a site where political change were to find its future blueprints in. The turn to culture as a site to constitute a new political order showed them both to embrace the Platonic trope of shaping the political body – transnational or national – as a plastic art.[59] The war was in the name of history.

By 1941, the Ministry of Education had set up a temporary editorial section for the overview of national history, putting those who held the emperor-centered view in charge.[60] Under this editorial supervision history textbooks characterized the war as a Holy War of defense against the West. They also suggested that the people were to work diligently toward the goal of building a New Asian Order and by extension, a New World Order under the benevolent protection of the Emperor.[61]

In her study on Pan-Asianism and Japan's war, Eri Hotta argues that the significance of Miki's work lies in the extent of legitimacy his texts gave to Japan's war and shaping of the historical narrative. Because of the efficacy of this newly defined war aim, it subsequently made it difficult for Japanese leaders to back out of the war short of winning this unwinnable war of liberation.[62] Following Miki, in the 1940s, the war as war realizing a new kind of order was reified by others not involved in the SRA. The Kyoto School philosophers – Masataka Kosaka, Iwao Koyama, and Masataka Suzuki – were conservative scholars who later participated in the conference, "Overcoming Modernity" and "Japan and its World Historical Standpoint".[63] In postwar years, the Kyoto School philosophers were criticized for glorifying Japan's war in the 1940s. The conference on overcoming modernity identified the objective of the war to be the making of a new world order – yet as Yonetani notes, the context in which the argument was made was vastly different from the context in which Miki made such a claim. With the war occurring between Japan and the United States, the glorification of war as war against the West was far easier to legitimate in the 1940s than in the period when Miki's pieces were written, for when the war broke out between Japan and China, the Western powers were not directly involved.[64] Japan opened war against England and the United States, and with the inclusion of the two as the enemy, many intellectuals felt a sigh of relief in part because the characterization of war as a war of resisting and repelling Anglo-Saxon domination finally became possible.[65] Historian Ryuichi Narita notes how the narration of war up until Pearl Harbor was mainly characterized as documentary and reporting of what is going on in the war front, and it was after the attack that war narratives began embodying higher aims.[66] In this sense, historical meaning of war slides from the first phase where in the name of pursuing socialist utopia differences were to be overcome, to another phase where the meaning of war turns into that of an East-West confrontation: when the war was between Japan and China, the kind of legitimation Miki endowed for intellectuals to join the project was akin to a last-ditch effort at potentially affecting the course of history by shaping the meaning of the Marco Polo Bridge Incident. Still, the fact of Chinese resistance and the prolongation of the war despite Japanese military victory made obvious the limitations of conceiving of the war as war with higher ends.[67] It was when the war expanded against Western powers these higher ends became more potent as war propaganda. The Kyoto School and the two conferences on "Overcoming Modernity" and "World Historical Position and Japan", formulated the project of "Overcoming Modernity" in these terms as overcoming Western modernity.[68]

Despite the caveat Miki added in the *Principles I* that Japan should not merely substitute the Western hegemonic position, in the end, the war became a war of establishing Japanese dominance in the region. This replication of oppressive dynamics suggests that we need to examine further the problematic of answering the Western denial of Asian agency with the claim that, to right such wrong, we must render the formerly oppressed and colonized as the subject of history, beginning anew. Why are responses to Western denial of historical agency susceptible to appropriation toward imperialist ends? Here, we return to wordings on methods proposed to resist the West in the *Principles I* and *II.*

There is merit in considering why the treatise was not named *The Principles of Japan* but *The Principles of New Japan* – for why the emphasis on beginning anew? Because the attempt to critique Eurocentric norms relied on poiesis as means to overcome the preexisting limitations in practical terms, this meant that there is a likening of Asia as a kind of malleable plastic art *and* the conception of Japan as both subject and maker of history. Moreover, the treatise itself is named as *The Principles of New Japan*, which reflects an emphasis on initiating a new beginning, a new order. Because the *Principles* rejected any return to the past, the turn to culture meant a *making* of new culture. Making requires a maker. Although Miki continuously warned that Japan should not merely replace the Western powers in

Asia, he nonetheless identified a special leading role for Japan as the beginner of this new culture. For positing of new order, there must be an agent who brings about this change, and one who is free of the ideological domination that is supposedly total. The appropriation of this call for new order into legitimating Japanese imperialism was bound to happen as the theoretical underspecification of "who" the subject of history is was to be answered by practical political concerns. In the name of political realism, those who asserted that Japan should be this agent of history claimed so in light of how Japan was the only country that fully escaped the predicament of being colonized by the West.

The notion of actualization of autonomy via the making of a new culture, a notion inspired from Kant, assigns Japan the role of the poet-creator and thereby an embodiment of autonomy unavailable before, when under inculcation of others. If, as Kant says, freedom is the freedom from any exogenously derived law, this freedom must depart from both Western derived law as well as "traditional" law. The treatise cannot be merely critical or derivative, but productive. This insistence on absolute endogeneity posed Kant with the question of how to make freedom incarnate in the natural world, the world governed by mechanistic causal law. In the two *Principles*, there is no mention of Kant, although Miki's very first writing on philosophy of history begins from his acknowledgment of Kant in providing a framework with which to critique history.[69] The point which I am trying to consider is whether this insistence on absolute autonomy from the given via emphasis on beginning anew is not conductive to a kind of blindness to plurality, intersubjectivity, and voices of people *from* Asia, not "Asia". Likewise, Shin'ichi Yamamuro points that discourse on culture and imperial policy was more potent when culture was not to refer to tradition but to a making of something anew.[70] Return to tradition would mean working with what is given to us. Making of *new* culture in contrast opens itself to a precarious claim, that anything is possible and no reference to actual Asia is necessary.

As Matsumoto documents, the discourse on Asia in Japan at the time of war tried to reconcile the fact that the resistance movement in China was directed against Japan. Other members of the SRA, such as Masamichi Royama and Hidemi Ozaki, like Miki, also tried to interpret the meaning of Chinese resistance.[71] The fact that the republicans and communists formed a cease-fire in order to unite their effort against Japan still was interpreted as Chinese people holding false consciousness and remaining ignorant about the worldwide historical trend toward regionalism and anti-Eurocentrism. This is to say that linear history, or civilizational history, was problematic as it naturalized Eurocentrism, yet the Japanese response crafted in the 1930s nonetheless continued to conceive of Asia as a theoretical problem whose solution lay in the construction of New Asian Order at the expense of Asian voices and dissent. Indeed, the *Principles* lack any account of the facts on the ground, of any voices or critiques from Asia. This very absence speaks to how the theorization of new Asia in the end remained as a theoretical issue having little to do with politics on the actual ground of Asia.

What is one to make out of this fact of collaboration and total mobilization, of potency of Miki's reformulation of historicism? As sketched out earlier, the hidden thematic here is how resistance against Eurocentrism took the form of cultural reconfiguration of historical significance, of how cultural production of new order came to legitimate and reproduce the kind of imperial violence which Miki originally sought to critique. The politicization of culture in the name of resistance in Chinese and Korean eyes was merely a new form of domination.[72] The shift from the "civilizing mission" discourse to cultural governance, while framed differently, nonetheless remained a colonialist discourse. The concept of culture, which was supposed to offer a site of resistance against civilizational discourse, in the end legitimated violence waged in the name of instating a new culture. Were there other possibilities of politicizing culture, and what does the lack of resistance among intellectuals in the period say about the proper relation between politics and culture? This weight of how agency-enabling historicism underwrote and legitimated colonialism and imperialism continues to implicitly bind the post-1945 discourse on the subject of history.[73] Yoshimi Takeuchi poses the question: if "Asia" becomes a subject through resistance, how could we theorize resistance otherwise?[74]

With the end of the war, there was a swift forgetting of this convergence among socialists, right-wing activists, militarists, and ordinary populace in sustaining the war effort in Japan. The U.S. Occupation force's policy of absolving the emperor and the people and casting the blame on the militarists in order to secure support from the Japanese did not help, either.[75] Kyoto School's Kosaka, who, during wartime elaborated on the significance of Japan's position in world history, would soon begin discussing the dawn of new historical movement led by the United States and Soviets as the new regional hegemon.[76] Miki died in prison a little after the end of war. With the advent of Cold War geopolitics and U.S. effacing of "Asia" from Japanese political thought, and the de facto delegitimation of Japan's war aim, the state of history in Japan is concealed.

The easy narrative out was to characterize the wartime period of 1930s and 1940s as a period in which the militarists oppressed and tricked the people into collaboration, which was the American script. Asianism was a taboo immediately after the war, and multiethnic Japan which legitimated Japanese imperialism was disavowed and the myth of homogenous Japan took root, thereby occluding former "non-Japanese" imperial subjects and their existence.[77] The Holy War became the wrong-headed war, and with the end of war, it became easy to critique wartime policy. Yet the collusion of the interests between Japanese establishment and U.S. Occupation forces meant that while what occurred in war against Western powers were subject to heavy criticism, much of the vexed relation between empire, colonialism, and Western imperialism in broader historical span was left out. In Kuang-Hsing Chen's formulation, the process of de-imperialization and decolonization of history was, therefore, suspended under the Cold War.[78] This meant that with the thawing of Cold War tensions, the question of how to write and speak of history returns, a literary critic named Norihiro Kato who pits the postwar literary debate into a political one in 1995 opens the debate. The return and haunting of postwar debate on the subject of history with memories of the wartime era is the subject of the last chapter.

Notes

1 I employ the term "nationalism" with reserve, as it confines the use of cultural historicism to the idea of the nation.
2 Katsunan Kuga, "Kokusairon [Theory of the International]", in Masanao Shikano ed., *Nihon no Meicho [Japanese Classics]*, Vol. 37 (Tokyo: Chuo Koronsha, 1971): 180–182.
3 Kiyoshi Miki, "Toa Shiso no Konkyo [Ground of Asian Thought]", in Hiroshi Uchida ed., *Miki Kiyoshi Toa Kyodotai Ronshu [Essay Collections of Kiyoshi Miki's Theory of East Asian Cooperative Body]* (Tokyo: Kobushi Shobo, 2007): 43.
4 Wataru Hiromatsu, *Kindai no Chokokuron: Showa Shisoshi he no ichi shikaku [Theory of Overcoming Modernity: A Perspective on Political Thought of Showa Period]* (Tokyo: Kodansha Gakujutsu Bunko, 2006): 126–127.
5 Even to this day, the adjacent museum within Yasukuni Shrine which commemorates the war dead, the *Yushukan*, narrates the meaning of war as a Holy War against the West. Every time a prominent politician or Prime Minister of Japan pays a visit to the shrine, it raises discomfort among survivors and victims among Japan's neighboring states. This is what is known as the contemporary "history problem" in East Asia.
6 Osamu Nishitani, *Sekaishi no Rinkai [Limit of World History]* (Tokyo: Iwanami Shoten, 2006): 141–164.
7 Gim was a friend and disciple of Fukuzawa, who sought to reform Choseon Korea along the model of Meiji Japan and seek national independence away from its suzerain, Qing China. The assassination was ordered by Queen Min, who formed the Sadae faction within the dynasty which pursued the policy of continuing Korea's adherence to the Sinocentric order. Masafumi Yonetani, *Ajia/Nihon [Asia/Japan]* (Tokyo: Iwanami Shoten, 2007): 41–56.
8 Turan Kayaoglu, *Legal Imperialism: Sovereignty and Extraterritoriality in Japan, the Ottoman Empire, and China* (Cambridge: Cambridge University Press, 2010).
9 On the Japanese state's use of civilizational logic to justify the colonization of Korea, see Alexis Dudden, *Japan's Colonization of Korea: Discourse and Power* (Honolulu: University of Hawai'i Press, 2006). On the development of Japanese Orientalism see Stefan Tanaka, *Japan's Orient: Rendering Pasts into History* (Berkeley: University of California Press, 1995).
10 Kevin Doak, *A History of Nationalism in Modern Japan* (Leiden, The Netherlands: Brill, 2007): 170.
11 Ibid., 184.
12 On the genealogy of altering Japanese self-images, see Eiji Oguma, *A Genealogy of "Japanese" Self-Images* (Melbourne: Trans Pacific Press, 2002).
13 The role of Chinese character was similar to Latin in medieval Europe – it was the language of the elites. This institute is the predecessor to today's Aichi University, the most prestigious university for China studies.
14 Tanaka, *Japan's Orient*; indeed, it is ironic that it was not scholars from Tokyo Imperial University but those from the Kyoto Imperial University who were employed to justify Japanese imperialism in the 1930s and 1940s.
15 Barucha, *Another Asia*; Eri Hotta, *Pan-Asianism and Japan's War: 1931–1945* (New York: Palgrave Macmillan, 2007): 32.
16 Michael Adas, *Machines as the Measure of Men: Science, Technology, and Ideologies of Western Dominance* (Ithaca, NY: Cornell University Press, 1990).
17 Hotta, 32.
18 Partha Chatterjee, *Nation and Its Fragments: Colonial and Postcolonial Histories* (Princeton, NJ: Princeton University Press, 1993): 6.
19 Ibid., 6.
20 Ibid., 6–13, 26–27.
21 Yamamuro Shinichi, *Shiso Kadai to shite no Ajia [Asia as a Theoretical Problem]* (Tokyo: Iwanami Shoten, 2001): 83.

22 Pheng Cheah, *Spectral Nationality: Passages of Freedom from Kant to Postcolonial Literatures of Liberation* (New York: Columbia University Press, 2006): 6.

23 Ibid., 5.

24 Stephen Toulmin, *Cosmopolis: The Hidden Agenda of Modernity* (Chicago: University of Chicago Press, 1992): 114–115.

25 Cheah, 64.

26 William E. Connolly, "Pluralism and Time", in *Pluralism* (Durham and London: Duke University Press, 2005): 114–116.

27 Hannah Arendt also treats Kant's *Third Critique* as his unwritten political philosophy because of the role attributed to community and *sensus communis*. Cf. Hannah Arendt, *Lectures on Kant's Political Philosophy* (Chicago: University of Chicago Press, 1989).

28 Cheah, "Human beings, Kant argues, have certain naturally given, original predispositions . . . such as reason and freedom of will that are directed toward rational activity. But these predispositions are not instincts. They are germs *(Keime)* that need to be developed *(entwickeln)* through our own efforts. These capacities remain dormant and ineffectual if they are not frequently exercised. But because we are finite and they take a long time to develop, they can only be fully developed in the species *(Gattung)*. Culture *(Kultur)*, as an objective realm broadly defined to include legal and political institutions and the arts and sciences, is the historical medium for the development of our rational capacities. Culture is thus a power for transcending the mechanism of nature found in nature itself. It is the prosthetic compensation for the limitation human finitude imposes on our development." 75.

29 Cheah, also Martin Heidegger, "Age of World Picture", in *The Question Concerning Technology, and Other Essays* (New York: Harper & Row, 1977).

30 Robert Young, "Disorienting Orientalism", in *White Mythologies: Writing History and the West* (New York: Routledge, 1990): 134.

31 Kiyoshi Miki, "Hihan Tetsugaku to Rekishi Tetsugaku [Critical Philosophy and Philosophy of History]", in *Miki Kiyoshi Rekishi Tetsugaku Korrekushon [Kiyoshi Miki's Collected Essays on Philosophy of History]* (Tokyo: Shoshi Shinsui, 2012).

32 Tetsuya Sakai, "Sengo Gaikoron no Keisei [Formation of Postwar International Relations Theory]", in *Kindai Nihon no Kokusai Chitsujoron [Genealogy of Modern Japanese International Order]* (Tokyo: Iwanami Shoten, 2007): 23–42.

33 Toshikazu Inoue, *Nicchu Sensoka no Nihon [Japan under Sino-Japanese War]* (Tokyo: Kodansha Sensho Metier, 2007): 14–15.

34 On Prime Minister Konoe's China policy, see Inoue, 14–15 and Hotta, 156–164. On the relationship between intellectuals and fascism, see William Fletcher, *Intellectuals and Fascism in Prewar Japan: The Search for a New Order* (Chapel Hill: The University of North Carolina Press, 1982); Harry Harootunian, *Overcome by Modernity: History, Culture, and Community in Interwar Japan* (Princeton, NJ: Princeton University Press, 2001).

35 Hiromatsu, 128.

36 Ibid., 134.

37 Kiyoshi Miki, "Nihon no Genjitsu [On the Reality of Japan]", in Hiroshi Uchida ed., *Miki Kiyoshi Toa Kyodotaironshu* (Tokyo: Kobushi Bunko, 2007): 7–28.

38 Hiromatsu, 141.

39 Sakai, 33.

40 Principle 1, 176. While Hiromatsu claims that the Principle could be considered as Miki's own writing, there is recent research indicating that while Miki was involved, he was not the principal author. Therefore, I will cite only as Principle and not as Miki.

41 Principle 1, 175.

42 Ibid., 177–178.

43 Ibid., 177.

44 Principles I, 179.

45 Ibid., 179, 183, 190.

46 Ibid., 182, 191.
47 Ibid., 179–180.
48 Ibid., 181.
49 Principle, 185–187.
50 Ibid., 185.
51 Ibid., 192.
52 Ibid., 193.
53 Principles II, 194.
54 Ibid., 198.
55 Ibid., 202.
56 Ibid., 212.
57 Inoue, 68.
58 Ibid., 108. Also, Louise Young, *Japan's Total Empire: Manchuria and the Culture of Wartime Imperialism* (Berkeley: University of California Press, 1998); Prasenjit Duara, *Sovereignty and Authenticity: Manchukuo and the East Asian Modern* (Lanham, MD: Rowman & Littlefield, 2004).
59 On the aestheticization of politics and how praxis is rendered into oblivion, see Dana R. Villa, *Arendt and Heidegger: The Fate of the Political* (Princeton, NJ: Princeton University Press, 1996): 246–253; Philippe Lacoue-Labarthe and Jean-Luc Nancy, "Overture: The System-Subject", in *The Literary Absolute: The Theory of Literature in German Romanticism*, trans. Phillip Barnard and Cheryl Lester (New York: State University of New York Press, 1988): 27–37.
60 Ryuichi Narita, *Rekishigaku no Pojishonariti: Rekishi Jojutsu to sono Shuhen [Positionality and Historiography: Surrounding Historical Narrative]* (Tokyo: Azekura Shobo, 2006): 108.
61 Ibid., 112.
62 Hotta, 174–176.
63 Miki himself was also a disciple of Nishida and Tanabe, but he is differentiated along with Jun Tosaka for his Marxist sympathies. The other disciples are grouped as Kyoto School conservatives.
64 Yonetani Masafumi, "Miki Kiyoshi no 'Sekaishi no Tetsugaku': Nicchusenso to 'sekai' [Kiyoshi Miki's 'World History: Sino-Japanese War and the 'World']", *Hihyo Kukan [Critical Space]*, Vol. 19, No. 2 (1998): 42.
65 Osawa, 202.
66 Narita, 59.
67 The limitation was sensed by Miki himself, too. In a note written after his trip to Manchuria, Miki observed that the different races within Manchukuo were not walking along side by side or spending time together despite Manchukuo's utopian project, the project of five races coexisting. This note is particularly poignant, as he was in the same passenger car as the Jews who obtained visas to escape to the United States by Sugihara. He was noting how the officers offered sake to the fellow passengers and they got drunk together – Miki observes and notes this, and reinforces the import of the Manchukuo and Japan's war aim, which for him is to provide minorities with places to exist. Yet he also notes that the Japanese and the Manchurians do not live together or share meals together. This writing subtly identified the gap between the aim and reality of Japan's war in Asia.
68 Sun Ge, "In Search of the Modern", in Thomas Lamarre and Kang Nae-hui eds., *Impacts of Modernities* (Hong Kong: Hong Kong University Press, 2004).
69 Kiyoshi Miki, "Hihan tetsugaku to rekishi tetsugaku [Critical Philosophy and Historical Philosophy]", in *Miki Kiyoshi Rekishi Tetsugaku Korekushon* (Tokyo: Shoshi Shinsui, 2012).
70 Yamamuro, 80–81.
71 Sannosuke Matsumoto, "'Toa Kyodotai' ron wo megutte [Over 'East Asian Cooperative Body']", in *Kindai Nihon no Chugoku Ninshiki*, 228–236, 268–285.

72 Japanese colonial policy on Korea shifts from the discourse of "civilizing" mission toward that of acculturation and assimilationist policy during the 1940s. This is the period when Korean subjects were forced to change their names into Japanese names and to learn the Japanese language and were drafted into Japanese military toward the end of the war campaign.
73 With the notable exception of the works by Japanese Sinologist Yoshimi Takeuchi.
74 Yoshimi Takeuchi, *Nihon to Ajia [Japan and Asia]* (Tokyo: Chikuma Gakugei Bunko, 1993).
75 On this, see James J. Orr, *Victim as Hero: Ideologies of Peace and National Identity in Postwar Japan* (Honolulu: University of Hawai'i Press, 2001).
76 Tetsuya Sakai, "Kaku Ajia Kindai no Chokoku – 1950 nendai nihon seiji shiso no ichidanmen [Nuclear Weapon, Overcoming Asian Modernity: A Segment of Japanese Political Thought in 1950s]", *Shiso [Thought]*, Vol. 1043 (2011): 7–26.
77 Eiji Oguma, *Genealogy of "Japanese" Self-Images*, trans. David Askew (Melbourne: Trans Pacific Press, 2002).
78 Kuang-Hsing Chen, *Asia as Method: Toward Deimperialization* (Durham and London: Duke University Press, 2010).

References

Adas, Michael. *Machines as the Measure of Men: Science, Technology, and Ideologies of Western Dominance*. Ithaca, NY: Cornell University Press, 1990.

Arendt, Hannah. *Lectures on Kant's Political Philosophy*. Chicago: University of Chicago Press, 1989.

Barucha, Rustom. *Another Asia: Rabindranath Tagore & Okakura Tenshin*. New Delhi: Oxford University Press, 2010.

Chatterjee, Partha. *Nation and Its Fragments: Colonial and Postcolonial Histories*. Princeton, NJ: Princeton University Press, 1993.

Cheah, Pheng. *Spectral Nationality: Passages of Freedom from Kant to Postcolonial Literatures of Liberation*. New York: Columbia University Press, 2003.

Chen, Kuang-Hsing. *Asia as Method: Toward Deimperialization*. Durham and London: Duke University Press, 2010.

Doak, Kevin. *A History of Nationalism in Modern Japan*. Leiden, The Netherlands: Brill, 2007.

Duara, Prasenjit. *Sovereignty and Authenticity: Manchukuo and the East Asian Modern*. New York: Rowman & Littlefield Publishers, 2004.

Dudden, Alexis. *Japan's Colonization of Korea: Discourse and Power*. Honolulu: University of Hawai'i Press, 2006.

Fletcher, William. *Intellectuals and Fascism in Prewar Japan: The Search for a New Order*. Chapel Hill: The University of North Carolina Press, 1982.

Ge, Sun. "In Search of the Modern." In *Impacts of Modernities*, edited by Thomas Lamarre and Kang Nae-hui. Hong Kong: Hong Kong University Press, 2004.

Harootunian, Harry. *Overcome by Modernity: History, Culture, and Community in Interwar Japan*. Princeton, NJ: Princeton University Press, 2001.

Heidegger, Martin. *The Question Concerning Technology, and Other Essays*. New York, NY: Harper & Row, 1977.

Hiromatsu, Wataru. *Kindai no Chokokuron: Showa Shisoshi he no ichi shikaku [Theory of Overcoming Modernity: A Perspective on Political Thought of Showa Period]*. Tokyo: Kodansha Gakujyutsubunko, 2006.

Hotta, Eri. *Pan-Asianism and Japan's War: 1931–1945*. New York: Palgrave Macmillan, 2007.

Inoue, Toshikazu. *Nicchu Sensoka no Nihon [Japan under Sino-Japanese War]*. Tokyo: Kodansha Sensho Metier, 2007.

Kayaoglu, Turan. *Legal Imperialism: Sovereignty and Extraterritoriality in Japan, the Ottoman Empire, and China*. Cambridge: Cambridge University Press, 2010.

Kuga, Katsunan. *Kokusairon [Theory of the International]*. Nihon no Meicho [Japanese Classics] 37. Edited by Masanao Shikano. Tokyo: Chuo Koronsha, 1971.

Lacoue-Labarthe, Philippe and Jean-Luc Nancy. *The Literary Absolute: The Theory of Literature in German Romanticism*. Translated by Phillip Barnard and Cheryl Lester. New York: State University of New York Press, 1988.

Matsumoto, Sannosuke. *Kindai Nihon no Chugoku ninshiki [How the Japanese Recognized China in the Modern World]*. Tokyo: Ibunsha, 2011.

Miki, Kiyoshi. *Miki Kiyoshi Toa Kyodotai Ronshu [Essay Collections of Kiyoshi Miki's East Asian Cooperative Body]*. Edited by Hiroshi Uchida. Tokyo: Kobushi Shobo, 2007.

Miki, Kiyoshi. *Miki Kiyoshi Rekishi Tetsugaku Korrekushon [Kiyoshi Miki's Collected Essays on Philosophy of History]*. Tokyo: Shoshi Shinsui, 2012.

Narita, Ryuichi. *Rekishigau no Pojishonaritii: Rekishi Jojutsu to sono Shuhen [Positionality and Historiography: Surrounding Historical Narrative]*. Tokyo: Azekura Shobo, 2006.

Nishitani, Osamu. *Sekaishi no Rinkai [Limits of History]*. Tokyo: Iwanami Shoten, 2006.

Oguma, Eiji. *A Genealogy of 'Japanese' Self-Images*. Translated by David Askew. Melbourne: Trans Pacific Press, 2002.

Orr, James J. *Victim as Hero: Ideologies of Peace and National Identity in Postwar Japan*. Honolulu, HI: University of Hawai'i Press, 2001.

Osawa, Masachi. *Sengo no Shiso Kukan [Atmosphere of Postwar Political Thought]*. Tokyo: Chikuma Shinsho, 2005.

Sakai, Tetsuya. "Kaku Ajia Kindai no Chokoku – 1950 nendai nihon seiji shiso no ichidanmen [Nuclear Weapon, Overcoming Asian Modernity: A Segment of Japanese Political Thought in 1950s]." *Shiso*, no. 1043 (2011): 7–26.

Sakai, Tetsuya. *Kindai Nihon no Kokusai Chitsujoron [Genealogy of Modern Japanese International Order]*. Tokyo: Iwanami Shoten, 2007.

Takeuchi, Yoshimi. *Nihon to Ajia [Japan and Asia]*. Tokyo: Chikuma Gakugei Bunko, 1993.

Tanaka, Stefan. *Japan's Orient: Rendering Pasts into History*. Berkeley: University of California Press, 1993.

Toulmin, Stephen. *Cosmopolis: The Hidden Agenda of Modernity*. Chicago: University of Chicago Press, 1992.

Villa, Dana. *Arendt and Heidegger: The Fate of the Political*. Princeton, NJ: Princeton University Press, 1996.

Yamamuro, Shin'ichi. *Shiso Kadai To Shiteno Ajia [Asia as a Theoretical Problem]*. Tokyo: Iwanami Shoten, 2004.

Yonetani, Masafumi. "Miki Kiyoshi no 'Sekaishi no tetsugaku': Nicchusenso to 'sekai' [Kiyoshi Miki's 'World History': Sino-Japanese War and the 'World']." *Hihyo Kukan [Critical Space]* 19, no. 2 (1998): 40–68.

Yonetani, Masafumi. *Ajia/Nihon [Asia/Japan]*. Tokyo: Iwanami Shoten, 2006.

Young, Louise. "Introduction: Japan's New International History." *American Historical Review* (2014): 1117–1128.

Young, Robert. *White Mythologies: Writing History and the West*. New York: Routledge, 1990.

4   On the postwar palimpsest subject of history

At a symposium on East Asian history education held among Chinese and Japanese scholars in 1994, historian Gong Qizhu asserted that

> scholars of both countries must condemn the war of invasion instigated by the Japanese militarism, inflicting tremendous damage on China, Korea, and Asia; [and scholars] must contribute towards the formation of accurate historical consciousness which formulates recognition that "Japan is the aggressor" about the past war.[1]

Opinion polls in China and Korea both presume that the Japanese people's understanding about the past war is unrepentant and nationalistic, therefore requiring correction.[2] This assumption has become widespread, largely because the standoff over how to write history is driven by sensationalist media reports, rather than by actual analyses of the postwar politics of history textbooks in Japan.[3] Such characterizations of what makes history writing problematic – that it is nationalistic – in turn shapes the assumption that the solution to this standoff is to reconfigure history in a "correct" manner. I will argue that this response is too simplistic, and that it exacerbates mutual misunderstanding and animosity. The "history problem" continues to persist because it inevitably raises questions of how to deal with the subject of history, and whether this subject has agency and thereby the ability to respond to Asian victims' demands.

An ahistorical analysis of the persistence of Japanese history problem results in a study littered with countless caveats. This is ineluctable because what is meant by "Japan" or "Korea" or "China" or "Dutch Indies", to take a few examples, does not hold consistent boundaries throughout history. There were governments in exile, such as the Korean government in Shanghai under Japanese colonial rule, which was not legally recognized as a sovereign by the international community but nonetheless enables contemporary Republic of Korea to point to the resilience of the Korean sovereignty and its continuity in museums.[4] Spiritual sovereignty in light of material domination, legal sovereignty pitted against national liberation movements, sovereignty won and sovereignty given from above, such multiple faces and shapes of sovereignty elucidate the limit of what Roxanne Lynn Doty calls the orthodox mainstream international relations which takes as given a fixed and stable understanding of sovereignty (1996: 121). Still, this leaves one with a question: how does the awareness of the constructed nature of state sovereignty and the demand for the state to face its past stand in tension with one another?

As a representative of a legally sovereign state, figures such as Chief Cabinet Secretary Kiichi Miyazawa, who later became the Japanese Prime Minister, could only issue a statement with regards to the history problem that awkwardly presupposes the givenness of the boundaries, yet implicitly leaves a trace of a nod to the historicity of the issue involved. In 1982, which is a point when the history problem garnered international attention, as a response to South Korean and Chinese protests over how Japanese history textbooks depicted its wartime past, Miyazawa issued a statement acknowledging the effect that history writing has on the stability of inter-Asian relations. He stated that "Japan is keenly conscious of the responsibility for the serious damage that Japan caused", and this sense of responsibility was reflected in the "spirit in the Japan-ROK Joint Communiqué and the Japan-China Joint Communiqué".[5] Moreover, the spirit of the two communiqués was to be reflected in education as well. Consequently, Miyazawa stated, the government of Japan would take any necessary measures to revise the Ministry of Education's textbook authorization guidelines.[6] As a result, the textbook authorship guidelines included a clause on "kinrin shokoku joko (neighboring state clause)" which instructs textbook authors to consider the impact that historical narration might have on neighboring states.[7] This statement clearly conceived of the problem of history not as a matter of respecting sovereignty and non-intervention, but as a matter of international relations and implicitly of decolonization hastily dictated under American hegemony since 1945. The history of Korea and China are far more intimate than that of a neighbor,[8] though what is notable in this statement is also how North Korea and Taiwan are both left out.[9] The statement marks how, in the context of East Asia, the advent of Cold War politics, despite its supposed end, continues to limit decolonization of history.[10] But so also is this assumption, that the contour of the sovereign state is a given.

Noting how wanting a static account of sovereignty is, drawing on critical and post-structural accounts of international relations, Doty suggests a concept of sovereignty that is an illusion that "[focuses] on the conditions that lead to attempts to fix meanings and identities, and thereby to produce the foundations presumed by conventional understandings of sovereignty"(Doty, 1996: 123–124). To flesh out what she calls the "sovereignty effect", she examines the discourse on New Commonwealth immigration and how British national identity is produced in post-World War II Britain. The dilemma she sketches out is the following: in the post-World War II period, there is a need to navigate between different imagined communities associated with the idea of Britain, "little England", and that of the "Commonwealth ideal" and the need to "[resolve] Britain's dilemma of having to choose between being reduced to the status of a mere European power *or accepting some form of American hegemony*" (1996: 124 italics mine). There are few points that both Japan and Britain share in post-World War II. What would translate to "little England" in the context of Asia is "mainland Japan [hondo – which in Chinese character is spelled as the real soil]" or "inside land [naichi – which in Chinese character is spelled as inside land]", and the "Commonwealth ideal" to some extent could be likened to the Japanese wartime notion of New Cultural Order and the "Greater East Asia Co-Prosperity

Sphere". What is different is the ability to provide a way to resolve the dilemma for Japan – unlike the British and the French, also a former empire, with the dropping of the two atomic bombs by the United States, decolonization for Japan was swift and gave little space for acrobatic appropriation of the meaning of the end of war and decolonization in history.[11] Such state of history remains visible in the archives and museum in contemporary Japan as the ink-covered textbook *(suminuri kyokasho)*, conveying the radical sense of uncertainty about the acceptable form and shape of the sovereign subject of history.

The phenomenon known as ink-covered textbook refers to the textbooks used by schoolchildren briefly after 1945 and before new textbook production supply could reach the schools. Paper supplies were short, yet education had to continue, but the time has radically changed, rendering many of the sections in textbooks used during wartime as a problem to be dealt with on the ground. These are considered the raw remnant that attests to the radical overturning of values and morals where the state of history is simultaneously there and not there, existing beneath the ink, yet rendered invisible to the eyes.

Images of the state of war saturated the surface of news reports, as well as the magazines consumed on a daily basis. Military planes and images of soldiers were commonplace and reached children's textbooks. However, it was not only in songbooks, where one would expect patriotic lyrics, and in the national language *[kokugo]*, where stories of empire would complement the expanding image of the state. Rather, images of war even made their way to math textbooks (Figures 4.1 and 4.2).

Figure 4.1 Covers of math textbooks published in 1941

Photo taken by Hitomi Koyama, permission to take photo granted by Dr. Syuichi Suga, Hanazono University, Japan

Figure 4.2 Math textbooks, showing calligraphy ink coverage of warplanes

Photo taken by Hitomi Koyama, permission to take photo granted by Dr. Syuichi Suga, Hanazono University, Japan

The images are of two identical math textbooks, published by Nihonshoseki in 1941. On the upper right corner, there is an image of warplanes and students are asked to compare the number of planes and determine which side is greater than the other. This illustration reveals the extent to which the study of elementary mathematics was affected by the state of history. While produced in the same year, the illustration of the warplanes is covered by calligraphy ink in the left, while it is still visible in the right. Any patriotic or militarist images, including these warplanes, had to be "deleted", and the form of deletion took various forms, including this painting over with low-quality calligraphy ink.

The second set of images is all from textbooks on Japanese national language *(kokugo)* published and printed by Tokyo Shoseki in 1942. The titles in the table of contents covered up (Figure 4.3), to name a few, are "Melting of Ice in the Amur River", "Nagahisaou", a name of a Japanese imperial family member who was also a politician and a military leader, "The Tale of Genji", "The Ocean Battle in the Sea of Japan", which is on the Battle of Tsushima in Russo-Japanese War, and the entire appendix section whose subsections are entitled "The Scenery of Java", "Bismarck Archipelago", "Rural Sulawesi", and "Impression of Sarawak" – all pertaining to South Asia. Figure 4.4 shows the page where the story of "Melting of Ice in the Amur River" is entirely covered thoroughly in ink. Upon closer inspection, one can note how the next page after the covered section on the Amur River does not match with the textbook intact in the left side of the photo. As Figure 4.5 shows, this is because several pages have been ripped out, resulting in the page skip. A similar phenomenon can be observed on the page pertaining to the Russo-Japanese War in Figure 4.6, where the illustration of the Battle of Tsushima – famed for a non-white power defeating a white power in modern history. Figure 4.7, as seen from the side view of the bottom of the same textbook, shows the gap left by the tearing out of entire appendix pertaining to South Asia – where

Figure 4.3 Table of Contents of textbook with inked-out chapter titles

Photo taken by Hitomi Koyama, permission to take photo granted by Dr. Syuichi Suga, Hanazono University, Japan

Figure 4.4 Ink coverage of section on China's Amur River (Heilong River)

Photo taken by Hitomi Koyama, permission to take photo granted by Dr. Syuichi Suga, Hanazono University, Japan

over several pages description of the inhabitants and their custom as well as "exotic" fruits are introduced to the Japanese children (Figure 4.8). This version of the textbook is *shotoka kokugo nana* [elementary national language seven], a textbook that neither the Ministry of Education nor the Supreme Commander of Allied Powers (SCAP) ordered to be deleted appropriately.[12] What the remaining text in the present therefore conveys is the ad hoc initiatives taken by educators in local school districts in anticipation of what the state and the new actual ruler of the state may instruct next.[13] The coverings were done sometimes by the children themselves as instructed by the teachers, at others, by parents following the instruction the children brought home, and others by the teachers themselves

Figure 4.5 Close up of ripped pages on Amur River

Photo taken by Hitomi Koyama, permission to take photo granted by Dr. Syuichi Suga, Hanazono University, Japan

Figure 4.6 Ink-covered section of a textbook that narrates the battle of Tsushima in Russo-Japanese War

Photo taken by Hitomi Koyama, permission to take photo granted by Dr. Syuichi Suga, Hanazono University, Japan

Figure 4.7 A bottom view of a textbook where the appendix about South Asia is ripped out entirely

Photo taken by Hitomi Koyama, permission to take photo granted by Dr. Syuichi Suga, Hanazono University, Japan

Figure 4.8 A page in the textbook used during wartime of an appendix where the peoples of Southeast Asia are introduced

Photo taken by Hitomi Koyama, permission to take photo granted by Dr. Syuichi Suga, Hanazono University, Japan

because children could not be entrusted with following order properly. According to testimonies collected by Suga of those who recall the period, some delighted at the idea of the amount of study being visibly reduced, others could not but help note the torn look on the face of the teacher – some are thoroughly inked, others, merely a light cross over, others are covered by a different sheet of paper being glued over the section to be deleted (2012: 95–98). The term deletion was interpreted variously and creatively. The works done upon these books by various hands render the object into a three-dimensional textured debris, with rough patches, folding, tearing, and sudden gaps marking the uncertainty and beginning of a new era: the (post)war period.

The ink-covered textbooks are usually not what is discussed as being part of the history textbook issue, which has become a subcategory of the history problem in contemporary East Asia. What is under international scrutiny in the present is the textbook evaluation guideline issued by Ministry of Education, Culture, Sports, Science and Technology (MEXT, the former Ministry of Education) and how political pressure by various Prime Ministers through the political appointment of the head of the MEXT, affect the content of the textbooks. It is also worth noting that while the deletion executed on the aforementioned textbooks are prompted by the United States, both imagined (and, therefore, anticipated) and real, the recent controversy's demand to deal with history comes from Asia instead. Nonetheless, the question haunting the controversy remains the same. In what form and shape is the state of history acceptable for the world, after empire, after decolonization, and under occupation and after? Since 1945, attempts at fixing meaning of war and imperialism have abound, but have continually failed.

Just as Algeria is an indispensable part of French national history, so are the former colonies of Japan. Korea is at once both part of and outside of Japan. A more accurate and objective history alone, while equally important, cannot grapple with this theoretical paradox at hand – leaving the history problem in a standstill. What is this paradox? Simply put, after the dual deaths of grand narratives – which in the case of world history was the history of Europe, and in the context of Asia was the grand narrative of Japan as the subject of history as we have seen in the previous chapters. With the postmodern awareness of how grand narratives have operated through the exclusion of Others, how can one navigate the demand by postcolonial critics to acknowledge them also as sovereign? In this vein, the question of the place of sovereignty becomes crucial, especially for a palimpsest illusionary sovereign, where the ability to fix the meaning of identity is radically compromised, although the demand for recognition by Japan's Asian Other necessitates clarity of the state of history. This in part has to do with how, in contrast to Britain or France, Japanese decolonization was a decolonization started and halted under the new hegemony, America. To further build on the architectural debris, I argue that the persistence of the history problem cannot be understood by skipping the politics of history that took place between 1945 and 1952, the period under U.S. Occupation. This chapter shows how the palimpsest state of history is formed by the constellation of American hegemony, domestic politics of history, and the disavowal and yearning for grand narrative in post-1945 period, implicating the impasse over historical responsibility.

This chapter has three parts. In the first part, I offer a summary contextualization of how the "history problem" has been understood in East Asian international relations since 1945. In the second part, I address a widespread misperception stemming from the assumption of the nationalistic nature of postwar Japanese history textbooks, specifically through a discourse analysis of such textbooks themselves. I then examine the ambivalent shape of the sovereign state and its implication for theorizing responsibility for war to demonstrate that pursuit of empirical evidence and truth alone cannot address the persistence, we need to consider the place and meaning of the subject of history, as literary critic Norihiro Kato submitted in 1990s. Such recurrence of the notion of the subject in turn has resulted in a stalemate within Japan, as evinced in the "postwar debate on the subject of history" that took place between Norihiro Kato and academic-activist Tetsuya Takahashi in the 1990s. This debate, as I will demonstrate, elucidates many of the more fundamental stakes and relationships between understandings and practices of history writing, decolonization, and international relations. In the third part, then, I engage with a closer analysis of the debate between Kato and Takahashi. Here, I highlight the significance of the fact that, in the course of the debate Takahashi labeled Kato as a neo-nationalist and dismissed his thesis about how Japan might overcome the postwar identity split. This is because, I argue, it demonstrates the extent to which we cannot discuss the moral imperative to decolonize history while simultaneously circumventing who the subject of history *is*.

I. The "history problem" in inter-"national" context

Although contentions over history is not limited to the postwar period, historians of Japanese international relations such as Iokibe identify the 1980s as the point in which the "history problem" became widely recognized as an international issue (2017: 10). The Chinese and South Korean governments' demand for the Japanese state to take action on history education arose from a 1982 report in the liberal newspaper *Asahi News* that the Ministry of Education's textbook evaluation committee instructed a certain textbook author to change the term "invasion" to "advancement".[14] The South Korean and Chinese leadership took this instruction as an attempt to downplay the impact of the war.[15] Still, Chinese and South Korean diplomats' criticism of Japanese history textbooks in the 1980s was relatively contained. The demand from former victim states to address the history problem became more prominent toward the end of 1980s, as Cold War tensions in the region eased and democratization took root in South Korea and Taiwan. In the early 1990s, two Korean women publicly identified themselves as survivors of the military sexual slavery system – euphemistically known as "comfort women" – and demanded an apology from the Japanese state. Around the same time, historian Yoshimi Yoshiaki discovered evidence in the Defense Agency archive of the Japanese military's involvement in running the military brothel system. In response, the Japanese state claimed that the normalization treaty between South Korea and Japan foreclosed the right of the survivors to legal restitution. Nevertheless, under the leadership of socialist Prime Minister

Tomiichi Murayama, a public-private hybrid institute called the Asian Women's Fund was established that disbursed compensation to women who were identified by the NGOs of respective states as survivors.[16] Additionally, in the mid-1990s, Iris Chang's publication of *The Rape of Nanking* intensified anti-Japanese demonstrations by both Chinese American and Chinese citizens. The demonstrations were so significant that the Chinese state had to take them into consideration when engaging with Japan diplomatically.[17] Neither the South Korean nor the Chinese state could contain domestic movements' demands for redress any longer. In the words of the Taiwanese cultural critic Kuan-Hsing Chen, the process of decolonizing and de-imperializing history by the people's hands had finally resumed with the end of the Cold War.[18] Since then, the issue of how to write in history textbooks about "comfort women" and the Rape of Nanjing continues to be the center of contentions in East Asian international relations.[19]

The solution to the history problem appears straightforward: In general, the state is understood to be an enduring corporate actor/subject/agent in international politics. In this vein, the state ought to be able to offer an apology and to address the history problem by exercising its powers to regulate the textbooks that narrate its national history. Nevertheless, the history problem persists to this day. All nine of the high school history textbooks from 1993 and all seven of their middle school counterparts from 1996 assigned by Japanese public schools had passages or lines mentioning the "comfort women".[20] Under Prime Minister Shinzo Abe's new textbook evaluation guidelines, however, there is now pressure to reduce the length of the description of the existence of the women.[21] There is also a revisionist movement that seeks to rewrite history in an affirmative, positive light and downplay the atrocities committed by Japan.[22] A textbook authored by this group has passed the textbook evaluation system. While this particular textbook has been assigned only in rare cases, the Japanese states' willingness to approve of the text nevertheless remains a cause of concern for the country's neighbors. A few Prime Ministers have made statements of remorse and apology, but politically appointed ministers seem to contradict these statements. In 1995, the Socialist Prime Minister Tomiichi Murayama proposed a resolution titled "Resolution to Renew the Determination for Peace on the Basis of Lessons Learned from History". If the resolution had been successful, it would have become a formal collective statement of apology. In the end, however, the resolution merely indicated "a deep sense of remorse". The Murayama initiative was watered down by Diet members and interest groups, signaling the degree to which the state was divided.[23]

This attenuation of the resolution's potential apology reflects a deep divide among Japanese leadership, and indeed, the Japanese people, about how to come to terms with history writing. Of course, this problem was not isolated to Japan alone. Following World War II, there was a widespread international consensus that nationalistic and patriotic history textbooks had played an ideological role in legitimating and glorifying warfare.[24] In this context, a diverse array of critics went to great lengths to debunk the claim that in a democratic state one is entitled to view history in whatever light one wishes. Whatever differences may separate

such critical positions, shared among them is an expectation that extremely problematic views of history should be condemned and should not be permitted, even
as a matter of private opinion. The outright denial of massacres, and/or the mini-
malizing depictions of war crimes, has been widely rebuked and resisted by a
variety of historians, activists, and survivors. Therefore, the lack of severe sanc-
tions on politicians who deny that the Rape of Nanjing happened, or that the
Japanese state had any role in the drafting of "comfort women", has come to be
viewed in Asia as a sign of a lack of Japanese sincerity about facing its history.[25]
While several Prime Ministers have issued a statement of apology on Japan's
behalf, they are consistently plagued by some high-level counterpart who is eager
to deny or downplay Japanese responsibility.

This pattern has prompted the literary critic Norihiro Kato to refer to Japan as
schizophrenic. For Kato, this state of schizophrenia is caused by the absence of
a coherent subject, and specifically, a subject who can admit to having been the
agent of war. In his exchange with philosopher Osamu Nishitani, Kato argues:
"The postwar problem lies in how the Japanese never constituted the subject that
committed war and ran away from the task of becoming a subject that can be criticized by others".[26] For Kato, Japan needs to become a subject if it is to respond to
the history problem adequately.

But what warrants such claim that there is no subject as such in postwar Japan?
This is because since 1945, the status of the state, which is the subject of history,
has been compromised under two distinct, yet interrelated, influences: the pre-
dominance of geopolitics and the social science view of history and the socialist
rendition of history.[27] The view of history informed by geopolitics, as evinced
in prominent international relations scholars such as Hikomatsu Kagawa, reinforces a belief that the war was a structurally determined outcome and that the
state, therefore, had neither agency in nor responsibility for the war or how it
unfolded. In the first three of his articles in *International Politics [Kokusai Seiji]*,
Kagawa explains away the cause of war to natural cycle of state expansion into
empire, and likewise for Japanese colonialism (1957: 6). According to him, the
Japanese state was merely following its naturally dictated behavior, just as any
living organism would.[28] In this vein, naturalization and denaturalization of state
behavior was implicitly at stake over how the colonial question was occluded
from sight. The socialist rendition of history, on the other hand, seeks to reconfigure history as a site of politics, where men make history and exercise agency.[29] Yet
this socialist rendition of history as empowerment was suppressed in Japan under
the indirect control of the United States and, as a result, international history
was depoliticized according to Cold War geopolitical imperatives. In a sense, as
Sebastian Conrad has recently argued, the notion of imperial amnesia and prompt
forgetting of a state's imperial past is too simplistic (2014: 5). Rather, a layered
resonance of the imprints of imperial memory as they are juxtaposed against the
advent of Cold War American hegemony is due.

Put differently, an important consequence of the postwar politics of history was
the absence or erasure of a subject who could respond to Asian victims. This is
different from historiography, which has witnessed, and continues to witness, a

significant outburst of accounts. In light of this absence or erasure, Kato argued in (1995) that Japan must constitute a subject of history capable of such a response. This argument culminated in the "*sengo rekishi shutai ronso* [postwar debate on the subject of history]" between Kato and Tetsuya Takahashi in the mid-1990s. While Kato and Takahashi both shared the aim of addressing the history problem in order to reconcile relations with Asia, the debate resulted in an impasse over Kato's call to constitute a subject which, Takahashi argued, echoed the rhetoric of the 1930s and 1940s when Japan sought to assert itself as the subject of world history. While, in the context of the debate, the call to constitute a subject was meant to relate Japan back to Asia in such a way as to assume responsibility for the war, this call was met with ambivalent reluctance within Japan, not least because the lingering memory of Japan's previous attempt to fashion itself as the subject of history recurs and continue to haunt the postwar discourse on the subject of history.

In this sense, I will next demonstrate how the persistence of the history problem in postwar Japan is ineluctably bound up with the problem of how to theorize agency in history. The history problem cannot be attributed solely to a matter of empirical correctness. Rather, it has to do with how to come to terms with the two different ways in which modern Japan engaged with History. In the early Meiji period, history was conceived by way of Eurocentric civilizational history which denied Asian agency. As a response to this exclusionary history in the 1930s and 1940s, Japanese theorists sought to reconfigure Japan as the subject and agent of history – the maker of a New Cultural Order. As a result, these theorists legitimated Japanese imperialism in Asia. Both kinds of history are mired in problems: the first kind offers no place for non-European subjects, while the second kind also entails violence. These two relations to history frame and bind the postwar discourse over how to live with history.

II. The palimpsest state of history in 1945

There was a term for the classroom in postwar Japan: the classroom of blue sky, *aozora kyoshitsu*. This term suggested that the building and its attendant roofs were nonexistent. Supplies were short. So was paper. Under Allied Occupation command, education continued, but without any patriotic passages in the texts. *Sakujo* [deletion] was the term used in the command to eliminate any militaristic passages or figures from textbooks by both the Ministry of Education and SCAP. The nation was to be concealed out of, and in, history. Given the shortage of supplies, printing new textbooks was out of question, so children studied instead with ink-covered textbooks. Any passage deemed problematic by the censoring branch was redacted, some pages barely saying anything at all. Yet others were merely crossed over lightly with the text beneath remaining readable, while others were torn off, leaving the binding of the text with gaps (Figure 4.9). This was the state of history in 1945: a palimpsest.[30] The state of history and the history of the state reflected one another: beneath the thick cover of calligraphy ink the original text remained, although concealed. Patriotic passages were redacted,

Figure 4.9 Calligraphy textbook that valorizes the support for the empire in war that is crossed out by ink

Photo taken by Hitomi Koyama, permission to take photo provided by Dr. Syuichi Suga, Hanazono University, Japan

rendering some pages completely illegible. Still, the text itself remained in existence, despite the alteration in its appearance. The state was simultaneously present and absent. Indeed, this remains the case, such that the "history problem" is stirred every time the question of history's relation to war and apology is raised.

The question of how to narrate the history of war was shaped to a significant degree by the American army under the U.S. Occupation that lasted between 1945 and 1952.[31] At the outset, in order to subdue resistance against U.S. rule, U.S. military planners orchestrated a narrative which, according to James Orr, exonerated ordinary people from responsibility and participation in the war. Orr quotes from a secret document dated April 1945, issued by the U.S. Army:

> If people could be made to believe that they themselves are not to blame for disaster but rather that it is the fault of the military clique, it will ease their mental burden. As a scapegoat, the military clique is made to order.[32]

The strategy here was to distance the ordinary Japanese people from the military establishment and emperor. In other words, in order to prevent potential resistance to U.S. occupation by the Japanese people, a distinction of who had agency and was, therefore, responsible and who lacked agency and was, therefore, a passive victim of historical forces was deemed necessary. Such distinction according to Orr has constituted the foundation that on the one hand valorizes the pursuit of peace and renouncing of war, and on the other is a rigorous social science approach to the study of the past.

In addition to this "pragmatic" American decision, with military defeat, Japanese education became the site of experimentation for socialist-oriented U.S. Occupation staff at the outset of its rule. Although Japanese bureaucrats had drafted a reformed version of the constitution, this version was plainly rejected by the occupation force.[33] Instead, Japan was to accept a new constitution, which was written by U.S. staff members in a matter of few days.[34] Reflecting the experimental nature of this new constitution, clauses such as the rights of women were more progressive than even what were available in the United States at that time.[35] Japanese law was deemed a blank slate. The same attitude was reflected in the directives issued on education. Under occupation, the Ministry of Education was to be directly supervised by the General Head Quarter's subdivision, Civil Information and Education Section (CIE).[36]

During wartime, school textbooks were to align its contents toward the end of promoting the spiritual mobilization of the people.[37] After World War I, and more notably after the Manchurian Incident, the content became ultranationalistic and militaristic. There was only one state-designated textbook available for use by educators, and any expression of political thoughts which might promote dissent – here mostly the communists – were suppressed by the thought police. In 1936, the Ministry of Education issued a directive to educators that any content that would infringe upon the sanctity of national polity (kokutai) is to be corrected and deleted.[38] School textbooks were appropriated by the Ministry of Education as a tool to promote patriotism and war mobilization, and this complicity was also noted by the occupation force.[39]

Under the U.S. Occupation force's three-"D" (3D) policy – democratize, demilitarize, and decentralize – it was the sanctity of national polity that was to be corrected and deleted.[40] Patriotic passages which valorized Japan's world historical mission were erased, and in particular, any wordings which implied national security, promotion of war, or content which might impede international cooperation between Japan and the world, or embodied anti-democratic value were subject to deletion. Subject to erasure also were sections named "heitai gokko [military simulation game]", "sensuikan [submarine]", "niisan no nyuei [my brother joined the military]", "kamino ken [Godly sword]", "Chosen no Inaka [Rural home in Korea]", and "Dairen karano tayori [Letter from Dalian]".[41] By December 1945, the occupation force had issued directives to purge militaristic educators from schools, implement the separation of Shinto religion from public education, and temporarily suspend the teaching of three subjects: ethics, Japanese history, and geography.[42] The use of the Imperial Rescript on Education, which begins with the phrase, "Know ye, Our Subjects", was banned in March 1947, and in place of ethics, history, and geography, a new discipline of social science (shakaika) was substituted.[43] As in Germany, in the language of social science "the status of the nation . . . changed from a 'natural' form of social organization to one that is grounded in 'rational' arguments for its existence".[44] In the first postwar guidelines for education issued by the Ministry of Education in 1947, politics is explained as "an institution organized for the citizen's welfare".[45] The guidelines explicitly stated that textbook authors must apply kyakkanteki gori ninshiki [objective and rational recognition] of social phenomena.[46] Instead of narratives of the Japanese empire as an ever-expanding living entity, this new mode of narration employs functional and causal explanations to rationally legitimate the existence of the nation-state. For example, the title of a subsection of a textbook by Tokyo Shoseki characterizes the Japanese state as an institution which provides welfare.[47] The reason of state is no longer premised on its mythical nature but as an institution set up to serve its people.

Not everything was dictated by the United States, however. Before the occupation forces ordered the purge of militarist educators, Japanese historians themselves also took initiatives to revamp the study of history toward socialist, Marxist, and modernist ends.[48] During the war, the study of history was heavily censored, critical writings on the emperor system taboo, and by the end of the war, special police began monitoring the activity of Rekishigaku Kenkyu-kai [Historical Studies Association], resulting in the decision of the leaders to terminate its activity in 1944. In November 1945, while the resurrection of the Historical Studies Association was not yet set, a forum to reexamine and debate national history education was held, which saw advocacy for the urgent need to reform history education.[49] This was the first forum held among historians in the immediate postwar years. In 1946, the Historical Studies Association was reconvened at the University of Tokyo. The Association encompassed scholars with diverse perspectives on the study of history, drawing together scholars ranging between Marxist, modernist, and the democratically scientific views of history.[50] Meanwhile, Kiyoshi Hiraizumi, the leader of the traditional view of history that valorized the imperial household during the war, silently retired from the University of Tokyo. Among socialist, Marxist, and modernist scholars, a common issue was how to identify the agent, or the subject of history who might bring about democratic revolution.[51] For all three visions of history, however, the subject was understood to be the agent for change. Historical narratives were thus, obliquely, imbued with political stakes.

Historians' efforts to take back history were reflective of a larger intellectual movement that took place immediately following the war. Writing on this brief period between 1945 and advent of the Cold War and "reverse course" of U.S. Occupation policy, Victor Koschmann observes that "Marxism-Leninism, liberalism, proletarian literature, the naturalist 'I-novel' and social science – converged in an articulate concern for human agency, [and] manifested in a debate on active subjectivity".[52] This concern for human agency was projected against both the U.S. Occupation force and the conservative Japanese bureaucracy.

The antagonism between U.S. Occupation forces, educators, and Japanese bureaucrats now under American rule was further reflected in the bureaucrats and educators' reluctance to comply with the American directive to purge militarist educators from schools. Merely 0.5% of educators were removed from their positions, which meant that despite drastic alterations to education policy in theory, the figures responsible for teaching remained the same.[53] Nevertheless, school teachers who, during the war, had taught children about kichiku beiei (Anglo-American devil animals) and the virtue of emperor worship altered their stance and started preaching the virtue of American-style democracy, spreading the sense among students that while the ruler may have changed, the demand to be submissive persisted.[54] Amid the ashes of devastated homes and widespread poverty, the swift turn toward the glorification of the United States by bureaucrats stirred resentment among both educators and intellectuals against both the Japanese and the United States.

Among intellectuals, the kind of education valorized by a bureaucracy subservient to the United States had little to offer, as it failed to address the actual material conditions of Japan. Unlike the United States, Japan was devastated by war and poverty – the economy was likened to one in the Third World rather than the First World. In light of the multiple inabilities of liberalism and individualism to address class struggle and inequality, and by further consequence of these ideologies' role in justifying inequality as a matter of merit, they were roundly dismissed by Japanese intellectuals. According to these intellectuals, what was needed was not the further indoctrination of school children under the American model (which had little to do with the material conditions of Japan), but rather the constitution of subjects who aspired to social change and revolution.[55]

The emphasis on creating an active subject resonated with the worldwide fight for self-determination in a shifting international context. News of the return of the British and French to Asia revived Pan-Asianist and anti-American nationalism among educators who sought to teach history as the unfolding of revolutionary subjects who would bring about change.[56] Under the logic which equates creation of active subject to promoting resistance, the bureaucracy's push for American-style educational reform appeared as a mere guise for supporting imperialism once again – this time under U.S. leadership. The Asian war of independence was being suppressed by the return of former colonial rulers in South Asia too, and socialists and intellectuals identified with the Asian population as "fellow victims of Anglo-Saxon domination", thereby displacing and distorting a sense of Japanese responsibility toward the Asian victims during its own imperial era.[57] In fact, educators saw ethnic Koreans residing in Japan and running their own language education programs as role models for Japanese children in cultivating ethnic pride and nationalism.[58] The rationale for instilling national pride in children was that without underscoring the importance of self-determination at home first, Japan could not help fellow Asian victims unite against the reassertion of the Eurocentric world order elsewhere. For socialists and communists, history was once again the terrain of active political contestation. "Needless to say, educators are laborers" was a statement passed during the meeting of the ninth Japanese Educator's Association in 1952, which prescribed that history education was to work toward the aim of bringing about socialist revolutionary change and ridding the nation of American imperial oppression.[59]

The U.S. Occupation force had initially liberated the communists and socialists from jails in 1945. With the advent of the Cold War, the aim of 3D, however, was altered. This primarily resulted in the repression of communists and socialists, the rehabilitation of conglomerates, and statements urging the Japanese state to rearm itself once again by 1948 and 1949. This series of reversal of policies has come to be known as the "reverse course".[60] In short, the socialist and communist slogan of teaching history toward anti-imperialist ends was no longer tolerable to the United States. With this "reverse course", the occupation force conducted a Red Purge from 1949 on, leading to the firing of 1,700 activist educators.[61] The outbreak of the Korean War in 1950 further consolidated the suppression of socialist and communist movements. Against the educators' movement to politicize history education with revolutionary and anti-imperial goals, the Japanese bureaucracy emphasized "objectivity" in education, thereby depoliticizing history and voiding its "subject" as an agent of revolutionary change. History was no longer made by the people, but rather the people were reduced once again to passive observers of what happened, and not active agents in history.

The new goal of depoliticizing history teaching, the narration of history was to make the field "objective" and "scientific". The authors of the 1953 textbook *Kuni no Ayumi [the Path of the Nation]* recollect that by that point, Marxist understandings of history were predominant and the descriptive nature of textbook was under criticism by socialists.[62] Descriptive history was criticized because it served to naturalize the status quo as what was considered normal, thereby reifying the worldview of those in power from a Marxist perspective. Authors, therefore, had to tread between the Ministry's dictate to write history objectively and apolitically on the one hand, and the Marxist pressure to use history toward emancipatory ends on the other. The subject of history was caught between these two diametrically opposing demands on how history is to be written and toward what ends. The first history textbook drafted and written by the Ministry of Education after the war changed the description of the nation's mythic origins to a strictly scientific description.[63] Turning away from the origin myth of the Sun Goddess Amaterasu who created the island, history textbooks explained Japan's creation with an earth science account of climate, arable soil, and the beginning of human community. History writing was thus secularized and rid of myths.

Ultimately, in 1954, following the reclamation of full sovereignty by the Japanese state, kyoiku nihou (Two Laws on Education) was passed, banning educators from acting politically altogether.[64] Koschmann identifies this brief period – between the immediate aftermath of war and the advent of "reverse course" as a time in which educators, socialists, and historians sought to reconfigure history education toward emancipatory aims.

The shift from a "subjective" standpoint to an "objective" and "scientific" standpoint in the description of history had implications for how the responsibility for war was understood. As mentioned earlier, the initial message of the U.S. Occupation to ordinary Japanese people was that blame was to be cast squarely on the militarists and the emperor. Yet, with following the reverse course, the militarists and bureaucrats who were purged returned to power. This shift was most notably symbolized by the return of Nobusuke Kishi, who was held in Sugamo Prison as a Class A war criminal for serving in the Hideki Tojo cabinet during the war, and banned from participating in public affairs. He was back in politics by 1952. Kishi became the Prime Minister of Japan from 1958 to 1960, resigning from this role after he pushed through the renewal of the U.S.-Japan Security Treaty despite massive large-scale protests.[65] Thus, cooperation with and rehabilitation of the image of former war criminals and the militarists became necessary for retaining U.S. military hegemony in the region.[66] The rationalization of the role and behavior of the state served to alleviate the militarists' responsibility for the war. This was done through the new emphasis on the anarchic nature of international relations. From 1968 on, in textbooks published under Tokyo Shoseki, there were two new headings which reflected the impact of the Cold War and the need to legitimate the renewal of U.S.-Japan Security Treaty: "Dangerous War" and "the World of Endless Strife".[67] The intention of depicting the world in such way was according to the publisher is "so that one can realistically recognize the severe condition of international strife and approach international relations accordingly".[68] By emphasizing the anarchic nature of international relations it in turn bolstered and legitimated the state under the U.S. umbrella as the guarantor of security.

This emphasis on the role of state as the guarantor of security in a dangerous and anarchic world also underpinned explanations as to why and how World War II had happened. For example, postwar Japanese history textbooks began attributing the outbreak of war to the imbalance of powers in Asia by 1967.[69] Naturalization of war by attributing law-like patterns to state behavior could also be observed in the writing of Hikomatsu Kagawa, who wrote that every nation goes through a growth pattern and that Japan was also no different from Europe; in the process, he naturalized colonialism and imperialism as well (1957: 6). What is notable here is that the behavior of an individual unit – here, the nation-state – is dictated by lebensraum or the structure of international politics which depicts world politics as anarchical. The first and foremost imperative of anarchy, of course, is that the state must pursue its own survival. To survive, the state is to adapt to a shifting international context, forming alliances and expanding militarily to avoid absorption by colonization. In the language of structural determinacy, even the agency of the state is shaped to a significant extent by the structure of international politics, thereby making it plausible to say that the outbreak of the war was structurally determined. Such depictions of historical causality evoke an image of international politics where the structure determines the agent's action – here, the agent being the nation-state – thereby effacing the question of whether the agent could have acted otherwise. There is an increasing emphasis on the bearing of this structural effect upon the behavior of the state.[70] Under this rationale, the military buildup of the Japanese state and its expansion into Asia may be explained as a balancing act determined by exogenous forces. For example, the Japanese invasion of China is explained in history textbooks as an act of filling the power vacuum left by European powers, following the latter's retreat to their home continent in order to fight World War I.[71] The military buildup is explained as an outcome of the growing power of America and Britain and their respective encroachments into Asia. In other words, the Japanese militarists' behavior is viewed as fully rational and obedient to a balancing theory and its imperative to survive. Driven by the imperative to pursue survival and balance, the Japanese state had no agency over what subsequently happened. Historians also began emphasizing the effect of a balance of power to explain war, resulting in what Ryuichi Narita depicts as a "gap between the experience of war and explanation of war".[72]

The political reinstatement of those who were once held responsible for the war and the explanation of the war as the result of an imbalance of power meant that no single entity in international history had agency, and therefore no one was responsible for what had transpired. Herein lies the issue if state behavior is theorized as if it does follow a law-like pattern. To elucidate the implication of a metaphor, if a rock falls from a cliff and hits your head, you cannot demand of the rock that it not follow the law of gravity. Even if you die as a consequence, the rock cannot be blamed. Explanation and prediction here lie in tension with description and understanding. Phrased another way, a so-called objective account of the past ironically rendered the state an object without responsibility, only inertia. If the cause of war was structurally determined, it was similar to a natural disaster over which no one had any control. To be asked about one's responsibility for the destruction of crops by a natural disaster appears absurd. In this sense, such "objective" explanation makes the questioning of responsibility for what had happened difficult because it diffuses the role of agency.

This is a point which has been lost in contemporary debates over how to find solution for the history problem in East Asia as critics focus on the word choice and omissions of war accounts in history textbooks. While the choice of terminology used to describe the war matters, so too does the explanatory method and levels of analysis.[73] As John Hobson notes, there is a stark degree of difference in state agency conceived by liberals and realists: whereas liberal IR theorists would attribute strong state agency to mitigate uncertainty by setting up institutions, realists would emphasize the determinative influence of the structure of anarchy in shaping state behavior regardless of the individual state's intent (Hobson, 2000: 1). State international agency and national agency are different. Nonetheless, American news reports continue to depict Japan as a state holding onto nationalistic account of history. Yet postwar Japanese history textbook writing is far from "nationalistic" if nationalism is blatant glorification of war. Patriotic passages have been inked out, and in the newly printed textbooks, images of warplanes in math textbooks were nowhere to be seen. If an antidote to nationalistic history is "scientific" history, as the occupation force deemed, then the postwar Japanese history textbooks have been overwhelmingly "objective" and "scientific". Therefore, to focus on nationalism and glorification of war and amnesia alone are insufficient – although postwar textbooks do not endorse war, they do naturalize war and detach the ordinary people's relation to the world as a subject of history, thereby negating the possibility of one being a causal-agent of history.

To be sure, nationalism takes many forms and is not limited to pro-militarism. Pro-peace nationalism is also a form of nationalism that has exercised a significant influence in postwar Japan (Oguma, 2005). Yet if one were to focus on the state of history, resistance to taking responsibility as a Japanese subject is not attributable solely to nationalism as it is to "objective" accounts of history which portray it as flows and processes that are not of individual making. The effect is depoliticizing – one distances oneself from what took place in the past. This "objective" method of accounting for the past absolves people of responsibility because they are told that they had no agency in the making of history.

Yet, as William Connolly reminds us, in Kantian terms, in order for moral imperative to be an imperative, "dictates of morality require us to act *as if* history is morally progressive; but the embodied character of human being also means that the end-point can never be reached in history" (2005: 115). And a developmental view of history, as we have seen in the previous chapters, demands us to navigate through this ambivalent state of subject that is at once progressive and that is neither solely endogenously nor exogenously driven. Rearing its ugly head once again is the problematic of how to conceive of political agency against an overbearing structuralist logic and rationale. As in late nineteenth century Germany, increasingly rationalistic and mechanistic explanations of social phenomena have given rise to the dilemma of conceiving of political agency.[74] While postwar history textbooks no longer glorify the nation-state as the subject of history, the shift to an objective account of history inadvertently creates a different kind of difficulty, that of sensing responsibility. To theorize responsibility, or to speak of moral decision, there must be at least a possibility of choice, the potential for one to exercise agency in the course of history. A so-called objective account serves instead to depoliticize history. This is why so-called objective and scientific accounts of the past are also, perhaps despite their best efforts, imbued with political consequences.

In this sense, to attribute the persistence of the history problem between Japan and its neighbors is the fault of Japanese state's adherence to nationalistic account of history risks obscuring the implicit stakes of discussing the possibility of the people of being a causal-agent of history who responds to the world. What the focus on deconstructing the nation-state could obfuscate is the inadvertent effect of "objective" history neutralizing any possible sense of agency, and therefore the possibility of assigning the nation and the state any responsibility for what had happened.

Indeed, recent comparative studies on national history textbooks in East Asia observe that the content of Japanese history is one of the most "objective" among Asian nations in the sense that it does not portray history in patriotic terms.[75] The comparative study seems to presume objectivity is the standard by which properly "decolonized" and "demilitarized" history will be judged.[76] The persistence of the history problem in East Asia, therefore, must also take into account the place of agentic subject in history. This leads us to consider the relation between history and the subject.

As we have seen, after 1945, there was an extension of state control over how history was to be narrated thenceforth. The initial goal was to diffuse the sense of agency in the making of history in ordinary Japanese people. Redacted passages of history textbooks seem an apt metaphor for the state of history in postwar Japan – the state is there, but postwar Japanese politics has covered over the center, or the subject.

Ironically, this state of history – or the absence of it – invokes two interrelated and diametrically opposed moves in the 1990s: The first is the call to constitute a subject of history who can apologize and respond to Asia. The second is the consolidation of a conservative movement within Japan that valorizes the sense of nation – a push for instilling patriotism. In light of the concealment of the subject under Cold War geopolitical logics and epistemological imperatives, the problem of the subject recurs once more as it did in the 1930s.

III. The postwar debate on the subject of history as impasse

In the widely read *Darakuron [Discourse on Decadence]*, the novelist Ango Sakaguchi wrote the following words on history:

> Who committed this war, is it Tojo and the militarists? Such is the case, yet simultaneously, it must have been this large monstrous creature called history and its will. In front of this history the Japanese people were mere children obedient to fate.[77]

Here, Prime Minister Tojo and the militarists are to blame, yet Sakaguchi also depicts history as a monster, and the Japanese people as "mere children". Historical force as a monster casts a diminished sense of agency upon the Japanese people, who in the last instance are obedient children. Such an infantilized stance toward history results in a politics of history which keeps on attributing the causes of war to exogenous causes and forces, rendering the child a blameless victim of fate. During the Cold War, such a sense of history was cultivated by the confluence of compromise between Japanese leadership as well as by the American Occupation's objective to demilitarize and depoliticize history writing. Such was the state of history at the end of the Cold War when movements to decolonize history within Asia resumed.

Although there were efforts to remember and commemorate the war prior to the 1990s, the appearance in 1992 of two Korean victims of Japan's wartime policy of holding "comfort women", or military sexual slavery system, shocked the Japanese society and vividly symbolized the inadequacy of postwar Japan's capacity to deal with its own history.[78] This was the first time that victims had publicly identified themselves, and putting a human face to what was discussed in texts amplified a sense of urgency to deal with Japanese responsibility for wartime atrocities. That these women were well into their senior years added a sense of gravity to Japan's crime of omission. Prior to these victims coming forward, many people could imagine military sex slaves as youthful girls: the image of these women as harumoni [grandmother] who had suffered through decades of silence and neglect under Cold War geopolitics, Japanese indifference, Korean Confucian patriarchy, and the stigma often attached to victims of sexual violence in a society that (like its Christian counterparts) continues to places a premium on virginity, changed the very stakes of and made impossible to dismiss these and other victims' demands for recognition, not least because they might not have many years left.

The emphasis on the gendered dimension of the war was a strategic choice made by activists in 1990s. Etsuro Totsuka recalls that the NGO he led chose to call the victims as "sex slave" instead of "comfort women" in order to enact a paradigm shift.[79] The rise of feminism, transnational activism, and international legal scholars' move to define forms of gendered violence war crimes in 1990s all converged to render the history problem in 1990s as an issue which not only scholars and policymakers, but also ordinary Japanese people, were forced to reconsider.

The diffusion of Cold War tensions allowed voices from Asia to be heard, demanding that Japan atone and take responsibility for the war. Simultaneously, the United States was demanding that Japan abide by the U.S.-Japan Security Treaty and send its Self-Defense Force to the Middle East in order to assist American warfare in Iraq.[80] The U.S. demands necessitated a revisitation of Article 9 of the constitution, which forbids Japan from employing military force to resolve international disputes, but it also invigorated conservatives. Aided by U.S. pressure on Japan to take on a fair share of the cost in sustaining American hegemony, political figures such as Ichiro Ozawa advocated that Japan become a "normal" nation-state – normal in the sense that it functions as a full sovereign entity, instead of what Peter Katzenstein calls a "semi-sovereign" state which continues to be dependent on a guarantee of U.S. military protection for its own security.[81] "Normalizing" Japan meant for conservatives the promotion of a "healthy" sense of the nation in its children, too. For conservatives, postwar history textbooks failed to promote nationalism and was too "colored" in the sense that history education was tainted by communist influences. Conservative policymakers have lamented the dearth of children proud of their nation for over half a century, so much so that many of the statements politicians made were titled along the lines of, for example, "on the lamentable state of history textbook (ureubeki kyokasho mondai)". Conservatives took advantage of American policymakers' renewed pressure upon Japan to participate in war. For conservatives, the impending war served as an excuse to create patriotic children and thereby soldiers willing to die in the name of the state. As preparation for potential involvement in war, policymakers pushed through legislation that mandated the singing of the national anthem and raising of the Japanese flag in public schools by end of the1990s.[82]

It was in this context that, between 1993 and 1994, three Japanese cabinet level ministers made contentious statements regarding the meaning of World War II and resigned: one claimed that the Rape of Nanjing was a hoax, another claimed that the Greater East Asia War was fought without the intent to invade, and the third stated that there is no point in clinging to a constitution made more than half a century ago.[83] Each statement was made immediately following a Prime Minister's offer of apology with regard to the war. Kato likens this phenomenon to *The Strange Case of Dr Jekyll and Mr Hyde*, where one character makes a statement of apology only to have the other appear and contradict the statement. "Japan", in Kato's view, is schizophrenic.[84]

How does the past in theory bind the present? It is worth noting the strategic use of the term "mirror" by Chinese leaders in reminding Japan about the import of the past. In Asia prior to Westernization, major historical texts contained the Chinese character "mirror" in their titles – history was presumed to serve as a mirror that provoked self-reflection.[85] One learns from the past so as not to repeat similar mistakes in the future. In this sense, regardless of where a war is conducted, an instant association is made: how one debates about war in the present reflects how one learned lesson from the wars of the past. In this light, victim states saw Japanese discussions about providing logistical support for the American war in the Middle East in the 1990s as another disturbing sign of the lack of repentance about past wars.

From the perspective of the victims, the intended recipients of the apology, the Japanese state's split stance toward Japanese colonialism and the Fifteen Years War in the Asia-Pacific and contemporary war remains ambiguous at best, and unapologetic at worst.

The appearance of the elderly former "comfort women" added a sense of urgency that the history problem be debated within Japan. Identifying that this personality split – as reflected in the cycle of Prime Ministerial apology and politically appointed minister's negation of it – is a split that needs to be overcome if Japan were to apologize to Asia, Kato argues in his book, *Haisengoron [After Defeat]* that "first, what is necessary is . . . to establish the subject who can apologize".[86] In making this argument, he initiated the "*sengo rekishi shutai ronso* [postwar debate on the subject of history]" in the mid-1990s.

In the first half of this chapter. we examined how the U.S. Occupation policy shaped postwar Japanese history writing practices both directly and indirectly.

Kato, too, has written extensively on the extent and depth of the U.S. influence but in the realm of Japanese literature. In *Amerika no Kage [The American Shadow]*, he examines postwar Japanese literature which metaphorically engages with U.S.-Japan relations and the literary criticism of Jun Eto to elucidate how, throughout the postwar years, Japanese literature has been bound by a particular taboo. This is the taboo of facing the fact that Japan is dependent upon Amerika.[87] Kato asks why there is a tremendous gap in the reaction among literary critics and the Japanese and Korean reading public to a novel written by Yasuo Tanaka, *Nantonaku Kurisutaru [Somehow, Crystal]*. *Nantonaku Kurisutaru* became a best seller among Japanese and Korean public, although the majority of the Japanese literary establishment, with the notable exception of Eto, had condemned the novel as trash.[88] The plot of the novel is about a young trendy girl who gets a gig as a model and is cohabiting with her boyfriend. While the boyfriend is out of the house, the protagonist sleeps around with other men only to realize that in the end her boyfriend is the best person for her. Because the novel was littered with endless references to brand name products, literary critics widely agreed that the novel was a commentary on the ills of materialism and capitalism, albeit a bad one. Still, these critics could not pinpoint why such a bad novel became a best seller among the people. The same novel was translated into Korean and the pirated version was enormously successful, despite the fact that this was during a period when Korean authorities were censoring Japanese publications. Kato asks, what made the novel so convincing when the experts saw little value in the work? He claims that what resonated with the audience was the immense weakness and dependence of the protagonist. The protagonist is a model and has enough income to feel like she is making her own decisions and choices, unlike a housewife, yet in the end, what she comes to realize is that she needs her boyfriend and with that, an anxiety of when he might leave her. Like the protagonist model who has an independent income, postwar economic growth, which was made possible with the conclusion of the military security treaty that capped Japanese military spending to less than 1% of GDP, gave the Japanese the illusion that they are independent and on par with the United States. Such an illusion, according to Kato, concealed the shared feeling of pathos and emptiness embedded in postwar Japanese political thought.[89]

The emptiness of the discourse, according to Kato, stems from its failure to adequately meditate on the war dead and to write about war, namely because it is grounded on an illusionary premise that the American direct and indirect presence has had no impact on what Japan can and cannot do. While Eto in his critique does not frame this novel as a novel about U.S.-Japan relations, Kato references Eto's other writings on the presence of U.S. military base to show that what Eto finds valuable in the novel is this coming to terms with the grim reality, that Japan cannot live without Amerika. What the novel vividly exposes, and therefore what makes it so resonant to the reading public, is a postwar Japan absented of a subjectivity capable of exercising agency. Therefore, the idea of postwar that ignores this dependence on the U.S. triggers a symptom where one partial view that valorizes the U.S. and completely denies Japanese objection to Eurocentric world history is followed by another partial view that valorizes Japan's war as a war of liberation that in turn ignores Japanese aggression in Asian history.

For Kato, this avoidance of becoming the subject results in the haunting of the postwar discourse on how to respond to Asia and debate on the war in the Middle East.[90] Kato valorizes Eto's critique of military base novels because only Eto, in Kato's reading, does not lose sight of the fact that while the continued American subjugation of Japan is upsetting, Japan cannot seemingly live without Amerika.[91] Those who advocate for expelling the U.S. military base from Okinawa are naïve because, on this account, they do not understand how deeply dependent Japan is on the American presence. Those who oppose the American call for Japan to join the war in Iraq in the name of the sanctity of Article 9 of postwar constitution are naïve because they neglect how the imposition of Article 9, under the threat of another nuclear attack, was a nonnegotiable condition of the alliance treaty. At the heart of the emptiness of postwar political thought, therefore, lies a fundamental self-deception about the Japanese state and people as subject of history. Japan is fundamentally dependent on Amerika, yet postwar discourse on war in the past and the present brackets this fact. This is what Kato identifies as the taboo which permeates postwar Japanese political and literary discourse. And for him, the schizophrenic response to Asian demand for atonement is attributable to this forgetting of the bracketing of Japanese in-dependence to Amerika – in order to come to terms with Asia, Japan must come to terms with the forgetting of the forgetting, of the Occupation period.

Kato's *Amerika no Kage* was written before his publication of *Haisengoron [After Defeat]*, but according to his new preface, was crucial in formulating his thesis on how to overcome the personality split which characterizes postwar Japan's discourse on the history problem.[92] Between the publications of these two works, Kato makes a connection between the absence of subject with agency and the history problem. He argues that while under the American shadow, postwar Japan lacked agency, at the same time, it was postwar Japanese dependency on Amerika which enabled Japan to avoid being the subject of history, that is, a subject who can be held responsible by the Asian other. For Kato, this is also the reason why Japan failed to constitute a subject who can respond to Asia.[93] The Dr. Jekyll and Mr. Hyde phenomena recurs because the Japanese have yet to come to terms with the twisted extent to which this postwar condition was set to work. For him, Jekyll evokes Hyde when the rationale for Hyde is completely excluded from Jekyll's account. To counter the pattern, an account that also includes Hyde is necessary (Kato, 2010: 4). To take a case of complete denial of Hyde, in the face of absolute power disparity between Amerika and Japan, Japanese leaders sweepingly accepted the verdict of Tokyo War Crimes Trial as one of the conditions of regaining sovereignty in 1952. The war was deemed meaningless and so were those who died in war. Yet Hyde cannot be suppressed: the souls of the Class A war criminals have been silently added to the Yasukuni Shrine in 1978. The Japanese war dead who, in 1952, were declared guilty and irrelevant in front of Amerika, have since been declared martyrs by those who militate against American hegemony in East Asia. For Kato, the inconsistency of the Japanese political leadership and its people in their attempts to deal with history can be remedied only by recognizing this schizophrenia.

It is only in doing so that the personality split can be overcome and a coherent subject can be constituted – a subject who can admit to having committed war. This is to grapple with the course set by American occupation since 1945, where the explanation of who committed the war and who is responsible increasingly became diffuse. In the immediate aftermath of war, the military became the scapegoat for Japanese responsibility for war. With the onset of the Cold War, even this militarism came to be explained as the natural outcome of the state's necessary response to the anarchical conditions of international politics. Such "objective" account of the past led to the disappearance of a subject who can admit to having been the agent of war. For Kato, without an "I", one cannot meet the "other". This is why the original self-deception should not go on.

Others critical of the way the Japanese state deals with the history problem second Kato's identification of the source of the problem with the fragmented and inconsistent personality of the state. Masaaki Nakamasa, for instance, writes that the reason Japan cannot relate properly to Asia is because "the 'center' that made Japan a nation-state throughout the postwar years has remained in a state where one cannot even tell if it is alive or dead, rendering the 'subject' who is supposed to be responsible ambiguous".[94] Echoing Kato, Nakamasa argues that in order to meaningfully respond to Asian victims, Japan would need to be a kind of subject who can respond. The subject who responds is missing in the Japanese case – the majority of postwar Japanese living in Japan are aware that their nationality is Japanese, yet have little sense of how one might have agency over history because many have become accustomed to seeing history in a depoliticized manner.

Despite Kato's qualification that by the term subject he means a weak kind of subject, his insistence that the Japanese first acknowledge the Japanese war dead has been condemned in Japan.[95] The most pointed condemnation comes from Tetsuya Takahashi. Takahashi finds in Kato's thesis an echo of wartime national mobilization – a move to create willing and loyal Japanese subjects.[96] He points to how the mourning of the Japanese war dead directly replays the logic of war glorification and mobilization that the Yasukuni Shrine stands for. The Yasukuni Shrine was formerly a Shinto shrine which in modernity became a "device for the 'spiritual mobilization of the people'".[97] The ritualization of honoring the war dead by the emperor at Yasukuni Shrine turned their death into a joyous and honorable moment for their grieving families. Takahashi writes that according to Kato, "one should thus 'thank' the dead soldiers", whom Kato describes as having "died for our nation", "died so that we could be here now", and he asks, "but how does this logic differ from that of Yasukuni Shrine?"[98] Takahashi acknowledges that Kato's position is different from that of conservatives seeking to glorify war. Still, he finds Kato's thesis that Japan must constitute a subject who can respond unacceptable, largely because it would legitimate the assertion of Japan as a subject.

Takahashi's response to Kato is also informed by his academic works problematizing postwar Japanese society's historical amnesia on what Japan did to its Asian neighbors under colonialism and war.[99] For Takahashi, the Japanese people have the responsibility to remember and atone in perpetuity. This also means that one must not forget how war mobilization became possible in the first place. Takahashi shows how Kato's argument, while responding to the Asian demand for atonement, is nonetheless overtly framed in terms of the history of Japan-West relations. What he finds missing is a deeper consideration of the history of Asia-Japan relations. Indeed, in relation to Amerika, the postwar Japanese state's historical agency has been rendered negligible. Yet from the perspective of the victims in Asia, the same state has been actively silencing and refusing to acknowledge the existence of the Asian war dead. Depending on the emphasis one chooses to privilege, the state as the subject of history was both present and absent. With the conservative politicians' push to reconfigure Japanese history writing in an affirmative tone and their attempts at normalizing Japan from a semi-sovereign into a fully sovereign nation in background, Kato's call to constitute an agentic national subject reminded many of how similar the political climate of the 1990s was to the 1930s.

Indeed, in the 1930s, too, there was a debate on Japan as the subject of world history. Arguing that civilizational history is about Europe and not the rest, figures such as Masaaki Kosaka advocated for and supported Japan's war in Asia as a worthy mission, leading some to characterize Japanese imperialism as a Holy War against the West.[100] Sociologist Masachi Osawa notes how the discourse on history writing in the 1990s and the 1930s were both shaped by the question of how to reconfigure history writing in a way that would constitute political agency.[101] What is different about the 1990s discourse on the possibility and legacy of Japan as a world historical agent is, namely, that the memory of having to refashion Japanese society and law to live up to Eurocentric standards of "civilization" so as to gain Western recognition, equal treatment, and the repeal of humiliating unequal treaties is only faintly remembered. Instead, what is more vividly associated with the discussion of history writing is how, throughout the 1930s and 1940s, history writing became complicit with war mobilization and the legitimation of Japan's Greater East Asia Co-Prosperity Sphere – the connection socialist educators have insisted on making despite the attempt by MEXT to depoliticize history teaching throughout the Cold War period.[102] As Thomas Berger notes in this regard, the discourse on history and war in the 1990s continues to be shaped by the political battle over history fought in the 1940s and 1950s, which resulted in a combination of Japanese institutional dependence on America with persistent cultures of inconsistent anti-militarism.[103] The educators' motto throughout the Cold War period was "to never send one's student to the war front". Despite conservative politicians' moves to "normalize" the Japanese security posture, the Japanese public has consistently disavowed war in postwar period.[104] With this partial hindsight, subject formation is a bad idea.

Still, responsibility for war, so long as it was fought in the name of Japan in the past, "remains a 'national' question".[105] As Wendy Brown reflects on the feminist hesitation toward postmodern sensibility about the subject as being constructed, while the awareness of socially constructed nature of the subject serves to denaturalize and expose the workings of power, it nonetheless also unintentionally renders it impossible to demand that the Other take responsibility for the injury caused by deconstructing the subject. To quote, the irony is evident especially in a period that is considered as after grand history: "[e]ven as the margins assert themselves as margins, the denaturalizing assault they perform on coherent collective identity in the center turns back on them to trouble their own identities" (1995: 53). The trouble haunts back by,

> [c]ontrary to its insistence that it speaks in the name of the political, much feminist and anti-postmodernism betrays a preference for extrapolitical terms and practices: for Truth (unchanging, incontestable) over politics (flux, contest, instability); for certainty and security (safety, immutability, privacy) over freedom (vulnerability, publicity); for discoveries (science) over decisions (judgments); for separable subjects armed with established rights and identities over unwieldy and shifting pluralities adjudicating for themselves

– in other words, the emphasis on truths and facts corrode the ground of politics (1995: 37). This is a point that Japanese progressives such as Takahashi and Ueno, who condemned Kato for being a neo-nationalist, often miss. From the Korean perspective, Japanese feminists who demanded recognition from the Japanese state and emperor for the survivors of the military sexual slavery system, while also calling for all feminists to overcome national distinction for the sake of gender justice, was also problematic because it risked erasing and thereby silencing the different historical experiences of Japanese and Korean feminists. For critics like Kim, "feminism is an idea that does not occur and survive in a vacuum, feminism, in particular a postcolonial one, should not transcend nationalism".[106] Similar to the U.S. debate on white privilege, the Korean and Chinese demand for recognition and apology from the Japanese "calls them back to their bodies" in an unpleasant way, because it "conflicts . . . with ideals of self-invention and self-reliance, meritocracy and quick fixes".[107] Positionality and identity matter. So long as one is to theorize the history problem as a problem of responsibility and a collective – not individual – one at that, the national question cannot be circumvented.[108] Takahashi himself also flounders on this question of "who" the "Japanese" are, as he layers qualification over qualification on "who" must take responsibility "as Japanese". While he defines this "Japanese" as legal Japanese citizens who benefit from the continued existence of the state and its services it provides, he also finds it necessary to make a distinction between ethnic Korean Japanese and Japanese, and between Okinawans and Japanese.[109] The floundering points to both the necessity and inadequacy of seeing Japan as the agentic subject of history. While the idea of the nation is a modern social construct, pointing to the arbitrary nature of such construct does not do much for the victims of those who were killed in the name of the Japanese empire – for the effect is real. An apology must be made as a Japanese subject – not as a universal world citizen. Kato is right insofar as he identifies that postwar Japanese history writing has a self-deceptive and evasive relation between the Japanese people and the state, and whether the state had agency in the making of history. Yet, as Takahashi emphasizes, constituting a subject is suspect, as it could repeat the gesture of war mobilization in the 1930s and 1940s.

Conclusion

In sum, the impasse between Kato and Takahashi shows that while postwar Japan's history problem continues because under the Cold War, the subject of history disappeared, association of subject formation to memories of the 1930s and 1940s informs many in postwar Japan that becoming a subject of history is also violent.[110] Modern Japan dealt with history in two different ways in the past: when civilizational history arrived from Europe, such history denied agency for the Japanese, in Showa period Japanese intellectuals sought to reconfigure history writing toward the end of asserting Japanese political agency in the world. The memory of the 1930s and 1940s casts a bind on postwar debate on the subject of history because the second type of engagement with history was complicit in legitimating Japanese imperialism. Therefore, the argument that Japan must constitute a subject of history who can apologize, while it made sense theoretically speaking, could not be politically viable. This is why "since then [the war], sorrow no longer unites us. It shatters us apart".[111]

In reflecting on the controversy over the postwar subject of history Kato instigated, Osawa points out that thus far no one has produced a viable response to Kato's thesis.[112] His thesis that Japan evaded being a subject of history who can be scolded and be held responsible touched nerves of postwar Japanese people and intellectuals. The fact that the debate ended with Takahashi labeling Kato as a neo-nationalist elucidates the limits of liberal and postcolonial approaches to decolonizing history. A structurally determined account of history eliminates one's sense of having agency in the making of history – and with that, too, goes the sense of responsibility, because responsibility presumes the ability to respond, to be an agent. Yet as our daily experience and calling of others reminds us, we do not make history, either. To associate all discussions that attempt to rethink the relation between agency and history writing to neo-nationalist and implicitly colonialist knowledge is to ignore the contentious relationship that history writing and the concept of agency have had in modernity. Not all historicism produces the same effect, and this is why history writing is political.

Notes

1 Yorihisa Namiki, "Chugoku Kyokasho no sekai miraizo [Chinese Textbook's Vision of the World and Japan]", in *Kingendai no Nicchukankei wo tou [Reflection on Contemporary Japan-China Relations]* (Tokyo: Kenbunshuppan, 2012): 133.
2 Kan Kimura, *Nikkan Rekishininshiki mondai towa nanika; rekishi kyokasho, "ianfu" popurizumu [What Is the History Recognition Problem between Japan and Korea? History Textbook, "Comfort" Women, and Populism]* (Tokyo: Minerva Shobo, 2015); also see Ryuji Hattori, *Gaiko Dokyumento: Rekishininshiki [Diplomatic Documents: History Recognition]* (Tokyo: Iwanami Shinsho, 2015); Thomas Berger, *War, Guilt, and World Politics after World War II* (Cambridge: Cambridge University Press, 2012).

3 Hiroshi Mitani, "Japan's History Textbook System and Its Controversies", in Daqing Yang ed., *Kokkyo o okeru rekishi ninshiki [Toward a History beyond Borders: Contentious Issues in Sino-Japanese Relations]* (Cambridge, MA: Harvard University Press, 2012): 261. As a response, the Ministry of Foreign Affairs took upon itself the task of translating the content related to war in Chinese, Korean, and English and made it publicly available on the Ministry of Foreign Affairs website in 2008.

4 Such is a narrative displayed in the Independence Museum in Republic of Korea.

5 Ministry of Foreign Affairs of Japan, "Statement by Chief Cabinet Secretary Kiichi Miyazawa on History Textbooks", www.mofa.go.jp/policy/postwar/state8208.html (Accessed August 26, 2014).

6 History textbooks can be authored by anyone, but it must be submitted to the Ministry of Education (present-day MEXT) for evaluation. Generally, the authors would receive instructions (mandatory) and recommendations (nonmandatory) for revision, which is followed by another evaluation. Upon approval, the textbook would become part of the list of eight or nine textbooks which local education board and school teachers can select from for their classroom use. Local teachers technically can subvert the state-approved narrative by use of sub-textbooks to create a more complex narrative of the war. Still, the symbolic weight of which textbooks do get approved has an impact on East Asian international politics. On the textbook evaluation system and its postwar politics, see Mitani, 246.

7 Mitani, 252; "Monbukagakusho Kokuji Dai 166 Go [Ministry of Education, Culture, Sports, Science and Technology Japan Instruction on Textbook Evaluation Rules No. 166]",www.mext.go.jp/b_menu/hakusho/nc/1284728.htm (Accessed August 21, 2014).

8 See Jun Uchida, *Brokers of Empire: Japanese Settler Colonialism in Korea, 1876–1945* (Cambridge, MA: Harvard University Asia Center, 2011); Leo Ching, *Becoming "Japanese": Colonial Taiwan and the Politics of Identity Formation* (Berkeley, CA: University of California Press, 2001).

9 Under the tide of international isolation, the Republic of China also signed normalization accord with Japan after People's Republic of China did so to avoid alienating Japan which became an ally of the United States. The only state to this day that has not normalized relations with Japan is the Democratic People's Republic of Korea.

10 On de-Cold War and de-imperialization, see Kuan-Hsing Chen, *Asia as Method: Toward Deimperialization* (Durham, NC: Duke University Press, 2010).

11 On the French, see Todd Shepard, *The Invention of Decolonization: The Algerian War and the Remaking of France* (Ithaca and London: Cornell University Press, 2006).

12 The first order for deleting problematic sections were issued by the Ministry of Education on September 20, 1945. The second order for deleting pro-military, patriotic, and anti-democratic values, to name a few – was issued by SCAP on January 25, 1946. On the details of these specific orders, see Suga (2012).

13 On the significance of this specific textbook, see Suga (2016: 146–147).

14 Kimura, 80–82.

15 This report turned out to be ungrounded, yet it nonetheless triggered intensive scrutiny over how the state evaluates and thereby affirms these depiction of wartime Japan.

16 Yasuaki Onuma, *"Ianfu" mondai to wa nanndattanoka [What Was the "Comfort Women" Problem About?]* (Tokyo: Chuko Shinsho, 2007); Yuki Tanaka, *Japan's Comfort Women: Sexual Slavery and Prostitution During World War II and the US Occupation* (London and New York: Routledge, 2002); Chunghee Sarah Soh, *The Comfort Women: Sexual Violence and Postcolonial Memory in Korea and Japan* (Chicago and London: The University of Chicago Press, 2008).

17 Joshua A. Fogel ed., *The Nanjing Massacre in History and Historiography* (Berkeley: University of California Press, 2000).

18 In addition, the contended question between Republic of China (Taiwan) and People's Republic of China over who the rightful China is remains an issue in the region. This

casts a particular impact over how Taiwanese see the history problem in contrast to South Korea or mainland China. Chen, *Asia as Method.*

19 The issues under contention are not limited to these alone. For example, there remains the question of how to address the history of biological warfare unit 731 and the living vivisection committed against mostly Chinese victims, the use of forced labor in factories, how to account for the massacre of Koreans in the aftermath of the Kanto earthquake, and the legality of Japanese colonization of Korea – and there are disputes between South Korea and China over claiming of ancestral lands. Cf. Alexis Dudden, *Troubled Apologies among Japan, Korea, and the United States* (New York: Columbia University Press, 2014); Berger, *War, Guilt, and World Politics after World War II*; Tessa Morris-Suzuki, Morris Low, Leonid Petrov and Timothy Y. Tsu, *East Asia beyond the History Wars: Confronting the Ghosts of Violence* (New York: Routledge, 2013).

20 Mitani, 253–254. Private school is attended by 6% of the population. Japanese history is optional and not mandatory in high school in Japan while it is compulsory at middle school level. Because it is an elective at high school level, this has structurally led to many Japanese college-age students having little knowledge of Japanese history altogether.

21 Of the 15 textbooks evaluated in 2012, 14 contained explanation of the "comfort woman", yet the overall length of the description has been reduced.

22 Mitani, 254–255, 259; The employment rate in its first printing was 0.039%, in 2011 it was 0.6%. Cf. Jiyu Minshuto Seimu Chosakai Monbukagakubukai [Liberal Democratic Party Political Affairs Research Committee MEXT Subdivision], "Rekishiteki Bunya Kentei Gokaku kyokasho hikaku [Comparative Study on History Textbook That Passed Evaluation]", www.shindo.gr.jp/教科書比較(歴史).pdf; also see the website run by the group www.tsukurukai.com/

23 Franziska Seraphim, "Negotiating War Legacies and Postwar Democracy in Japan", *Totalitarian Movements and Political Religions*, Vol. 9, No. 2–3 (June–September, 2008): 203–224; also Norma Field, "War and Apology: Japan, Asia, the Fiftieth, and After", *Positions*, Vol. 5, No. 1 (1997): 1–50. Duke University Press.

24 Soysal and Schissler write: "The process of decolonization, the increasing dominance of the rights discourse, the social movements from the 1970s on, and the end of the Cold War have challenged political configurations on national as well as transnational levels . . . . [laying] the ground for important changes in the organization of societies. While the nation-state was affirmed as the universal mode of polity formation, the closure of societies and their definition as purely national collectives has become increasingly difficult to sustain, ideologically as well as institutionally. With these changes, 'what counts as history' has also changed . . . Accompanied by epistemological crises, major changes in the historical and social sciences took place . . . [on] two main issues. First, the question of agency: who has subject status and who acts in history? Second, the question of direction: where are we going, is history moving us into a certain direction?" Hanna Schissler and Yasemin Nuhoglu Soysal eds., *The Nation Europe and the World: Textbooks and Curricula in Transition* (New York and Oxford: Berghahn Books, 2005): 4. In Japan textbook historian Saburo Ienaga represents this view. Ienaga initiated a court case challenging the constitutionality of textbook evaluation system for over three decades to dissociate state control from education. Thus far, the legal challenge has been unsuccessful. Cf. Saburo Ienaga, *Senso Sekinin [War Responsibility]* (Tokyo: Iwanami Shoten, 1985).

25 Cf. Laura Hein and Mark Selden eds., *Censoring History: Perspectives on Nationalism and War in the Twentieth Century* (New York: Routledge, 2000).

26 Norihiro Kato and Osamu Nishitani, "Sekai Senso no Torauma to 'Nihonjin' [The Trauma of World War and 'Japanese']", *Sekai [The World]* (August, 1995): 51.

27 One might ask why the focus on education instead of collective memory. Indeed, there is a question of the extent to which historical narrative taught in school shapes

individual understanding about the war. I focus on education because how narrative is used here is deemed by victim states to be representative of Japanese people's view of history because this is evaluated and thus shaped by the state, unlike other venues of writing.

28 Hikomatsu Kagawa, "Kindaikokusaiseijishi ni okeru nihon [Modern History of International Politics and Japan]", *Kokusai Seiji [International Politics]*, No. 3 (1957): 1–21.

29 This notion of agency is a particular reading of Marx by particular historians who call themselves socialist. Marx himself qualifies this notion of making history: "Men make their own history, but they do not make it as they please; they do not make it under self-selected circumstances, but under circumstances existing already, given and transmitted from the past. The tradition of all dead generations weighs like a nightmare on the brains of the living". Karl Marx and D.D.L. trans., *Karl Marx: The Eighteenth Brumaire of Louis Bonaparte* (New York and Berlin: Mondial, 2005).

30 On palimpsest as presence of an absence, see Avery Gordon, *Ghostly Matters: Haunting and the Sociological Imagination* (Minneapolis, MN: University of Minnesota Press, 2008).

31 For a thorough account in the English language, see John Dower, *Embracing Defeat: Japan in the Aftermath of World War II* (Australia: Penguin Books, 1999).

32 Quoted in James J. Orr, *The Victim as Hero: Ideologies of Peace and National Identity in Postwar Japan* (Honolulu: University of Hawai'i Press, 2001): 17.

33 Norihiro Kato, *Amerika no Kage: Sengo Saiken [The American Shadow: Reexamining Postwar]* (Tokyo: Kodansha Gakujyutsubunko, 1995): 296–297.

34 Ibid.

35 Dower, 355–364.

36 Tokyo Shoseki, *Kindai Kyokasho no Hensen: Tokyo Shoseki Nanaju-Nenshi [Genealogy of Modern School Textbooks: The Seventy-Year History of Tokyo Shoseki]* (Tokyo: Tokyo Shoseki, 1980): 338–341; on the tension between democratization initiative and technocracy in education, see Shigeru Nakayama, *Science, Technology and Society in Postwar Japan* (New York: Routledge, 1991).

37 Tokiomi Kaigo, Arata Naka, and Masao Terasaki, *Kyokasho de Miru Kingendai nihon no kyoiku [Education of Contemporary Japan as Seen through Textbooks]* (Tokyo: Tokyo Shoseki, 1999): 140–141.

38 Ibid., 142–143.

39 Dower, 80–84.

40 For a detailed account of history textbook reform under American Occupation, see Yoko H. Thakur, "History Textbook Reform in Allied Occupied Japan, 1945–52", *History of Education Quarterly*, Vol. 35, No. 3 (Autumn, 1995): 261–278.

41 Shashi Henshu Iinkai, *Kindai Kyokasho no Hensen: Tokyo Shoseki Nanajyu-nenshi [Genealogy of Modern Textbooks: Seventy Years History of Tokyo Shoseki]* (Tokyo: Tokyo Shoseki, 1980): 338–339.

42 Eiji Oguma, *<Minshu> to <Aikoku>: Sengo Nihon no Nashionarizumu to Kokyosei [<Democracy> and <Patriotism>: Postwar Japan's Nationalism and the Concept of the Public]* (Tokyo: Shinyosha, 2005): 354.

43 For the text of the Imperial Rescript on Education see "The Imperial Rescript on Education [Official Document]", in *Children and Youth in History, Item #136*, https://chnm.gmu.edu/cyh/primary-sources/136 (Accessed July 2, 2015). Annotated by Brian Platt.

44 Julian Dierkes, "The Decline and Rise of the Nation in German History Education", in Schissler and Soysal, *The Nation Europe*, 83.

45 Iinkai, 480–481.

46 Ibid., 518–521.

47 Ibid., 491.

48 There are two interrelated groups here: the professional historians, who concerned themselves with the wartime complicity of history writing to militarist ends, and the

educators, who were not historians but were nonetheless committed to socialist ends, as will be discussed ahead. In terms of how the historical movement is conceptualized, the socialists, Marxists, and modernists all diverge – the koza-ha Marxists conceive of the Meiji Restoration as a failed revolution and that in terms of stages of development feudalism remains to be undone – modernists such as Masao Maruyama see wartime Japan as embodying premodern elements – there are variations, but all three are similar in that there is a directional history assumed and efforts are made at identifying the agent who can bring about change.

49 Keiji Nagahara, *20 Seiki Nihon no Rekishigaku [Historiography of 20th Century Japan]* (Tokyo: Yoshikawa Kobunkan, 2009): 141.
50 Ibid.
51 A representative modernist would be Masao Maruyama.
52 J. Victor Koschmann, *Revolution and Subjectivity in Postwar Japan* (London and Chicago: University of Chicago Press, 1996): 1. On Japanese social science, see Andrew E. Barshay, *The Social Sciences in Modern Japan: The Marxian and Modernist Traditions* (California: University of California Press, 2004).
53 Oguma, 355.
54 Ibid., 356.
55 Ibid., 362–363.
56 In Japanese account of the period, America is equated to the United States. Canada is referred to as "kanada" and South America as "nanbei", and the same applies to the writings by Norihiro Kato on Amerika – Amerika here refers to the United States and does not implicate other Americas.
57 Oguma, 365.
58 Ibid., 368.
59 Ibid., 366–367.
60 Dower, 23.
61 Oguma, 363.
62 Iinkai, 515.
63 Ibid., 188–194.
64 Oguma, 358; Kaigo, 209.
65 The protest against renewal of security alliance encompassed 330,000 protestors surrounding the Japanese Diet building. After Kishi's gorging of the alliance against the Japanese people's will, Fukuda came into power and further tried to suppress social dissent by instating his double-digit income policy, paving ways to further diffuse the appeal of socialist and communist ideology.
66 Dower, 272–273.
67 Iinkai, 497.
68 Ibid., 492.
69 Ibid., 534, 544.
70 Ibid., 542, 544, 547.
71 Tokyo Shoseki Henshubu Kikaku, *Atarashi Shakai Rekishi [New Social Science History]* (Tokyo: Tokyo Shoseki, 2006): 159; Shimizu Shoin, *Shin Chugakko Rekishi [New Middle School History]* (Tokyo: Shimizu Shoin, 2006): 166–167; also note how the excerpt of the Potsdam Declaration which singles out the militarists for war blame is emphasized in 174.
72 Ryuichi Narita, *Senso Keiken no Sengoshi [Postwar History of "War Experience"]* (Tokyo: Iwanami Shoten, 2010): 144.
73 On the contestation over terminology in postwar Japan, see Takashi Yoshida, "A Battle over History: The Nanjing Massacre in Japan", in Joshua A. Fogel ed., *The Nanjing Massacre: In History and Historiography* (Berkeley: University of California Press, 2000).
74 As Pheng Cheah makes the case, this likening of state to a living organism instead of an artifice is marked and haunted by this dilemma. Pheng Cheah, *Spectral Nationality:*

Passages of Freedom from Kant to Postcolonial Literatures of Liberation (New York: Columbia University Press, 2003).

75 Daniel C. Sneider, "Textbooks and Patriotic Education: Wartime Memory Formation in China and Japan", *Asia-Pacific Review*, Vol. 20 (2013).

76 In fact, it is this objectivity that is invoking a backlash domestically, manifesting as a political movement to envision history in more nationalistic manner. On domestic revisionist movement, see Eiji Oguma and Yoko Ueno, *<Iyashi> no nashionarizumu: Kusa no ne Hoshu Undo no Jissho Kenkyu [<Healing> Nationalism: Empirical Study on Grassroots Conservative Movement]* (Tokyo: Keio Gijyuku Shuppankai, 2003).

77 Ango Sakaguchi, *Darakuron [Discourse on Decadence]* (Tokyo: Kadokawa Bunko, 1993–initial publication 1957): 93.

78 The term "ianfu" was used by military staff under wartime, but the term "ianfu seido ['comfort' women system]" is a postwar lexicon. The term "jyugun ianfu ['comfort' women who follow the military]" is a term first used by Senda Kako who authored one of the first pioneering studies on the system. The term sexual slavery came to be used by legal scholars and transnational activists in 1990s. The "comfort" women at times under war were not even referred to as human, but as objects to be transported in military documents, or as "communal toilet". On the terminological variations, see Soh, 29–42. On detailed analysis of military documents and how the bodies were objectified, see Tanaka, *Japan's Comfort Women*. Also, Soh differentiates the condition of *ianjo* into three periods: post-Manchurian invasion 1932–1937, post-Nanking massacre 1938–1941, post-Pearl Harbor attack 1942–1945 and note the need to attend to the complex interplay and difference between the political economy of human trafficking and prostitution under wartime and the condition of rape camp. Soh, 132–140. American Occupation forces' neglect of the Asian war victims has been noted before, and to this I would also add the need to account for the colonial exceptions which rendered Korean victims without rights even during wartime. See 1921 International Convention for the Suppression of the Traffic in Women and Children, Treaty Series, League of Nations, Vol. 9, p. 415.

79 Etsuro Totsuka, "Kokusai Jinken Jindoho to Jyosei Kokusai Senpan Hotei [International Human Rights Discourse and International Women's Tribunal]", in VAWW-NET Japan ed., *Sabakareta Senji Seiboryoku: Nihongun Sei Doreisei wo Sabaku Jyosei Kokusai Senpan Hotei to wa Nande Attaka [Judging Wartime Sexual Violence: What Was the Meaning of the International Women's Tribunal That Judged Japanese Military Sexual Slavery System?]* (Tokyo: Hakutakusha, 2001): 149.

80 The U.S.-imposed postwar constitution forbid Japan from using military force to resolve international conflicts – in Article 9 of the constitution, it stipulates that Japan will not use military force (clause a) and to this end it will not have any military (clause b). Given that Japan is not allowed to remilitarize, the security treaty between America and Japan was formed as a way to ensure Japanese national security. American policymakers changed their mind as the Cold War intensified in East Asia and demanded that Japan remilitarize again, which led to a compromise of formation of the Japanese Self-Defense Force and establishment of the Defense Agency. Under Prime Minister Shinzo Abe, this Defense Agency was revamped into Defense Ministry in 2007.

81 Peter J. Katzenstein ed., *The Culture of National Security: Norms and Identity in World Politics* (New York: Columbia University Press, 1996).

82 This became law in 1999 as "Kokki Kokkaho [On Law Concerning National Flag and Anthem]", www8.cao.go.jp/chosei/kokkikokka/kokkikokka.html (Accessed August 20, 2015).

83 The three figures' names are Shigeto Nagano, Minister of Justice under Hata cabinet, Arata Sakurai, Murayama cabinet's Director-General of Environmental Agency; and Keisuke Nakanishi, Director of Defence Agency under Hosokawa cabinet. Norihiro Kato, *Haisengoron [After Defeat]* (Tokyo: Chikuma Bunko, 2005): 52.

84 Kato, *Haisengoron*, 52–54.

85 Georg G. Iggers and Q. Edward Wang, *A Global History of Modern Historiography* (Great Britain: Pearson Education Limited, 2008): 46–52.

86 Kato, *Haisengoron*, 110.

87 Because this is a section on how Japan sees America, I will use the Japanese term Amerika instead of following the distinction of America and the U.S. – in Japan, Latin America is referred to as nanbei and Canada as Kanada – when the term America is used it always refers to the United States, not to Canada or South America. Kato, *Amerika no Kage*, 28.

88 Kato, *Amerika*, 14–17.

89 Ibid., 43–60.

90 Nishitani and Kato, "Sekaisenso no torauma to 'nihonjin' [Trauma of World War and 'Japanese']", *Sekai* (August, 1995): 51.

91 Kato, *Amerika*, 37.

92 Ibid., 4; also Nishitani and Kato, "Sekaishi no torauma", 43.

93 Nishitani and Kato, "Sekaisenso no Torauma", 51.

94 Masaki Nakamasa, *Nihon to Doitsu Futatsu no Sengo Shiso [Japan and Germany: Two Postwar Thought]* (Tokyo: Kobunsha Shinsho, 2006): 129.

95 Kato, *Haisengoron*, 340.

96 Tetsuya Takahashi, "Japanese Neo-Nationalism: A Critique of Kato Norihiro's 'after the Defeat' Discourse", in Richard F. Calichman ed., *Contemporary Japanese Thought* (New York: Columbia University Press, 2005).

97 Tetsuya Takahashi, trans. and Philip Seaton, "The National Politics of the Yasukuni Shrine", in Naoko Shimazu ed., *Nationalisms in Japan* (New York: Routledge, 2006): 160.

98 Takahashi, "Japanese Neo-Nationalism", 201.

99 Tetsuya Takahashi, *Sengosekininron [Theory on Postwar Responsibility]* (Tokyo: Kodansha Gakujyutsubunko, 2005); Takahashi Tetsuya, Toko Kitagawa, and Takahiro Nakajima eds., *Ho to Boryokuno kioku: higashi ajia no rekishikeiken [Memory of Law and Violence: East Asian Historical Experience]* (Tokyo: Tokyo Daigaku Shuppankai, 2007); Takahashi Tetsuya ed., *<Rekishininshiki> Ronso [<Historical Recognition> Debates]* (Tokyo: Sakuhinsha, 2002); Takahashi Tetsuya, *Rekishi/Shuseishugi [History/Revisionism]* (Tokyo: Iwanami Shoten, 2001).

100 Satoru Ohsawa, "Fukuseisochi toshiteno 'Toakyodotai'ron", in Tomoaki Ishii, Hideo Kobayashi, and Masafumi Yonetani eds., *1930nendai no Ajia Shakairon: 'Toakyodotai'ron wo chushin to suru genzetsu kukan no shosou [Social Theories of Asia as Society in 1930s: On Discourse Surrounding "East Asian Collaborative Body" Theory]* (Tokyo: Shakaihyoronsha, 2010).

101 Masachi Osawa, *Sengo no Shiso Kukan [Atmosphere of Postwar Political Thought]* (Tokyo: Chikuma Shinsho, 2005).

102 Until 1995 – when Tomiichi Murayama exchanged the seat for Prime Minister for conceding the postwar socialist opposition to rearmament – the socialists consistently held one third of the Japanese National Diet seats. With the socialist concession to Liberal Democratic Party, the voters abandoned the Socialist Party altogether since then.

103 Berger argues that neorealist and neoliberal accounts fail to explain postwar Japanese military posture and that we must take into account the role of culture. On political-military culture and Japanese national debate on the Gulf War in 1990s, see Thomas U. Berger, "Norms, Identity, and National Security in Germany and Japan", in Peter Katzenstein ed., *The Culture of National Security: Norms and Identity in World Politics* (New York: Columbia University Press, 1996).

104 Berger, 340. This culture of anti-militarism is based on a self-deception of postwar Japan which Kato identifies, war is considered out of question and how postwar Japanese national security is intrinsically dependent on America is effaced from debates over U.S. military base deployment or whether to cooperate with America on the war in the Middle East.

105 Yoshikuni Igarashi, *Bodies of Memory: Narratives of War in Postwar Japanese Culture, 1945–1990* (Princeton, NJ: Princeton University Press, 2000): 208. He is referring to the debate between Korean and Japanese feminist scholars on whether feminism should transcend the national question – on this, see Hee-Kang Kim, "Should Feminism Transcend Nationalism? A Defense of Feminist Nationalism in South Korea", *Women's Studies International Forum*, Vol. 32 (2009): 108–119 which is response to Ueno Chizuko, *Nashionarizumu to Jendaa [Nationalism and Gender]* (Tokyo: Seidosha, 1998).
106 Kim, "Should Feminism Transcend Nationalism?", 117.
107 Parul Sehgal, "How 'Privilege' Became a Provocation", *New York Times*, July 14, 2015.
108 Igarashi, 208.
109 Takahashi, *Rekishi/Shuseishugi*, 28–29.
110 To be sure, Kato's characterization of disappearance of the subject, while metaphorically to the point, nonetheless fails to take into account the postwar struggle among ordinary Japanese people and historians to remember the war. On cultural memories of war, see Igarashi, *Bodies of Memory*; on detailed study on history of reconfiguration of war memory, see Narita, especially 154–189 on the debate among scholars of international relations and historians of war over methods of explanation, structural accounts of war, and depictions of war.
111 Kato, *Haisengoron*, 287.
112 Osawa, *Sengo no Shiso Kukan*, 26.

References

Barshay, Andrew. *The Social Sciences in Modern Japan: The Marxian and Modernist Traditions*. California: University of California Press, 2004.
Berger, Thomas. *War, Guilt, and World Politics after World War II*. Cambridge: Cambridge University Press, 2012.
Brown, Wendy. *States of Injury: Power and Freedom in Late Modernity*. Princeton, NJ: Princeton University Press, 1995.
Butler, Judith. *Giving an Account of Oneself*. New York: Fordham University Press, 2005.
Cabinet Office, Government of Japan. "On the Law Concerning National Flag and Anthem." www8.cao.go.jp/chosei/kokkikokka/kokkikokka.html (Accessed August 20, 2015).
Cheah, Pheng. *Spectral Nationality: Passages of Freedom from Kant to Postcolonial Literatures of Liberation*. New York: Columbia University Press, 2003.
Chen, Kuang-Hsing. *Asia as Method: Toward Deimperialization*. Durham and London: Duke University Press, 2010.
Connolly, William. *Pluralism*. Durham and London: Duke University Press, 2005.
Conrad, Sebastian. "The Dialectics of Remembrance: Memories of Empire in Cold War Japan." *Comparative Studies in Society and History* 56, no. 1 (2014): 4–33.
Dierkes, Julian. "The Decline and Rise of the Nation in German History Education." In *The Nation, Europe, and the World: Textbooks and Curricula in Transition*, edited by H. Schissler and Y.N. Soysal. New York: Berghahn Books, 2005.
Doty, Roxanne Lynn. "Sovereignty and the Nation: Constructing the Boundaries of National Identity." Chapter. In *State Sovereignty as Social Construct*, edited by Thomas J. Biersteker and Cynthia Weber, 121–147. Cambridge Studies in International Relations. Cambridge: Cambridge University Press, 2000. doi:10.1017/CBO9780511598685.005.
Dower, John. *Embracing Defeat: Japan in the Aftermath of World War II*. Australia: Penguin Books, 2000.

Gordon, Avery. *Ghostly Matters: Haunting and the Sociological Imagination.* Minneapolis, MN: University of Minnesota Press, 2008.

Hattori, Ryuji. *Gaiko Documento: Rekishi Ninshiki [Foreign Policy Documents: History Recognition].* Tokyo: Iwanami Shinsho, 2015.

Hein, Laura and Mark Selden eds. *Censoring History: Perspectives on Nationalism and War in the Twentieth Century.* New York: Routledge, 2000.

Hobson, John. *The State and International Relations.* Cambridge: Cambridge University Press, 2000.

Ienaga, Saburo. *Senso Sekinin [War Responsibility].* Tokyo: Iwanami Shoten, 1985.

Igarashi, Yoshikuni. *Bodies of Memory: Narratives of War in Postwar Japanese Culture, 1945–1990.* Princeton, NJ: Princeton University Press, 2000.

Iokibe, Kaoru, Kazuo Komiya, Yuichi Hosoya, and Taizo Miyagi eds. *Sengonihon no rekishininshiki [Postwar Japan's Recognition of History].* Tokyo: Tokyo Daigaku Shuppankai, 2017.

Jaeger, Sheila Miyoshi and Rana Mitter eds. *Ruptured Histories: War, Memory and the Post-Cold War in Asia.* Cambridge, MA and London: Harvard University Press, 2007.

Kagawa, Hikomatsu. "Kindaikokusaiseijishi ni okeru nihon [Modern History of International Politics and Japan]." *Kokusai Seiji [International Politics],* no. 3 (1957): 1–21.

Kaigo, Tokiomi, Naka Arata, and Masao Terasaki. *Kyokasho de miru kingendai nihon no kyoiku [Education of Contemporary Japan as Seen through Textbooks].* Tokyo: Tokyo Shoseki, 1999.

Kato, Norihiro. *Amerika no Kage [The American Shadow].* Tokyo: Kodansha Gakujyutsubunko, 1995.

Kato, Norihiro. *Haisengoron [After Defeat].* Tokyo: Chikuma Bunko, 2005.

Kato, Norihiro. *Sayounara, Gojiratachi – Sengo kara toku hanarete [Goodbye, Godzilla: From Far Away from Postwar].* Tokyo: Iwanami Shoten, 2010.

Kato, Norihiro and Osamu Nishitani. "Sekai Senso no Torauma to 'nihonjin' [The Trauma of World War and 'Japanese']." *Sekai* 611 (1995): 42–64.

Katzenstein, Peter ed. *The Culture of National Security: Norms and Identity in World Politics.* New York: Columbia University Press, 1996.

Kim, Hee-Kang. "Should Feminism Transcend Nationalism? A Defense of Feminist Nationalism in South Korea." *Women's Studies International Forum* 32 (2009): 108–119.

Kimura, Kan. *Nikkan Rekishininshiki mondai towa nanika; rekishi kyokasho, 'ianfu' popurizumu [What Is the History Recognition Problem between Japan and Korea? History Textbook, 'Comfort' Women, and Populism].* Tokyo: Minerva Shobo, 2015.

Koschmann, Victor. *Revolution and Subjectivity in Postwar Japan.* London and Chicago: University of Chicago Press, 1996.

Marx, Karl and D.D.L. trans. *Karl Marx: The Eighteenth Brumaire of Louis Bonaparte.* New York and Berlin: Mondial, 2005.

Ministry of Education, Culture, Sports, Science and Technology Japan. "Monbukagakusho Kokuji Dai 166 go [Ministry of Education, Culture, Sports, Science and Technology Japan Instruction on Textbook Evaluation Rules No. 166]." www.mext.go.jp/b_menu/hakusho/nc/1284728.htm (Accessed August 21, 2014).

Ministry of Foreign Affairs of Japan. "Statement by Chief Cabinet Secretary Kiichi Miyazawa on History Textbooks." www.mofa.go.jp/policy/postwar/state8208.html (Accessed August 21, 2014).

Mitani, Hiroshi. "Japan's History Textbook System and Its Controversies." In *Kokkyo o koeru rekishi ninshiki [Toward a History beyond Borders: Contentious Issues in Sino-Japanese Relations],* edited by Daqing Yang. Cambridge: Harvard University Press, 2012.

Morris-Suzuki, Tessa, Morris Low, Leonid Petrov, and Timothy Y. Tsu eds. *East Asia beyond the History Wars: Confronting the Ghosts of Violence*. New York: Routledge, 2013.

Nagahara, Keiji. *20 Seiki Nihon no Rekishigaku [The Japanese Discipline of History in Twentieth Century]*. Tokyo: Yoshikawa Kobunkan, 2003.

Nakamasa, Masaki. *Nihon to Doitsu Futatsu no Sengoshiso [Japan and Germany: Two Postwar Political Thoughts]*. Tokyo: Kobunsha Shinsho, 2006.

Namiki, Yorihisa. *Kingendai no Nicchukankei wo tou [Reflection on Contemporary Japan-China Relations]*. Tokyo: Kenbunshuppan, 2012.

Narita, Ryuichi. *Rekishigau no Pojishonaritii: Rekishi Jojutsu to sono Shuhen [Positionality and Historiography: Surrounding Historical Narrative]*. Tokyo: Azekura Shobo, 2006.

Narita, Ryuichi. *'Senso Keiken' no Sengoshi [Postwar History of 'War Experience']*. Tokyo: Iwanami Shoten, 2010.

Oguma, Eiji. *<Minshu> to <Aikoku>: Sengo Nihon no Nashionarizumu to Kokyosei [<Democracy> and <Patriotism>: Postwar Japan's Nationalism and the Concept of the Public]*. Tokyo: Shinyosha, 2005.

Onuma, Yasuaki. *'Ianfu' mondai to wa nandattanoka [What Was the 'Comfort Women' Problem About?]*. Tokyo: Chuko Shinsho, 2007.

Orr, James. *Victim as Hero: Ideologies of Peace and National Identity in Postwar Japan*. Honolulu: University of Hawai'i Press, 2001.

Osawa, Masachi. *Sengo no Shiso Kukan [Atmosphere of Postwar Political Thought]*. Tokyo: Chikuma Shinsho, 2005.

Sakaguchi, Ango. *Darakuron [Discourse on Decadence]*. Tokyo: Kadokawa Bunko, 1993.

Schissler, Hanna and Yasemin Nuhoglu Soysal eds. *The Nation, Europe, and the World: Textbooks and Curricula in Transition*. New York: Berghahn Books, 2005.

Shashi Henshu Iinkai. *Kindai Kyokasho no Hensen: Tokyo Shoseki Nanajyu-Nenshi [Genealogy of Modern Textbooks: Seventy Years History of Tokyo Shoseki]*. Tokyo: Tokyo Shoseki, 1980.

Shepard, Todd. *The Invention of Decolonization: The Algerian War and the Remaking of France*. Ithaca and London: Cornell University Press, 2006.

Shimizu Shoin. *Shin Chugakko Rekishi [New Middle School History]*. Tokyo: Shimizu Shoin, 2006.

Soh, Chunghee Sarah. *The Comfort Women: Sexual Violence and Postcolonial Memory in Korea and Japan*. Chicago and London: University of Chicago Press, 2008.

Suga, Syuichi. "Kokumin gakko 'shotoka kokugo' 5–8 no suminuri kyokasho no jitsujo ni tsuite", in *Hanazono daigaku bungakubu kenkyu kiyou [Departmental Bulletin Paper Hanazono University]* No. 48: 143–173.

Suga, Syuichi. "Suminuri kyokasho <Showa Nijyu kara Nijyuichinen> no jitsujo ni tsuite [Rigid Censorship over School Textbooks by the Ministry of Education in 1945–46]", in *Hanazono shigaku [The Association of History Research Hanazono University]* No. 33 (November 2012): 52–105.

Takahashi, Tetsuya. *Rekishi/shuseishugi [History/Revisionism]*. Tokyo: Iwanami Shoten, 2001.

Takahashi, Tetsuya ed. *<Rekishininshiki> Ronso [<Historical Recognition> Debates]*. Tokyo: Sakuhinsha, 2002.

Takahashi, Tetsuya. "Japanese Neo-Nationalism: A Critique of Kato Norihiro's 'after the Defeat' Discourse." In *Contemporary Japanese Thought*, edited by Richard Calichman. New York: Columbia University Press, 2005.

Takahashi, Tetsuya. *Sengo Sekininron [Theory on Postwar Responsibility]*. Tokyo: Kodansha Gakujyutsubunko, 2005.

Takahashi, Tetsuya. "The National Politics of the Yasukuni Shrine." In *Nationalisms in Japan*, edited by Naoko Shimazu, translated by Philip Seaton. New York: Routledge, 2006.

Tanaka, Yuki. *Japan's Comfort Women: Sexual Slavery and Prostitution during World War II*. New York: Routledge, 2003.

Thakur, Yoko. "History Textbook Reform in Allied Occupied Japan, 1945–52." *History of Education* 35, no. 3 (1995): 261–278.

Tokyo Shoseki. *Kindai Kyokasho no Hensen: Tokyo Shoseki Nanaju-Nenshi [Genealogy of Modern School Textbooks: The Seventy-Year History of Tokyo Shoseki]*. Tokyo: Tokyo Shoseki, 1980.

Totsuka, Etsuro. "kokusai jinken jindoho to jyosei kokusai senpan hotei [International Human Rights Discourse and International Women's Tribunal]." In *Sabakareta Senji Seiboryoku: nihongun sei doreisei wo sabaku jyosei kokusai senpan hotei to wa nande attaka [Judging Wartime Sexual Violence: What Was the Meaning of the International Women's Tribunal That Judged Japanese Military Sexual Slavery System]*, edited by VAWW-NET Japan. Tokyo: Hakutakusha, 2001.

Ueno, Chizuko. *Nashionarizumu to Jendaa [Nationalism and Gender]*. Tokyo: Seidosha, 1998.

Yoshida, Takashi. "A Battle over History: The Nanjing Massacre in Japan." In *The Nanjing Massacre in History and Historiography*, edited by Joshua Fogel. Berkeley, CA: University of California Press, 2000.

Conclusion

I wanted to give texture to the hesitation about narrating history, to add local color to the transparent silence, to eke out such space amid the disciplinary language of international relations to think about the politics of history in East Asia. I wanted to think about what it means to stand at the limits of history after the death of grand narratives, to attend to the messiness of being-with-others rather than the clarity of logic, to ask what the impasse conveys. I wanted to think about the words that could be said, the words that ought to be said, and capture the moment of withholding of the words that should be said.

Repetition of a phrase, regardless of whether one understands the meaning, can be surprisingly effective. As the only East Asian student in an elementary school in Virginia, although I was promptly placed in the English as a Second Language class for a good three years, I was nonetheless repeating the pledge of allegiance every single morning along with the other students, and to this day after thirty-one years, I am able to recite every single phrase. I finished the second half of elementary school education in Tokyo, and the contrast could not have been more stark. No one could sing the national anthem, let alone remember the lyrics. On the rare occasions when the anthem was sung, I could feel the uncertain fizziness in the air as the music began, as if one is attempting to listen to an old radio that is barely audible. A kind of collective endurance happens, and a sigh of relief could be heard when the music was over. But how can one convey this atmosphere?

This was the 1990s. The first Gulf War was going on, and against the U.S. demand for Japan to participate, a constitutional crisis was avoided by providing monetary contribution instead of men. The crisis in simple terms meant that Article 9 of the postwar U.S.-drafted constitution of Japan, which prohibits the use of force to resolve international disputes, would be violated should the Japanese have capitulated to the U.S. demand. For the second U.S. invasion of Iraq, monetary support alone no longer seemed to be an option, so men were sent to Iraq.

The contradictory presence of the "self"-"defense" force faraway from Japan, a country that renounced war, was realized by the nesting of the Japanese Self-Defense Force within the British and Australian compound in Iraq so that use of force could be avoided, and the leader of the Clean Government Party, which was in coalition with the ruling Liberal Democratic Party, insisted that he was not being hypocritical for supporting a war by stepping afoot on Iraqi soil to show that this was not a war zone. The absurdity is as clear as day. But this is Japan, in relation to the so-called West.

Let us return to the subject with which we started at the beginning of the book, which has to do with the so-called East. As I write, the "irreversible" clause in the December 2015 Japan-South Korea joint statement is being reviewed by the new leadership in South Korea (Sang-Hun, 2017). The mayor of Osaka is seeking to terminate the sister-city relationship with the city of San Francisco because the city has permitted another "comfort women" statue to be put up.

A few weeks ago, in a first for the Philippines, a new statue symbolizing the "comfort women" has been set up in that country, further disorienting the premise that the Asia Women's Fund, set up by former Prime Minister Tomiichi Murayama as a hybrid form of reparation, could steer the states that are economically more disadvantaged than South Korea to toe the line that the Japanese state is attempting to finalize.

More than three quarters of a century ago, when Japanese women in the mainland were turned into child reproduction machines, many others were turned into what advocates for the victims, such as Totsuka, has called military sex slaves.[1] It has now come to light that during the negotiations with South Korea, Japanese negotiators were demanding that the term sex slave also be no longer used to refer to these women (Sang-Hun, 2017).

The act of rendering the past into a statue reifies a particular image of the past. The statue admits of certain narratives of the past while denying others, although interpretations of such works of art are by no means predictable. These are the materializations of past injury into tangible forms, and the period of existence of a bronze statue is far longer than the life span of the living humans they symbolize, whose numbers are dwindling by the year. In this sense, the act of setting up a statue is an antidote to forgetting, silencing, and whitewashing. It is also an act of reifying a particular positionality in an era that increasingly has become identified as postmodern.

The two previous paragraphs both refer to the state of Japan, showing the limits of comprehending the politics of history in either bilateral or dichotomous terms. Even if the analysis involves more than two parties, it would be along the lines of how South Korea and Japan must get along in light of pressures from the United States, which both states depend upon for their security: the calculation of national interest and the chain of effects that follow. While such analysis could capture some rationale on the way state behavior is dictated, it nonetheless cannot convey the texture of hesitation that colors the impasse over the history problem. Such analyses also presume clear contours of the state of history.

The time in which we live in today is what Wendy Brown calls the time of "being after" a grand narrative (1995: 31). Our time, she writes, is the time that is disoriented. Regarding history, Brown says, the refusal

> to self-define or write a single origins story also reflects a late modern or postmodern consciousness of the exclusions and violations accomplished by

master narratives, the oppressiveness of closure on identity, and the vulner-
ability to colonization and regulation presented by definitive meaning.

(1995: 30)

There is a general unease with totalizing history and the consequence of positing a semblance of order at the expense of those who become eliminated in order
to endow reality a sense of coherence. While Brown's writing reflects on the contours of the North American political landscape, the interweaving of the discussion about disorientation and disavowal of master narratives also elucidates the
political contours of the post-1945 Far East, or the dis-oriented Orient.

In *Rekishi no dekonsutorakushon [Deconstruction of History]*, the philosopher
Yasuo Kobayashi writes that philosophy's task for the humanities is to interrogate
the very idea of the subject of history: of what it effaces and the power it presupposes.[2] Yet, history writing in postwar Japan and decolonized and democratiz-
ing Asia has witnessed a flourishing of multiplied subjects of histories. In Frank
Ankersmit's understanding, while such flourishing is often interpreted as the end
of political history – the history of kings and states in the narrow sense – and the
democratization of history for the formerly excluded, this also is a triumph of the
politicization of history into the realm heretofore excluded (2001: 268).

Suspicion of the subject and the aspiration to constitute oneself as a subject
precariously commingle in the same (post)war space. In a world that is ever more
mired in the arms race, the Japanese state since 1945 (or 1952, if we are to mark
the restoration of sovereignty) has sought to resignify its world image as a peace-
loving nation and as a progressive state that has constitutionally renounced the
use of military means to resolve international disputes. Yet such resignification
was made possible under the U.S. nuclear umbrella, thereby rendering the sense
of Japanese state agency and the actual commitment to peace suspect. It is one
thing to commit to peace on one's own terms, and another to commit to peace on
the terms of the other.

The presence of the United States on Japanese soil, therefore, serves as a guarantor of peace for East Asia in the sense that Japanese militarism will be kept
under check of the United States, yet it also means that the figure of Japan as the
sovereign agentic subject of history is also enigmatic. Disavowal of the state as the
subject of history and ambiguity of the state as the subject of history has become
entrenched in U.S.-Japan relations. But this is not so for Asia-Japan relations.

Counterintuitively, for Asia, the ambiguity of Japan as a subject is often deemed
an issue that must be concretely addressed, although in terms of security, an issue
that is preferred not to be addressed, for it could easily dovetail into Prime Minister Shinzo Abe's move to normalize Japan into a sovereign state that can exercise
international political agency by changing Clause B of the Article 9 of the Peace
Constitution.[3]

Let us return to the specific issue of the "comfort women". While the discourse
on "comfort women" cannot solely be characterized as a feminist movement, let
us take up Brown's exposition of the feminist hesitation toward the postmodern
sensibility. The postmodern sensibility at once denaturalizes the preexisting social

order, and simultaneously prohibits one from making a subject-centered claim, thereby dissolving "a relatively bounded formulation of the political and disintegrates the coherence of women as a collective subject" (Brown, 1995: 38–39).

The proliferation of statues resembles the politics of *ressentiment* insofar as it develops "a righteous critique of power from the perspective of the injured, it delimits a specific site of blame for suffering by *constituting* sovereign subjects and events as responsible for the 'injury' of social subordination" (1995: 27, italics mine). Furthermore, such politics of *ressentiment*

> fixes the identities of the injured and the injuring as social positions, and codifies as well the meanings of their actions against all possibilities of indeterminacy, ambiguity, and struggle for resignification or repositioning . . . [casting] the law in particular and the state more broadly as neutral arbiters of injury rather than as themselves invested with the power to injure . . . powerfully [legitimizing] law and the state as appropriate protectors against injury.
>
> (ibid)

To demand that the Japanese state respond, therefore, re-centers the state. While Brown is speaking in terms of identity politics *within* North America, in the case of the Far East, decolonization and an ahistorical conception of the nation as always having been sovereign, at least in spirit if not always in reality, renders the politics of history into that of politics of *ressentiment* which at once contests and reifies the state as the sovereign subject of history. The persistence of Japan's history problem evinces the simultaneous disavowal and desire for a sovereign subject toward an effective resolution.

On the one hand is the awareness of the socially constructed nature of the categories in which we speak and upon which we depend, such as the idea of a homogenous nation-state that is an agent-actor in world politics. On the other, it seems, there is the need for a concrete and sovereign state that is to both reckon and arbitrate about injury, even one that its predecessor has inflicted and which it has inherited.

As Judith Butler reminds us in her reading of Nietzsche, response

> to allegation must, from the outset, accept the possibility that the self has causal agency, even if, in a given instance, the self may not have been the cause of the suffering in question . . . [t]he narrative does not emerge after the fact of causal agency but constitutes the prerequisite condition for any account of moral agency we might give.
>
> (2005: 12)

What she elucidates is how the politics of history cannot be solely grounded upon determination of facts and truths, but on the possibility of having had causal agency, too.

There is a difference between having agency and possibly having had agency, just as there is a difference between the Japanese state being the sovereign subject of history and possibly having had agency in such name. Still, if acceptance of the possibility is necessary, the distinction alone cannot settle the matter. The reason why I have traced the place of agency in history and historicism throughout the book was to show how the texture of the impasse over the history problem could be felt if we were to broaden the matter beyond truths and facts, and to include also the pursuit of the possibility of exercising agency in history as part of the imperial debris.

To think of the place of responsibility, one must track back the place of agency in history, and the multiple conceptions of where historical agency resides, and how they remain pitted against one another. History and politics are far more intertwined and implicates the discourse on responsibility because it pivots around the supposition of agency. Throughout, I have attempted to place history back into politics and politics back into history in the Asian theater.

Chapter 1 historicizes historicism by placing the development and differentiation of the meaning historicism took into its late eighteenth century European political context. Contra Chakrabarty, I argue that historicism played the role of both denying and asserting political agency. For the sake of conceptual clarity, I identify two different versions of historicism at play: agency-denying historicism, civilizational historicism which conceives of history as progressive history, and agency-enabling historicism, cultural historicism which envisions history as an autonomous unfolding of sovereign subjects.

Chapters 2 and 3 examined how different historicisms were intertwined with modern Japan's reconfiguration of its place in world history and its relationship to the West and Asia. In early Meiji, there was a brief flirtation among Japanese thinkers with civilizational historicism. This lasted only until the 1890s, when many realized that this kind of agency-denying civilizational historicism was inherently Eurocentric and offered little space for those who belong to the "stagnant" Orient. The now-familiar trope of "First in the west, then in the rest" identified by Chakrabarty was visible at the turn of the century.

This trope prompted a search for alternative ways of conceiving of history. This reaction to progressive history was not limited to the "rest". Within the peripheral west, Germany (in what Mandelbaum identifies as the Romantic rebellion against the Enlightenment) envisioned a historicism that could affirm the individuality and autonomy of diverse cultures – *kultur* was pitted against civilizational historicism. In Asia, this valorization of culture was used by theorists such as Kiyoshi Miki and later the Kyoto School philosophers to assert the import of Japan's "world historical" mission to constitute a new cultural order. In the strictly theoretical sense, not only in Europe, but in Asia, too, World War II was "nothing other than a disagreement about the nature of history".[4]

The denial of historical agency by Eurocentric progressive history is problematic, but so was the response by Japan, a response which sought to make Japan the subject of history yet also legitimated Japanese imperialism in Asia. I argue throughout that in order to understand postwar Japan's difficulties in facing history, we must take into account how there were two different kinds of historicism at work. The first was Eurocentric progressive history, and the second was a response to progressive history waged in the name of culture.

This leaves us to ask in what other ways one might counter Eurocentrism without replicating the violence that accompanies the assertion of oneself as the sovereign subject of history or seeking to overcome the west. When this question is asked, the study of Japanese rhetoric legitimating war in the name of making history and its similarity to contemporary postcolonial critiques of Eurocentrism and linear history is striking.

Having examined the way in which the two versions of historicism reconfigured Japan's relation to the world, Chapter 4 examines the aftermath. After witnessing the violence legitimated in both versions of historicism, what might one have to say about history?

Since 1945, Japan as a subject of history has assumed the form of a palimpsest being there and not there, simultaneously. As Cold War tension thawed and the movement to decolonize history and the demand for acknowledging the victims in the historical narrative in Japanese history textbooks surged, this ghostly palimpsest form of the state became an issue. If Japan were to be held responsible by Asian victims, it must be constituted as a response-able subject. Such was the thesis of literary critic Norihiro Kato. This thesis, despite being offered as a response to the Asian demand to face history, appeared all too similar to the rhetoric of the 1930s and 1940s, which legitimated Japanese imperialism in the name of asserting Japan as the sovereign subject of history and, therefore, was mired in an impasse. As a result, the "postwar debate on the subject of history" ended in a stalemate.

The politics of history and its persistence attest to the ineluctable ways in which our conceptions of agency and, thereby, of freedom and responsibility are implicated. Despite the attempt at separating politics from history by disavowing anachronism and appealing to the value of an objective study of the past, historically the desire for emancipatory ends – either that of freedom or of equality – have recolonized political identity despite itself.

The broad schematic contour of the history of Japan's engagement with world history are mired in these moments when it sought inclusion and recognition within the framework of universal history and liberal universalism, only to begin exercising the politics of resentment, of reinscribing differences into rigid identities with the dawning of the realization that liberalism continually fails to recognize how differences are socially (in this case, socially within the context of expanding European international society) inscribed while simultaneously presupposing it.

In terms of how the politicization of identity is implicated here, Brown's analysis of identity politics resonates with the mapping of what went awry in wartime Japan. While Japan challenged "liberalism's universal 'we' as the strategic fiction of historically hegemonic groups and [asserted] liberalism's 'I' as social – both relational and constructed by power – rather than contingent, private, or autarkic. Yet it [reiterated] the terms of liberal discourse insofar as it [posited] a sovereign and unified 'I' that is disenfranchised by the exclusive 'we'".[5] Brown echoing William Connolly elucidates the ways in which the politicization of identity that arises from exclusion culminates in the reiteration – in "its configuration of a sovereign, unified, accountable individual".[6] The persistence of the politics of history in postwar Japan and its viscosity are the properties of this anguish over the place of the sovereign in the state of history.

The geopolitical history of postwar Japan evinces how such a presupposition of power cannot quite stand, and never has stood, be it the place of the emperor or the state.[7] What we see here is the jutting of the partially shared conception of the place of sovereignty and the state as subject of history in postwar Japan, where theory, history, and memory of the theory of history are pitted against one and the other, registering to those outside of Japan as lack of repentance, as a still-shot frame, constituting the impasse over the state of history. What I showed was, in fact, the question of how the awareness of the constructed nature of the state (the postmodern awareness) and the demand for the state to face its past stand in tension with one another.

While Brown is referring to the grand narrative of the West, the grand narrative in this book refers to both the narrative of Europe as the subject of history and the narrative which became dominant in Japan after the attack on Pearl Harbor and British Malay: that the war had higher meaning, that Japan was the subject of history. In his study on narratives about the war in wartime and postwar Japan, historian Ryuichi Narita notes the shift in the ways in which war was reported back in the mainland after December 7, 1942.

Up until that point, the meaning of the war was unclear and the news consisted mainly of reporting what was taking place rather than attributing a grand story to it. After December 7, the reports sent back to the homeland more frequently became embedded in a larger narrative (2010: 44). Undeclared warfare had been ongoing in China for years, yet even for those who had been critical of Japanese activities in Asia, such as Yoshimi Takeuchi, this attack on the West held significance hitherto unexpected.[8]

In 1942, Takeuchi wrote:

> History was made. The world has changed overnight. We witnessed this . . . there is a surging sense which could not be named. On December 8th, the day the imperial declaration of war was given, the Japanese people's decision became one.
>
> (2006: 41)

The forums subsequently held in Japan were titled "World Historical Position and Japan" and "Overcoming Modernity" that attempted to theorize Japan as the subject of world history, which before had been European history.[9]

In this vein, the postwar hesitation to deal with history is informed, in part, by the extensive reflection on this affective dimension of history. For figures such as Yoshimi Takeuchi, it was this affective dimension of history that became an object of reflection in the postwar years. Takeuchi asks: what rendered that moment so special that it overcame the critical instincts?[10] To be sure, the representation of war as a world historical event in mainland Japan did not implicate everyone equally, and in much of postwar accounting done by intellectuals, ordinary people as well as militarists cannot be free of anachronism.

After the war, the reckoning took many forms. One notorious form was that of "*ichioku sozange* [all million repent as one]" which called for everyone to repent. Such a call served to flatten the different degrees of responsibility that different imperial subjects had during wartime and to equate the responsibility of the military top brass with those who were laboring in the warplane factory. For scholars, much of the military's doings were still withheld from scrutiny, and the immediate postwar response was to anchor research based on strictly empirical terms and to disavow ideology.

Yet the acceptance of American hegemony and the "scientific" explanation of the causes of war in terms of the balance of power or geopolitics, along with the suppression of socialist and Marxist educators in the postwar years, have also, in addition to the use of euphemism and deletion in regards to crimes committed in Asia, naturalized war and, to a large extent, absolved the militarist state as merely adhering to a natural behavioral pattern that every other great power followed. The subtle battle over whether to theorize the state as an agent-actor or as a unit also has implications for whether the state should be held accountable. As the awkward few minutes experienced during the playing of national anthem suggest, the awkward state of history is as much part of what constitutes the postimperial historical debris.

In reference to World War II, literary critic Norihiro Kato wrote in his essay *After Defeat* in 1995 that since then, "sorrow no longer unites us. Every time we mourn, it shatters us apart".[11] The line, written in his typically dense style, seemed to strike a chord with some, whereas others wholly dismissed his thesis.[12] What seemed to separate those who concurred with him from those who did not appeared to lie with the question of whether one considered the persistence of the history problem as a problem of political thought, or as a problem of depoliticization of historiography. Regarding World War II, Michael Allen Gillespie, in his study of the political thought of Hegel and Heidegger, writes that the war was "nothing other than a disagreement about the nature of history".[13]

The fault lines seem to fall along disciplinary boundaries, too. The treatment of the problem in philosophy is different from that in history, whereas those engaged in literary studies straddle the two. For historians who continue to document the war dead and the consequences for those left behind throughout the world, such a statement could amount to a testament to how out of touch philosophy is from history and reality. I maintain that the war had to do with a disagreement, but much more than that, rather than "nothing other than". Depending on who you ask, the meaning of history and its relationship to war is usually only partially shared in the sense that it does matter, but the way it does and should matter diverges.

Is one part of and an active maker of history or a passive victim of historical laws? Embedded beneath such a question is how the self, the state, and the world might relate without polarizing the answer into total mastery or total passivity. The stance which I hold is that there is no singular definition of history or historicism – both immensely contested terms – and that the persistence of the politics of history elucidates a broader global predicament about how to theorize being-in-common, after grand narratives have become suspect and master narratives are dead, yet where one also cannot throw up one's hands to claim that one had nothing to do with history.

Why did I focus on Norihiro Kato in the end? I did so because his position as a literary critic enables inclusion of the discussion on the limits of historical representation as well as how politics and history could not be detached from one another, and because he has been constantly pursuing the possibility of relating to the world and the self by attempting to put words to the texture of the postwar atmosphere. Kato's thesis in *After Defeat* straddles both historical archives and postwar literature, to treat them both as historical and as a problem of political thought.

But to locate how the impasse is constituted in the present context, I had to re-view the past discourse on historicism as a kind of debris. In the case of Japan, the resentment against the "West" for being both the "sovereign and subject of history", to quote Robert Young quoting Gayatri Spivak, culminated in the repetition of the same violence it sought to critique, implicating not only the West, but also predominantly Asia (1990: 17). To think of how to respond to Asia over what had happened, therefore, required the extension of the horizon to the hundred years before 1945 instead of fifteen, as most who treat the history problem as a problem of empirical evidence and violence of narrative would.

During the hundred years, which would cover the mid-nineteenth century to the mid-twentieth century, questions of the Enlightenment, civilization, empire, and how to respond to Eurocentrism's grand narrative of history became enmeshed with one another. And inflected amid these are questions of free will, determinism, and agency. This book is a response to Kato's call to theorize the politics of history that would be inclusive of the two halves that are supposedly schizophrenic.

When one apologizes and expresses remorse, the other half emerges to state the opposite; when one condemns the Japanese war dead for having fought a meaningless war, the other half retorts by hailing the war as a war against the West and, therefore, had meaning. To address both Jekyll and Hyde, a ground, which would place the cause of the split, had to be contextualized in the longer span of a hundred years, rather than the fifteen years of war alone. Doing so was to come to terms with the need for, as well as the limits of, resistance, claiming agency in history, and pursuing a politics of purity.

What could possibly alter the tension at hand is a shift from focusing on clarity, correctness, resolution, and purity to acknowledging how questions of responsibility are bound to raise uneasy questions about agency. As Butler notes, it is the "possibility" rather than the actuality that the subject is formed and navigates within the world. Butler asks if it would be impossible to ground a notion of responsibility when the self is ungrounded, or "schizophrenic", to use Kato's term. To this, she points toward an alternative possibility other than nihilism that could well be the consequence of deconstruction and post-structuralism. She shows how the acknowledgment of the limits of self-knowledge can "serve a conception of ethics and indeed responsibility" (2005: 19).

Historiography and narratives and responsibility are ineluctably intertwined in the sense that the attempt at responding to those who question the meaning of war and its aftermath is to think of the *possibility* of how the individual is located in this causal chain of events. There is a distinction between possibility and actuality. Nonetheless, narrative as historical representation short-circuits this distinction because it acknowledges the impossibility of representation but nonetheless pursues it. To ask how one is related to war is to account for and imagine the possibility of one having had causal agency even if it might appear implausible. What drives this?

As we saw in the final chapter, it is this attempt at responding to Japan's other that the place of the agentic subject appears to be a prerequisite. Yet it is a requisite that evokes a sense of déjà vu. Kato argued that in order to respond to the other, there must be an "I", and the history problem recurs because postwar Japan has evaded constructing this "I". The reason why a literary critic has pointed this out, I argue, is in part because he navigates between fiction and nonfiction. Of stories told, tellable and untellable. Unlike historians who adhere to that which is empirical, a literary critic identifies this need for a "I" – despite, and because of, its fictionality.

In a sense, this is a response to the post-structuralists who would deconstruct the "I" and to those who would correctly note that subject formation is necessarily violent. To examine the self that was drawn into the war and supported it is to trace how one comes to lose oneself in the grand narrative, to think of the war as the destined clash of the East vs. the West. Then the natural consequence would be to seek to establish an agentic subject that could critique and withstand the grand narrative.

Yet as Robert Young wrote on Edward Said's *Orientalism* and *Culture and Imperialism*, to ground an organic intellectual in the Gramscian sense that could identify the hegemonic structure of ideology is to reintroduce an agent (Young, 1990: 134–136). Here again, the question becomes this – if the ideology is as total as it is claimed, then there are no grounds for agency, and if there is agency, then the claim of the dominance of the ideology by definition no longer becomes total. For the emergence and possibility of the critical subject this becomes a circular issue. But the image of the state as the agentic subject is never total or clear.

In a sense, as Kato reflects more than two decades after *Haisengoron [After Defeat]*, the similarity between himself and Prime Minister Shinzo Abe, who is currently pushing for constitutional amendment, had to do with the presupposition that there must be a clear-cut subject (2010: 117). He writes, as a partial concession to his critics, that his call to straighten out and address the original contradiction that mires postwar Japanese society was intolerant of ambiguity. He now asks what it would mean to embrace the contradiction. He also adds the fact that, despite its theoretical impurity, postwar Japan has somehow made do clumsily, avoiding going to war to kill, although the Self-Defense Force was sent to Iraq. He suggests that because this has worked, there is a kind of resilience against the calls to amend the constitution to deal with the North Korean threat (2010: 141).

Perhaps this could be called the realism of the defeated – a reluctance to pursue theoretical righteousness underwritten by the skepticism of the strong, the victorious, and the righteous. Tellingly, it is the younger generation, with no experience of the war and who is more keen on and susceptible to conspiracy theory, who has less patience for the viscosity of the persistent history problem.

The book began with the issue of the "comfort women". Against the impatient moves which presuppose the solvability of the issue, the book sought to reframe and make cogent the politics of history as debris and to re-view the issue as clustered layers of divergent approaches toward history and its meaning. The politics of history is neither settled nor settle-able. Nonetheless, it is worth thinking about, precisely because it reflects our incessant articulation, hesitation, and yearning to ask what it means to be in common – to utter the term "we" – because of, and against, the liberal political discourse of our time.

This is because speaking about collective responsibility necessarily invokes the question of agency and the boundaries of the collective: how is one related to another? How do we think of the relationship of the now to the past without equating the past to sheer meaningless contingency? For if we do, then there is no point, there is no use, there is no politics. The persistence and existence of the politics of history, therefore, inversely attest to the thriving of the question, a striving toward an answer that cannot ultimately be found, yet which we seek nonetheless.

Collective guilt is different from responsibility, as collective responsibility is vicarious.[14] If guilt is predicated on one's action, responsibility is not, but rather, it arises as a result of our belonging to a collective not of our own choosing. In a world where individual political agency has come to feel ever more illusory, the discussion of how one is to relate to the past of the state ineluctably opens the way toward asking a question that invites entry *into* politics. To attend to these often contradictory forces that have led to the impasse over the history problem, I showed how philosophers and historians only partially share an understanding about the relationship between politics and history within the international context of modernizing Japan.

It is in this sense that I acknowledge that the history issue has yet to be settled. But the persistence of the politics of history in postwar Japan must be understood in light of this specific sensibility and memory of the ways in which the politicization of identity in history writing has come to embody clusters of reluctance and yearning surrounding the relationship between the state and history.

What the impasse elucidates is the indispensable and inadequate role that the idea of the agent/subject might assume in a world that is postimperial, postcolonial, yet presumed to be governed among and by sovereign nation-states, among the subject(s) of history. While Kato's thesis to constitute a subject was condemned within Japan, as Masachi Osawa observes, no one, thus far, has offered a proper engagement with the point that Kato implied: to speak of justice or morality or responsibility, one cannot circumvent answering the question – who is the subject/agent of history.[15]

This is because moral responsibility is applicable only *if* there is an agent that has the freedom to choose the course of action to take. Deterministic accounts of history or historical accounts which attribute the role of exogenous forces such as fate, chance, law of necessity, or contingency is inimical to the discussion of responsibility because such account offers no place for the exercise of agency and control in history. Those who could not have acted otherwise cannot be held responsible.

The problem of how to address history writing responsibly circles back to the question of what to do with this equation, that the sovereign is the agent and subject of history. There is more than one story behind this lack of perceivable and acceptable atonement, and in this lies the impasse over how to write history. While the silence surrounding history writing could be perceived as the exercise of power over history and narrative, and a staunch refusal to include others, attending to the discourse on the "postwar debate on the subject of history" illuminates otherwise. Japan's postwar silence surrounding history writing is weighted and bound by memories of past engagements with two versions of historicism, and the sovereign view of agency.

This book reflects on the predicament that contemporary Japan faces in light of its past when Japan claimed to also be the sovereign subject of history, to make new history. As Sharon Krause notes, in the liberal tradition, "alongside the idea of the sovereign state, there emerged . . . a quasi-parallel conception of the human being", who is presumed to be capable of exercising discipline and being in control of actions taken.[16] Experience tells us something else, that we are seldom in control of what happens. Nonetheless, the modern concept of agent is understood as having a rational will that can give law to nature – what Miki read in Kant, the sovereigntist view of agency that continues to animate these divergent approaches to historicism.

The issue to consider here is a question: in the postwar period where the historical subject as sovereign and agentic is suspect, how might one consider the demand to respond to historical injustice? In addition to the disagreement over epistemology, there is strident disagreement over how one is to relate the ambiguity of the status of the subject-agent to responsibility, because it evokes the necessity and inadequacy of the coherent, self-sufficient, autonomous liberal subject as the starting point of theorization.

Kato pointed to the Japanese state's incomplete political agency in the global context, whereas critics of revisionist history deconstructed the myth of the state as the subject of history. As a consequence, this deconstructionist approach provided a way for contemporary revisionists to claim that if all is constructed, then so is the notion of the Japanese people's responsibility for war, thus justifying the right to say "it has nothing to do with me". In other words, to attribute power to every dimension of politics inversely exonerates one from thinking of how to take action in time to make a difference. If power saturates, there is no place for agency, and so goes response-ability as responsibility.

To give cogency to this debris, much detail has been effaced. I defer to the cultural historians and specialists in their respective fields from which I have drawn and to whom I am much indebted.[17] The politics of history as a very broad stroke recurs and is animated and reenergized by our constant questioning as well as desire for a way to rethink of the relationship between the "we" and the "I", between the self and the state, and between the states of the world.

Many are unwilling to simply leave the matter of history by pointing to the obvious, that "I wasn't born then and, therefore, have nothing to do with it". There are works on history by generations born long after the war ended in 1945, and not all are purely for the purpose of discerning the facts and evidence, but are motivated by a question of how to relate to the world. It is such contentions over history that take place despite the awareness of the limits of history that a study of the persistence of the Japanese history problem that bases itself in terms of right or wrong would occlude.

Still, here I want to end this book with an exchange between Jacques Derrida and Emmanuel Levinas, on "Violence and Metaphysics". In this essay, Derrida responds to Levinas's characterization that all ontology is imperial. While Derrida agrees that the violence of light, the violence of re-presentation is problematic, he compares this to the violence of the night. This is a place where there is no language, no representation, no light, only silence and darkness, a world of stillness.

Derrida argues that notwithstanding the violence inflicted by the use of language, he would choose this violence of the light over the violence of the night.[18] To be sure, there are degrees of difference among the violence of the light – some are far more violent than others – yet, to forego all light, all acts of representation, appears too hasty a solution. It is in this sense that I side with Derrida at the end of this book, to take the risk of writing of the limits, as words.

While I have taken the path less trodden to think about the place of history in Japan and global politics, I insist that there is a use to approach this politics of history from the vantage point of a decidedly interdisciplinary international relations and its historicizing of the ways in which power constitutes the subject of history. There are reasons why we continue to resist ceasing to discuss the place of history in the world, and this is what also affirms our fact of being-in-common. History, in this sense, is communal, and it is about community, interconnection, and yearning to reflect on how one relates to the world.

As Nancy (1990) puts it, history is

> a decision about politics, about if and how we allow our otherness to exist, to inscribe itself as a community is to expose ourselves to the nonpresence of our present, and to its coming (as a "future" which does not succeed the present, but which is the coming of *our* present).
>
> (1990: 171)

The future is not predetermined or destined, it is rather born out of the momentum embodied in our cumulative decisions toward and surrounding history, the utterances, hesitations, and writings all despite the awareness of the very limits of history. Such is the politics of history after history in the globalized present.

Notes

1 There are Japanese "comfort women" as well, although the majority were non-Japanese. On the estimated composition of "comfort women", see Soh (2008).

2 Hideo Kobayashi's *Rekishi no dekonsutorakushon* is a collection of his essays surrounding history and theory where he often reflects on his sense of hesitation to speak of the subject of history (2010).

3 The Article 9, which is known as the no-war clause in the U.S. written constitution, has two parts. Clause A declares that Japan will renounce the use of military force to resolve international disputes, Clause B states that in order to realize Clause A, Japan will not use any military force. Therefore, the recent call to amend the constitution is geared toward closing the gap between the text of the constitution and the reality that Japan does have a Self-Defense Force, so it is Clause B, while Clause A is kept intact.

4 Michael Allen Gillespie, "The Question of History", in *Hegel, Heidegger, and the Ground of History* (Chicago and London: University of Chicago Press, 1984): 21.

5 Wendy Brown, *States of Injury: Power and Freedom in Late Modernity* (Princeton, NJ: Princeton University Press, 1995): 64–65.

6 Ibid., 65.

7 The chapters as a whole focused on the state rather than the imperial family. On the place of the emperor in sovereign thinking, see Takashi Fujitani, *Splendid Monarchy*; on the place of the emperor in the postwar context, Masachi Osawa's discussion of the ghostly presence is instructive. Cf. *Sengo no Shiso Kukan*.

8 Masafumi Yonetani's extensive reflection on Asia-Japan relations and various postwar thinkers on this matter is instructive. Pp. 1–6; Yoshimi Takeuchi, "Daitoasenso to warerano ketsui (sengen) [Greater East Asia War and Our Determination (A Declaration)]", in Tetsushi Marukawa and Masahisa Suzuki eds., *Takeuchi Yoshimi Serekushon I: Nihon e no/karano manazashi [Selected Essays by Yoshimi Takeuchi I: The Gaze from/toward Japan]* (Tokyo: Nihon keizai hyoronsha, 2006): 41–45 – original text written in 1942.

9 "Sekaishiteki tachiba to nihon [World Historical Position and Japan]" was published in 1943. The forum on overcoming modernity and the texts are collected and edited by Yoshimi Takeuchi in *Kindai no Chokoku [Overcoming Modernity]* and the meeting took place in July 1942.

10 Takeuchi, "Daitoasenso to warerano ketsui (sengen)".

11 Norihiro Kato, *Haisengoron [After Defeat]* (Tokyo: Chikuma Bunko, 2005).

12 Masachi Osawa, *Sengo no Shiso Kukan [Atmosphere of Postwar Political Thought]* (Tokyo: Chikuma Shinsho, 2005).

13 Gillespie, "The Question of History", 21.

14 I take the notion of collective responsibility from Hannah Arendt in her essay, "Collective Responsibility", in Jerome Kohn ed., *Responsibility and Judgment* (New York: Schocken Books, 2003): 147–158.

15 Osawa Masachi, *Sengo no Shiso Kukan [Atmosphere of Postwar Political Thought]* (Tokyo: Chikuma Shinsho, 2005): 26.

16 Sharon Krause, *Freedom beyond Sovereignty: Reconstructing Liberal Individualism* (Chicago and London: The University of Chicago Press, 2015): 2.

17 Ann Laura Stoler, *Duress: Imperial Durabilities in Our Times* (Durham, NC, and London: Duke University Press, 2016): 339.

18 Derrida, Jacques. "Violence and Metaphysics", in *Writing and Difference* (London: University of Chicago Press, 1978): 102.

References

Ankersmit, Frank R. *Historical Representation*. Stanford, CA: Stanford University Press, 2001.

Arendt, Hannah. "Collective Responsibility." In *Responsibility and Judgment*, edited by Jerome Kohn, 147–158. New York: Schocken Books, 2003.

Brown, Wendy. *States of Injury: Power and Freedom in Late Modernity*. Princeton, NJ: Princeton University Press, 1995.

Butler, Judith. *Giving an Account of Oneself*. New York: Fordham University Press, 2005.

Derrida, Jacques. *Writing and Difference*. London: University of Chicago Press, 1978.

Gillespie, Michael. *Hegel, Heidegger, and the Ground of History*. Chicago and London: University of Chicago Press, 1984.

Kato, Norihiro. *Haisengoron [After Defeat]*. Tokyo: Chikuma Bunko, 2005.

Kato, Norihiro. *Sayounara, Gojiratachi – Sengo kara toku hanarete [Goodbye, Godzilla: From Far Away from Postwar]*. Tokyo: Iwanami Shoten, 2010.

Kawakami Toru, Teruko Takeuchi et al. *Kindai no Chokokuron [Overcoming Modernity]*. Vol. 23, Edited by Yoshimi Takeuchi. Tokyo: Toyamabo Hyakka Bunko, 2006.

Kobayashi, Yasuo. *Rekishino Dekonsutorakushon: Kyosei no Kibo e mukatte [Deconstruction of History: Toward an Hope for Coexistence]*. Tokyo: University of Tokyo Press, 2010.

Kosaka, Masaaki et al. *Sekaishiteki tachiba to Nihon [World Historical Position and Japan]*. Tokyo: Chuo Koronsha, 1942.

Krause, Sharon. *Freedom beyond Sovereignty: Reconstructing Liberal Individualism*. Chicago and London: University of Chicago Press, 2015.

Nancy, Jean-Luc. "Finite History." In *The States of 'Theory': History, Art, and Critical Discourse*, edited by David Carroll, 149–174. New York: Columbia University Press, 1990.

Narita, Ryuichi. *'Senso Keiken' no Sengoshi [Postwar History of 'War Experience']*. Tokyo: Iwanami Shoten, 2010.

Osawa, Masachi. *Sengo no Shiso Kukan [Atmosphere of Postwar Political Thought]*. Tokyo: Chikuma Shinsho, 2005.

Sang-Hun, Choe. "Deal with Japan on Former Sex Slaves Failed Victims, South Korean Panel Says." *The New York Times*, December 27, 2017. www.nytimes.com/2017/12/27/world/asia/comfort-women-south-korea-japan.html?hp&action=click&pgtype=Homepage&clickSource=story-heading&module=first-column-region&region=top-news&WT.nav=top-news (Accessed December 28, 2017).

Soh, Chunghee Sarah. *The Comfort Women: Sexual Violence and Postcolonial Memory in Korea and Japan*. Chicago and London: University of Chicago Press, 2008.

Stoler, Ann. *Duress: Imperial Durabilities in Our Times*. Durham and London: Duke University Press, 2016.

Suga, Syuichi. "Suminuri kyokasho <Showa Nijyu kara Nijyuichinen> no jitsujo ni tsuite [Rigid Censorship over School Textbooks by the Ministry of Education in 1945-46]", in *Hanazono shigaku [The Association of History Research Hanazono University]* No. 33 (November 2012): 52–105.

Yomiuri, Shinbun. "Summary of Analysis of Japan-ROK Agreement on 'Comfort Women' Issue." December 28, 2017.

Young, Robert. *White Mythologies: Writing History and the West*. New York: Routledge, 1990.

Index

Note: Page numbers in *italics* indicate a photo on the corresponding page.